Keith Snider, one of the world's most distinguished experts on tone, provides an extremely useful, clear, and comprehensive introduction aimed at students, scholars, and field workers who want to know how pitch is exploited in African and other tone languages. Focusing first on methodological issues arising from the interpretation of pitch contrasts, the author then carefully guides us through questions of phonological and orthographic analysis. Drawing from his extensive research on Chumburung (Kwa; Ghana) and other languages, *Tone Analysis for Field Linguists* is a book that those venturing out into the world of tone will want to have on their home or office shelf and by their side in the field.

Larry M. Hyman
Professor of Linguistics, University of California, Berkeley
President, Linguistic Society of America (2017)

Anyone who is about to undertake fieldwork on a language they suspect might be tonal needs to have this book at their side. Snider leads the reader step-by-step through the questions they need to ask, the ways to control their data collection and analysis, and even how to represent their findings in a practical orthography. It also contains much of value for the desk-bound linguist working on the analysis of tonal languages, for whom it should raise an awareness of the potential pitfalls in interpreting tonal data gathered by others, not all of whom will have been as careful as Snider in their methodology.

Moira Yip
Emeritus Professor of Linguistics, University College London
Author of Tone *(Cambridge University Press)*

Students training to be linguists often find tone a scary topic. Reading about tone in some languages may make them feel they are facing a poorly discernible creature with uncontrollable tentacles reaching into every part of the phonology and morphosyntax. At a comfortable pace, this book will guide them through a methodologically explicit account of how to observe and analyse tone, by ear and through acoustic analysis, written from the perspective of the author's first-hand experience with describing one such language in detail.

Carlos Gussenhoven
Emeritus Professor of General and Experimental Phonology, Radboud University Nijmegen
Author of The Phonology of Tone and Intonation *(Cambridge University Press)*

Keith Snider's book addresses a major problem in learning how to do linguistic field work, that tone is seen as very mysterious. Taking the perspective of the student who knows nothing about tone, he demystifies the problem by explaining the steps of tonology from auditory discrimination to systematic phonological analysis. Students will learn the major factors known to be relevant to tone, such as how segmental structure, prosody, morphology and grammar can affect tone. Especially useful is the chapter on Chumburung, which gives an extensive model of how a tonal analysis should be done and documented.

David Odden
Professor Emeritus of Linguistics, The Ohio State University
Author of Introducing Phonology *(Cambridge University Press)*

Keith Snider is a widely-recognized authority on tone languages. This volume summarizes his decades of experience analyzing tonal systems from all over the world. A unique contribution of this manual is that it combines numerous practical suggestions and guidelines for unraveling tonal patterns with a profound understanding of the linguistic mechanisms driving them. Another highlight of his approach is that it applies this knowledge to the difficult issue of how to represent tone orthographically. The result is a synthesis of three aspects of dealing with tone languages that should be extremely helpful to academicians, fieldworkers, and native-speakers alike: (1) the methodology of gathering and analyzing tonal data, (2) the theory behind them (phonetic and phonological), and (3) orthography development.

Steve Parker
Associate Professor, Graduate Institute of Applied Linguistics

Snider's carefully described methodologies provide the field linguist with a powerful discovery procedure. Students and seasoned field workers alike will find answers for their questions and expert advice for eliciting, organizing, controlling, and analyzing data in tone languages. Snider's expertise and years of experience in the field and the classroom have produced a book that is both rigorous in method and accessible to all.

Michael Ahland
Assistant Professor of Linguistics, California State University, Long Beach

The volume offers a clear and detailed introduction to the exciting 'detective game' (2.2) of phonological analysis of African level-tone systems. It also offers a voyage through the immense diversity of the world's tone systems.

Alexis Michaud
CNRS-LACITO, France

Some years ago I participated in a tone workshop in Addis Ababa, in which Keith Snider introduced the principles of this book. In those six weeks I developed such a good knowledge of the tonal characteristics of the Majang language, starting from zero, that I felt confident enough to undertake a full description of the language. It quickly became clear that it would have been impossible to penetrate the system of grammatical relations of that language without this solid tonal foundation. I therefore recommend to anyone planning on describing a language that is suspected to be tonal to start out all research by following this methodology.

Andreas Joswig
Field linguist, SIL Ethiopia

It is no exaggeration to say that Keith Snider's teaching over many years, now distilled into the contents of this book, has transformed my professional career. It has inspired my involvement in tone description and orthography development in Niger-Congo languages. Whereas some perceive analyzing tonal phenomena to be intimidating, too complicated, and only for the experts, I have found that the methodology in this book has given me not only success and confidence, but enjoyment in the process. This book encapsulates Snider's three decades of extensive experience. It is easy to read, thorough, and solidly based on both theory and data. If you are engaged in, contemplating—or avoiding—tone analysis, it is well worth your investment.

Bruce Wiebe
Linguist, SIL International

For decades, tonologists in the Americas, Africa, and Asia have held divergent methodological and theoretical views related to tone. The beginning linguist approaching tone analysis often has trouble knowing where to start. Snider has experience analyzing tone systems around the world, and the methodology in this book is globally applicable, guiding the researcher clearly and logically through the discovery procedure. One of its strengths is the way Snider integrates important aspects of various phonological approaches (particularly autosegmental): he argues that the 'tonal phoneme' is best viewed as the pattern over a whole root or word, rather than the tone on individual segments. This understanding of tone is critical for the beginning researcher, as many of our transcription systems do not easily lead us to view the pitch patterns across multiple segments. These insights about the pitch patterns, along with others gleaned from lexical phonology and Optimality Theory, should prove very helpful in the design of pedagogical materials for new readers and writers of previously unwritten tonal languages.

Hugh Paterson III
Independent researcher

Tone Analysis for Field Linguists is everything I want in a handbook: comprehensive yet concise, clear but not simplistic, and anchored in real linguistic data. Snider provides a solid methodology sure to produce quality tonal data and analyses. As a field linguist, I count this book as absolutely essential.

Joshua Smolders
Linguistics field researcher, SIL International

I hope to work with Asian languages in the future, but nothing intimidated me more than tone, until I read Snider's *Tone Analysis for Field Linguists*. Detailed yet accessible, the book explains the theory of tone and offers a step-by-step guide to tone analysis in any given language. Snider's approach to tone makes more sense than anything else I have read. I will make sure to have this book beside me as I go to the field.

Lauren Schultz
Graduate student of linguistics, Trinity Western University

Before I read this book, I knew nothing about tone except that it existed. After reading this book, I feel prepared to successfully analyze tone in a real language! The concepts are clearly communicated and the focus is on providing a practical methodology, making it a great text for anyone working with a tonal language.

Maria Stølen
Graduate student of linguistics, Trinity Western University

There is a lot of confusion surrounding tone languages, and even experienced linguists may be daunted at the prospect of analyzing one. In this book, Keith Snider clears up a lot of the confusion and lays out a straight-forward procedure for analyzing the tone system of a language. Not being tethered to any particular linguistic theory, this book is a practical guide to any linguist wanting to analyze the tone system of a language.

David Barnes
Graduate student of linguistics, Trinity Western University

Tone Analysis for Field Linguists

Managing Editor
Susan McQuay

Copy Editor
Dirk Kievit

Proofreader
Eugene Burnham

Production Staff
Lois Gourley, Production Director
Judy Benjamin, Compositor
Barbara Alber, Graphic Artist
Barbara Alber, Cover Design

Cover Photograph
Cover image: https://pixabay.com/en/paper-colorful-color-loose-green-571938/, available under CC0 Creative Commons license: https://creativecommons.org/licenses/by-sa/3.0/legalcode.

Tone Analysis for Field Linguists

Keith L. Snider

Foreword by Will Leben

SIL International®
Dallas, Texas

© 2018 by SIL International®
Library of Congress Catalog Number: 2017959659
ISBN: 978-1-55671-422-1

All Rights Reserved

No part of this publication may be reproduced, stored in a retrieval system, or transmitted in any form or by any means—electronic, mechanical, photocopy, recording, or otherwise—without the express permission of SIL International, with the exception of brief excerpts in journal articles or reviews.

Instructors may access the accompanying online exercises. Register here: https://www.sil.org/resources/publications/toneanalysis_teachermaterials

Copies of this and other publications of SIL International® may be obtained through distributors such as Amazon, Barnes & Noble, other worldwide distributors and, for select volumes, www.sil.org/resources/publications:

SIL International Publications
7500 W. Camp Wisdom Road
Dallas, Texas 75236-5629 USA

General inquiry: publications_intl@sil.org
Pending order inquiry: sales@sil.org

Contents

Foreword ix
Preface xi
Acknowledgments xiii
Abbreviations xv
1 Introduction 1
    1.1 What is a tone language? 2
    1.2 Tonal contrast 6
    1.3 Contrastive tone height 11
    1.4 The concept of tone patterns 13
        1.4.1 Unity of underlying patterns though realized differently with different syllable profiles 14
        1.4.2 Stability of tone patterns regardless of segmental changes 18
        1.4.3 Non-recognition by native speakers of individual tones in a pattern 20
    1.5 Data collection 21
        1.5.1 Elicited vs. "natural" language data 21
        1.5.2 Conventions for transcribing pitch data 22
        1.5.3 Transcribing pitch accurately 25
2 Methodology for Phonological Analysis of Tone 29
    2.1 Setting up a database 31
        2.1.1 Grammatical word category 31
        2.1.2 Stem type 33
        2.1.3 Syllable profile of stem 37
        2.1.4 Surface tone patterns 40
        2.1.5 Underlying tone pattern 41
        2.1.6 Noun and/or verb class 42
        2.1.7 Consonant(s) 44
        2.1.8 Phonation type of vowels 46
        2.1.9 Syllable stress pattern 48
    2.2 Procedure for tone analysis 49

	2.2.1 Which words to analyze first 51

| | 2.2.2 Order of investigation .... 53 |

2.3	Words spoken in isolation 54
2.4	Words spoken in other morphological environments. 56
2.5	Words spoken in other phrasal environments 58

3 Phonetics of Pitch 63

3.1	The articulation of pitch 64
3.2	The acoustics of pitch 66
3.3	Acoustic analysis. 68
	3.3.1 Avoid measurements to the left of a TBU's mid-point. 69
	3.3.2 Measure at points in flat stretches 69
	3.3.3 Avoid measuring perturbations caused by obstruents 70
	3.3.4 Measure at points marked by peaks and valleys. 70
	3.3.5 Recognize TBUs that are only transitional 71
	3.3.6 Measure at points of syllable energy peaks 72
	3.3.7 Allow for declination 72
3.4	Acoustic studies 73

4 Tone and Orthography 79

4.1	Functional load 80
4.2	Failure of writing surface representations. 84
4.3	Critiques of some strategies for marking tone 85
	4.3.1 Zero marking. 85
	4.3.2 Distinguishing minimal pairs. 87
	4.3.3 Diacritic marking of grammatical constructions 88
4.4	Phonologically ideal orthography 90
	4.4.1 Tonal entity of representation 91
	4.4.2 Historical overview of orthography and phonological depth issues 91
	4.4.3 Lexical Orthography Hypothesis 93
4.5	Issues in representing tonal contrasts 96
4.6	Issues with teaching tone 98
4.7	Conclusion 98
	4.7.1 Linguistic analysis 99
	4.7.2 Orthography development 99

5 Phonological Analysis of Chumburung Tone 101

5.1	Setting up the database and entering data 104
5.2	Full analysis of preliminary words 114
	5.2.1 Analysis of isolation forms of preliminary words. 115
	5.2.2 Analysis of plural forms of preliminary words. 117
	5.2.3 Analysis of phrasal environments of preliminary words 120
5.3	Analysis of isolation forms of remaining words. 127
	5.3.1 Analysis of isolation forms of *kI-* class nouns. 127
	5.3.2 Analysis of isolation forms of *I-* class nouns. 129
	5.3.3 Analysis of isolation forms of verbs 130
5.4	Analysis of remaining words in other morphological environments 130
	5.4.1 Analysis of plural forms of *kI-* class nouns. 130
	5.4.2 Analysis of nominalized verbs 137
5.5	Analysis of remaining words in phrasal environments 139
	5.5.1 *kI-* class nouns in phrasal environments 139

  5.5.2 *I*- class nouns in phrasal environments 146
  5.5.3 Verbs in phrasal environments. 147
 5.6 Conclusions. 150
  5.6.1 Underlying noun root patterns. 150
  5.6.2 Less transparent matters 153

6 The Lexical Orthography Hypothesis Applied to Chumburung Tone 157

 6.1 Lexical and postlexical processes in Chumburung. 158
  6.1.1 High tone dissimilation (lexical) 158
  6.1.2 High tone spreading across word boundaries (postlexical, but phonemic) . 159
  6.1.3 High tone spreading within words (lexical) 160
  6.1.4 Automatic downstep (postlexical, allophonic) 160
  6.1.5 Non-automatic downstep (postlexical, but represents displaced contrast) . 161
  6.1.6 Prepausal floating low tone docking (postlexical) 162
  6.1.7 Prepausal falling low tones (postlexical, allophonic) 163
 6.2 LOH applied to Chumburung 164
  6.2.1 Surface representations 164
  6.2.2 Phonemic representations 165
  6.2.3 Underlying representations 167
  6.2.4 Lexical representations 167

References 171

Index 179

Foreword

In this foreword I want to share my enthusiasm for Keith Snider's new book, a complete course on tone. While it is laid out as a primer for beginners, I'm delighted to find that it also very well serves my own level by reviewing progress in the analysis and typology of tone covering the world's important linguistic areas, including Africa, Asia, the Americas and even a case from Papua New Guinea. While the book justifiably advertises itself to field linguists, it will prove just as useful for any armchair tonologist who wishes to crack a tone language or simply get an appreciation for the diversity of tonal systems around the world and for the tightly woven web of intricacies that come with tonal analysis.

Chapter 1 presents a far-reaching overview of phenomena found in the various types of tone language, along with a comparison of the different transcription systems for tone. Chapter 2 takes us through the procedures for the phonological analysis of tone, from setting up elicitation frames to completing an analysis, with many stops along the way at points that reveal how complex tonal interactions can be: influences from neighboring words and neighboring sounds, interactions with stress and phonation types, conditioning effects of grammatical categories and syntactic phrasing, and so on.

Chapter 3 takes us through the basics of pitch production and acoustic measurement. In chapter 4, we get an extensive treatment of factors in developing an orthography for unwritten languages, including a historical overview, with special attention to the problem of determining the functional load of tone and a section recommending an approach to tone in teaching materials.

Chapters 5 and 6 are case studies putting the content of the preceding chapters into practice for the phonological analysis and tonal orthography of Chumburung, a Kwa language of Ghana. Accompanying the book are a set of thirteen online exercises on the tone system of Chumburung nouns, including databases and sound files. Chumburung figures prominently among the languages Keith Snider has worked on in the three decades he has devoted to the theory and description of tone in a variety of languages. The present book also profits from his past publications and consulting work on developing practical orthographies for lesser known languages and from his career as an educator, again focussed on the study of tone. Some of the ideas in these pages received an early airing by Snider in 2011 as an invited participant at the *Workshop on how to study a tone language: From the first elicitation to the latest software* (University of California, Berkeley, 18-20 February 2011).

It is tempting to compare the present book to Kenneth Pike's 1948 landmark monograph *Tone Languages*. Both are organized as primers yet include data from a large number of languages from around the world as a way of illustrating how tone behaves and outlining optimal approaches to capturing that behavior. Both books take the student step by step through the procedures of analysis. Indeed, as Snider notes (p. 17), he adopts Pike's use of "frame" for the carrier phrase of a tone from Pike 1948. And the "Pike" system [Snider's quotes] is among those presented for transcribing pitch data in the current book. Both books also end with chapters applying the content of the book to the analysis of specific languages. In Pike's case, the languages were Mixteco and Mazateco, Otomanguean languages of Mexico, while the present book uses Chumburung.

More important to us than the similarities between the two works, published about seven decades apart, are the dissimilarities. Of course, we now know much more and have better frameworks for describing what we know, and this is thanks in part to Pike's pioneering work and continuing efforts by Keith Snider along with several generations of scholars in between. The present book also benefits from Snider's intimate acquaintance with the practical problems of orthography, an area in which we learn from this book that answers, while no easier to come by than in phonology, are available. Online access to the data, both the sound files and the transcribed data, from which this book's exercises are drawn is of course an incomparable asset.

Tone studies got a huge and lasting boost in 1948 with the publication of Kenneth Pike's *Tone Languages*, one of the key works that attracted many new experts to this field and gave us confidence that the mysteries surrounding tone were more tractable than first appeared. Pike's book served as a point of reference for many decades and still does to some extent. But thanks to the many advances that are well reflected in this new volume, we finally have a new kid on the block, a primer for anyone interested in analyzing tone and a serious, comprehensive review of the fundamentals of tone for the more seasoned tonologist.

Will Leben
Stanford, CA
April 27, 2017

Preface

The inspiration to write this book came when following publication of *The Geometry and Features of Tone* (Snider 1999), a theoretically oriented book on tone features, I was dismayed to discover that some of the students who had done well in my tone course were failing when it came to analyzing tone in the field. This prompted me to re-think the course, which, in turn, led me to emphasize practical matters more. Indeed, what was the point of turning out students who were able to account for every sort of tonal alternation imaginable in the classroom, but who then couldn't even establish proper tonal contrasts in the field? Moreover, it began to dawn on me that these students weren't alone. Judging from the descriptions of tone languages that appear in the literature, it would seem that many linguists have difficulty when it comes to carrying out basic fieldwork on tone.

As with any linguistic problem, the first thing most of us do is to survey the literature. But while there are many fine books available that describe how tone behaves (e.g., Fromkin 1978, Yip 2002, and Gussenhoven 2004—to name three that I have personally found very helpful), with the exception of Pike 1948, the shelf is quite empty when it comes to books that teach one how to actually analyze tone. The present book is therefore an attempt to help fill this lacuna.

As is everyone, I am a product of my "upbringing," and in this case, my graduate training in linguistics left me well schooled in the theory of Autosegmental Phonology. This—coupled with the many years I personally spent carrying out primary tone analysis, as well as the numerous opportunities my consultant job provided me to help others analyze tone—shaped my approach to tone analysis significantly. So I began asking myself how "my methodology" differed from that of others. The answer is two-fold: a) a greater emphasis on discovering the contrastive tonal patterns of morphemes, as opposed to the contrastive tones of tone-bearing units, and b) a greater insistence on keeping constant all factors that can potentially affect tone, so that utterances being compared are truly comparable. While the notion that phonological contexts need to be controlled for is not a new one (since it is regularly applied in other areas of phonology), in practice many linguists fail in the course of tone analysis because they don't recognize a similar need to control for relevant grammatical factors like word categories and grammatical constructions.

Few things give me more delight than watching people I have taught analyze tone well. In writing this "how to" book on tone analysis, it is my sincere hope that the approach presented in this book, which has proven helpful to many people in the past, will prove helpful to many more in the future.

Acknowledgments

The Chumburung data that appear throughout this book were gathered periodically from 1982 to 2016 in the Chumburung village of Ekumdipe, N.R. Ghana. I lived in Ekumdipe with my wife and young family from 1982 to 1987, and I have made several visits back to the village over the years since, the most recent one being for a period of four weeks in October 2016. Many Chumburung people contributed to my knowledge of their language, and I am most grateful to the Chumburung community for their welcoming spirit and gracious help. Two good friends stand out for having helped me significantly since I first began studying Chumburung: Isaac Demuyakor and his cousin Evans Demuyakor. Both men are mature native speakers of Chumburung who have lived their entire lives in the village of Ekumdipe. Isaac provided all of the recordings for the data in the online exercises, as well as for much of the data in chapters 5 and 6, and Evans has always helped me in every way possible. Thank you, Isaac and Evans, for your faithful contribution to my scholarship over many years, and for your patience with me. Thank you also Esther Demuyakor (Evan's wife) for your practical help and friendship when we lived in the village, and for your kind and gracious hospitality during different visits in the years since.

Many non-Chumburung people have also contributed significantly to this book, and I will do my best to acknowledge as many as possible. I have divided the help into categories and arranged the surnames in alphabetical order within each category. My apologies to anyone I may have unintentionally missed.

I am grateful to Larry Hayashi for his patience with me on computer-related matters, and for his technical assistance at various times as I was writing this book. In particular, I am grateful for his sketch of the vocal folds (figure 1, chapter 3). Bruce Wiebe very graciously agreed to help with the proofreading, and to the extent that this book is error-free, it will largely be due to Bruce's meticulous help. Good discussions with many people helped shape this book. Those who contributed in this way include: Steve Anderson, Rod Casali, Larry Hyman, Connie Kutsch Lojenga, and Jim Roberts. Many people provided written comments of an editorial nature on one or more chapters. These include: Alison Nicole, Hannah Olney, Rebecca Ouwehand, Hugh Paterson III, Ed Quigley, and Francine van Woudenberg. I also received written comments that were primarily substantive in nature on one or more chapters from: Joan Baart, Mario Chávez-Peón, Bruce Connell, Cathy Davison, Mark Donahue, Robert Hedinger, Steve Marlett, Dave Roberts, and David Weber.

These next two people, Phil Davison and Roselle Dobbs, deserve very high commendation. Both wrote extensive comments of both a substantive nature as well as an editorial nature on multiple versions of almost all the chapters. I am most grateful for their help and for their patience, as I'm sure both thought this book would have appeared long before it actually did. Thank you, Phil and Roselle, for your great help! And then what would this book be without the input of the publisher's reviewers, Inga McKendry and Mary Pearce? Thank you both for your helpful comments and your patience with me. I am also grateful to my many tone course students and tone workshop participants (too many to mention individually) for drawing to my attention typos, mistakes, inconsistencies, and places where more emphasis or clarity was needed.

I wish to thank Will Leben for kindly agreeing to write the foreword for this book. In it, Will compared and contrasted my work with that of Pike 1948, noting that my work exploits many of the advances in tone knowledge that have evolved since Pike's publication seven decades earlier. What he failed to mention was his own contributions to those advances! I asked Will to write this foreword because his seminal work on suprasegmental phonology (Leben 1971, 1973) greatly influenced the present work. I first became aware of Will's work in 1983 when I read his analysis of Mende tone in Leben 1978. By describing how five underlying tone melodies in Mende could account for the distribution facts of the surface tone patterns of monomorphemic nouns regardless of how many syllables were involved, Will convinced me and countless others that the tone melody, or tone pattern as I call it, functions as a phonological unit. The approach to tone analysis that I have found most useful on the field, and which I outline in the present work, rests solidly on the notion that establishing contrast between the tone patterns of morphemes yields a greater payoff than simply establishing contrast between the tones of tone-bearing units. So thank you, Will, for this insight and also for your constructive comments.

Finally, I am grateful to my wife, Ruth, for her patience and encouragement during the writing process and to God for giving me the strength and ability to bring this project to a conclusion.

As is evident, I have received a lot of help with this book, and I am most grateful to everyone who has contributed in one way or another to its success. I offer my sincere thanks to everyone. Undoubtedly there are inadequacies, and for these, I take full responsibility.

Abbreviations

1S	1st person singular
3S	3rd person singular
2P	2nd person plural
3P	3rd person plural
ADJ	adjective
AM	associative marker
ATR	advanced tongue root
C1, C2, C3, etc.	noun class 1, 2, 3, etc. marker
F_0	fundamental frequency
H	high tone
ꜛH	downstepped high tone
HORT	hortative
Hz	hertz
IPFV	imperfective
ITER	iterative
L	low tone
LOC	locative
LOH	Lexical Orthography Hypothesis
M	mid tone
N	nasal consonant
n.	noun
NC	noun class marker
NEG	negative
pl.	plural
POSS	possessive
Rd	round
S	sonorant consonant

TBU	tone bearing unit
UF	underlying form
V	vowel

1

Introduction

Tone, often viewed by many as "exotic," is one of the most fascinating topics in linguistics that one can investigate. Differences in pitch that might seem unimportant to speakers of non-tone languages often signal major differences in meaning in tone languages, and examples such as those in (1) never seem to lose their appeal.

(1) Four tones in Mandarin [cmn][1] (McCawley 1978:120)

mā	'mother'
má	'hemp'
mǎ	'horse'
mà	'scold'

Even for linguists, the different tonal alternations that some morphemes undergo in different contexts can be utterly baffling. For example, how does one explain the different placements of the high tones in (2)?

(2) Tone alternations in Mbololo Taita [dav] (Odden 2006:41)

mbanga	'cave'	mbangá mbaha	'big cave'
nganda	'wall'	nganda mbáha	'big wall'

Since the second word in each of the phrases *mbangá mbaha* and *nganda mbáha* is the same (viz. *mbaha* 'big'), the fact that the high tones are placed differently in the two phrases must mean that *mbanga* 'cave' and *nganda* 'wall' have different underlying tones. Yet tonally, these two words are pronounced identically in isolation. Seemingly unsolvable puzzles like these not only intrigue experienced linguists, but also sometimes frighten off beginning linguists. This is unfortunate because once one understands the true nature of tone, the general principles that govern its analysis turn out to be no different than those that govern segmental analysis. This book therefore seeks to help beginning linguists bridge that mysterious gap between analyzing segments and analyzing tone.

[1] At the first mention of each language name, the ISO 639-3 code for the language is provided between square brackets (e.g., Mandarin [cmn], English [eng]).

Although serious research into how to analyze tone languages is definitely taking place,[2] the fact remains that tone is still often poorly investigated and tone marking often ignored in publications that focus on other aspects of linguistics. Undoubtedly, the reasons for this are numerous and complex, but one stands out as being a major culprit: historically, at least, most serious linguistic research has been carried out by people who don't speak a tone language. While such speakers are comfortable transcribing and analyzing contrasts differentiated by consonants and vowels (elements common to all languages), many are distinctly uncomfortable transcribing and analyzing similar contrasts differentiated by tone, a device not employed in their own languages.

1.1 What is a tone language?

Since tone is not a characteristic common to all languages, it is important to understand what it is, and how tone languages differ from their non-tone counterparts, particularly since all languages do employ pitch contrastively in one way or another. Throughout this book, the term "pitch" is used to denote phonetic tone, or tone as it is perceived, while the term "tone" denotes phonological tone, or tone as it is realized in contrast with other tones (see section 1.2). Pitch is often described acoustically in terms of fundamental frequency (abbreviated F_0), which corresponds articulatorily to the rate at which the vocal folds vibrate at any point in time. When precise phonetic detail is not important, pitch is often represented graphically using the "bar" notation. In this notation, level pitches are represented with level bars that correspond to the pitch heights they represent (e.g., LH [_ ¯]), and contour pitches are represented with angled bars that slope from higher to lower in the case of falling pitches (e.g., falling [\]), or from lower to higher in the case of rising pitches (e.g., rising [/]).

Here are some examples of how pitch contrasts differentiate meaning in English [eng], a non-tone, intonation language.

(3) Contrastive intonation patterns in English

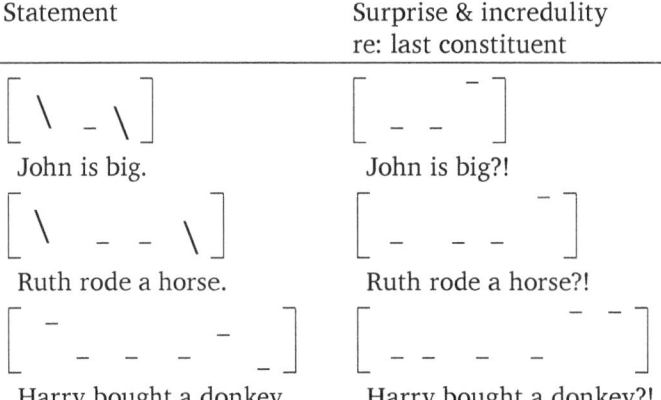

The examples in (3) illustrate two contrastive intonation patterns that are frequently used in English. Notice that for each pattern, when we substitute different nouns and verbs for the different sentence constituents, the pattern itself doesn't change, even when the number of syllables in the relevant constituents changes. This is because the intonation pattern is not identified with any particular morpheme or word, but rather with the greater overall construction.

---

[2] Examples of recent research on how to analyze tone languages include the Berkeley Tone Workshop (February 2011), the Australian National University Tone Workshop (December 2011), and the edited collection of papers (Bird and Hyman 2014) that was inspired by those workshops. Both Hyman 2014 and Snider 2014a were originally presented at the Berkeley workshop.

1.1 What is a tone language?

So what is the difference between "intonation" languages like English, Italian [ita], and Hungarian [hun] and "tone" languages like Mandarin, Zulu [zul], and Akan [aka]? The difference lies in the scope of the domains of the pitch patterns in each case, and also in the different functions of the phenomena. For intonation languages, the domain of the pitch pattern is a constituent greater than a single morpheme or word, and its function is to communicate "discoursal meaning," to mark boundaries, and to indicate attitudinal meaning (Gussenhoven 2004:24). On the other hand, for tone languages, the domain of the pattern is the morpheme (Ladd 2008),[3] and its function is to aid in the communication of lexical meaning. In this regard, Hyman and Leben (to appear), building on Welmers' 1959:2 definition, provides this very useful definition of a tone language: "The bare minimum to be considered a 'tone language' is that pitch enters as a (contrastive) exponent of at least some morphemes." So, regardless of how heavy or light the functional load of tone is in a language (i.e., the degree to which differences in lexical and/or grammatical meaning are distinguished solely by tone differences), all tone languages distinguish, to one degree or another, at least some morphemes by means of pitch contrasts. As the title of this book suggests, we will focus on providing a methodology for conducting tone analysis, not intonation analysis.[4]

We look now at examples from two tone languages, Kenyang [ken], a Bantoid language spoken in southwestern Cameroon with a "full" tone system, and Somali [som], a Cushitic language spoken in Somalia with a "reduced" tone system.

As may be seen in (4), the use of pitch in a tone language like Kenyang is very different from that in an intonation language like English.

(4) Minimal tone contrasts in Kenyang (personal field notes)

[/ \]
ba-te 'you (pl.) stood'
2P-stand

[/ ⁻]
ba-te 'you (pl.) drilled'
2P-drill

[⁻ \]
ba-te 'they stood'
3P-stand

[⁻ ⁻]
ba-te 'they drilled'
3P-drill

In this set of examples, we have four words with identical segments (i.e., *ba-te*). Each word, however, is comprised of two morphemes, the first being the person/subject marker and the second being the verb root. In the case of the person/subject marker, there are two morphemes distinguished solely by pitch contrasts: a low-to-high rising pitch on the 2P marker and a high level pitch on the 3P marker. In the case of the verb roots, again there are two morphemes distinguished solely by pitch contrasts: a high-to-low falling pitch on the root meaning 'stood' and a high level pitch on the root meaning 'drilled'.

As just discussed, the domain of the tone pattern contrast in tone languages is the morpheme. This does not mean, however, that the lexicon necessarily assigns tones to every morpheme. As the examples in (5) and (6) show, there is a three-way contrast between underlyingly high, low, and toneless verb roots in Kenyang. (These examples are discussed in detail further below.) In (5), when all three verb roots are preceded by the low-toned iterative affix /-màj-/, the toneless roots pattern with the low-toned roots. However, in (6),

---

[3] The situation is complicated by the fact that probably all tone languages also employ intonation. Ladd (2008) identifies three ways that tone languages employ intonation features: a) expansion of the pitch range to express emotions, b) modifications of certain tones to distinguish statements from questions, and c) modifications of overall contour shapes to distinguish statements from questions or to distinguish completed actions from incompleted ones.

[4] For studies related to the field of intonation, the interested reader is referred to Cruttenden 1997, Gussenhoven 2004, Ladd 2008, Xu and Xu 2005, and Liu and Xu 2007.

when these same roots are preceded by the high-toned hortative affix /-ń-/, the toneless roots now pattern with the high-toned roots, thereby demonstrating that they are neither low nor high underlyingly.

(5) Iterative verbs in Kenyang

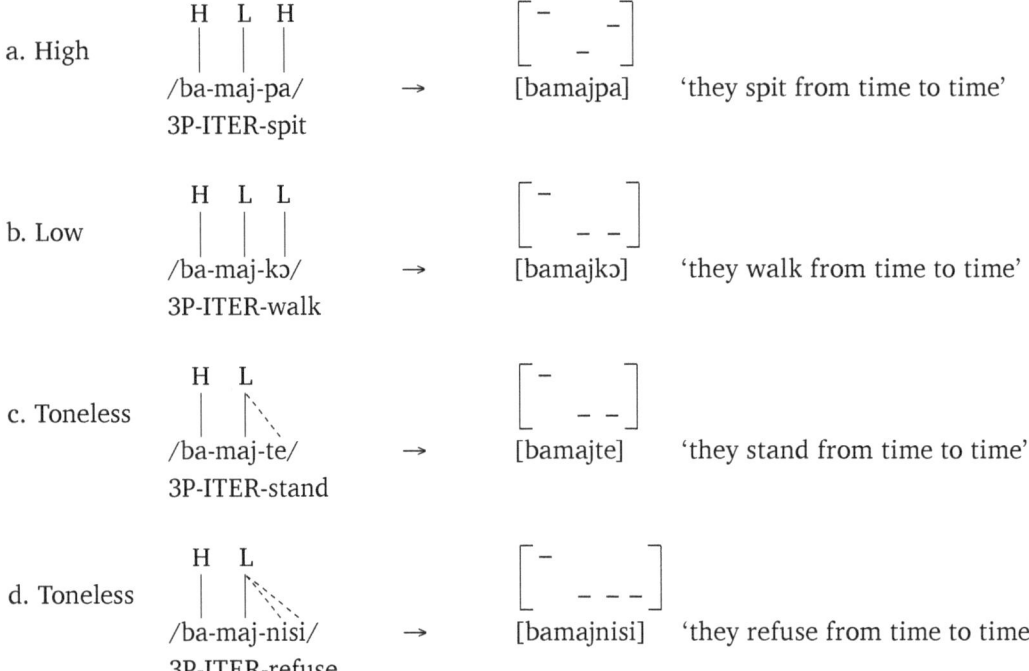

a. High
/ba-maj-pa/ → [bamajpa] 'they spit from time to time'
3P-ITER-spit

b. Low
/ba-maj-kɔ/ → [bamajkɔ] 'they walk from time to time'
3P-ITER-walk

c. Toneless
/ba-maj-te/ → [bamajte] 'they stand from time to time'
3P-ITER-stand

d. Toneless
/ba-maj-nisi/ → [bamajnisi] 'they refuse from time to time'
3P-ITER-refuse

In (5a), when the low-toned iterative affix precedes the high-toned root, as in bámàjpá, the second high tone is downstepped relative to the first high. (Downstep, irrelevant to the matter at hand and discussed in detail further below, is a register lowering phenomenon whereby a high tone and all tones that follow it are lowered following a low tone.) In (5b), when the low-toned affix precedes the low-toned verb root, as in bámàjkɔ̀, both are, not unexpectedly, pronounced with low tones. Finally, when the low-toned affix precedes the toneless verb roots in (5c) and (5d), both the affix and the roots are again pronounced with low tones. At this point, there is no reason to suspect that the toneless roots contrast tonally with their low-toned counterparts. As mentioned above, however, this changes in (6) when the verbs are preceded by a high tone.

1.1 *What is a tone language?*

(6) Hortative verbs in Kenyang

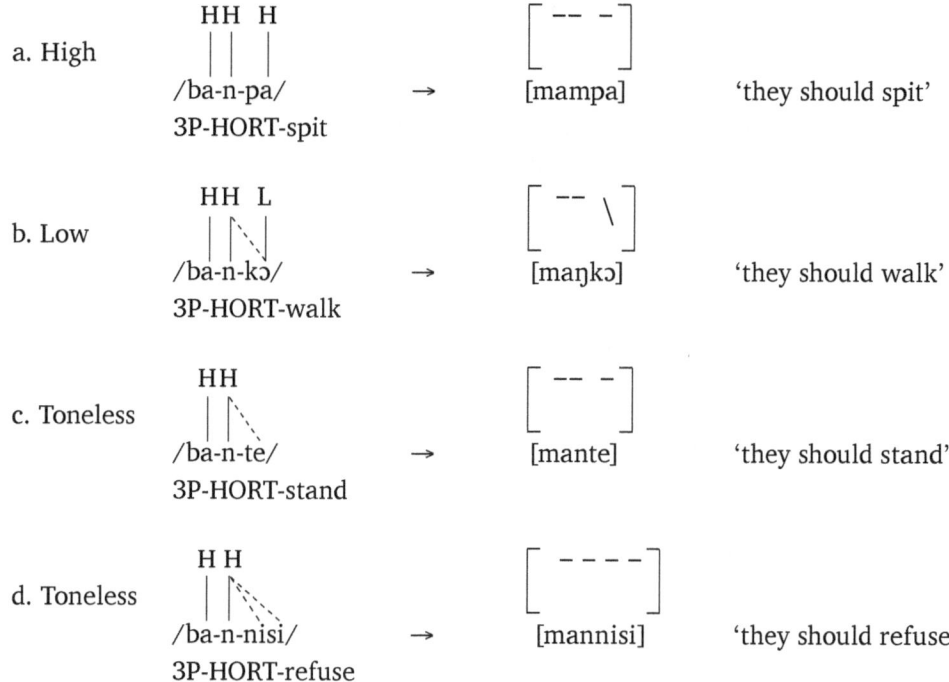

a. High	/ba-n-pa/ 3P-HORT-spit	→ [mampa]	'they should spit'
b. Low	/ba-n-kɔ̀/ 3P-HORT-walk	→ [maŋkɔ]	'they should walk'
c. Toneless	/ba-n-te/ 3P-HORT-stand	→ [mante]	'they should stand'
d. Toneless	/ba-n-nisi/ 3P-HORT-refuse	→ [mannisi]	'they should refuse'

As may be seen in (6a), when the high-toned hortative affix /-ń-/ precedes the high-toned root, as in *mámṕá,* both are, not unexpectedly, realized with high tones. In addition, it may be seen that the *b* of the subject prefix /bá-/ assimilates to the nasal quality of the hortative affix and that the hortative affix itself assimilates to the place of articulation of the following consonant. More germane to the discussion at hand, however, is that in (6b), the underlyingly low-toned root /kɔ̀/ undergoes high tone spreading from the preceding high-toned affix, and this results in a high falling pitch on *kɔ*, as in *báŋkɔ̂*. It's at this point that the difference between the low and toneless roots emerges. When one compares the behaviour of the low-toned root in (6b) with that of the toneless roots in (6c) and (6d), one finds that the toneless roots assimilate completely to the high tone of the preceding affix, unlike the low-toned root which, although it undergoes high tone spreading, nevertheless retains its underlying low as the rightmost element of the falling pitch.

To sum up this discussion of toneless morphemes, the examples in (5) demonstrate that those verb roots labelled toneless are different from those labelled high, while the examples in (6) demonstrate that they are also different from those labelled low. The fact that these roots are always realized with low tones when they follow low tones and with high tones when they follow high tones, without giving any indication of having inherent tones of their own, is a strong indication that they are indeed toneless.

In some languages, the use of tone to signal morphemic differences is more limited. Hyman 1981 and Saeed 1993, 1999 describe the tone system of Somali as marking mainly grammatical information like gender and number.

(7) Grammatical tone in Somali

Masculine		Feminine	
ínan	'boy'	inán	'girl'
náʕas	'stupid man'	naʕás	'stupid woman'
góray	'male ostrich'	goráy	'female ostrich'
darmáan	'colt'	darmaán	'filly'
ʕeesáan	'young he-goat'	ʕeesaán	'young she-goat'
daméer	'he-donkey'	dameér	'she-donkey'

In these examples, the placement of the high tone, indicated by an acute accent, is contrastive and appears on the penultimate vowel of masculine nouns and on the final vowel of their feminine counterparts. In all words, any vowels that precede the high tone are pronounced with mid pitch, while any vowels that follow the high tone are pronounced with low pitch. The placement of these secondary pitches is therefore totally predictable, and the pitches themselves serve only to help native speakers more easily identify which segment bears the contrastive high tone.

Finally, a number of languages have mixed tone-stress systems in which stressed syllables play a role in determining the surface realization of underlying tone patterns.[5] For example, Baart (2014) claims that stress plays a crucial role in the realization of tone in most, if not all, of the languages of northern Pakistan that are tonal. From another part of the world, Michael (2011a) describes Iquito [iqu], a Zaparoan language spoken in northern Peru, as having a mixed tone-stress system (cf. the description of Iquito in chapter 2).

1.2 Tonal contrast

Tone analysis is all about discovering contrast. In order for a language to be considered tonal, it must have morphemes whose surface pitch patterns contrast with each other in one or more comparable environments. The catch, of course, lies in what is meant by "comparable." At this point, an analogy with paint colours might prove helpful. Assume the following scenario.

There are two pots of paint with unmarked labels. We think both pots have the same colour of paint, but we're not sure. In order to determine if they are the same, we paint two samples—one from each pot of paint—and then compare the colours. After painting the first sample, we are interrupted and are only able to paint the second sample several hours later. Immediately after we finish painting the second sample, we compare its colour with that of the first one and discover that it is significantly darker than the first sample. Are we justified in concluding that the two pots have different colours of paint?

Anyone who has done any painting will know that this isn't a fair comparison because the two samples have not had equal drying times. As paint dries, its colour typically changes slightly, rendering invalid any colour comparisons made with paint that has just been freshly applied. So, in order to properly test whether two paint colours are the same, we need to ensure that their drying times are the same. Drying time, of course, isn't the only factor that affects paint colour. Other factors include the types of paints being compared (e.g., flat, semi-gloss, high gloss), the type and material of the surfaces being painted (e.g., rough vs. smooth), and the colour of the light under which each sample is viewed. Only when one controls for all the factors that can affect how paint colours appear can one say for sure whether or not any two paint samples were painted with the same colour.

---

[5] Earlier literature often referred to these as "pitch accent" languages (e.g., McCawley 1978, Van der Hulst and Smith 1988).

1.2 Tonal contrast

Applying this analogy to tone analysis, in order to determine whether two morphemes have the same underlying tone patterns, the morphemes being compared must be the same in all aspects that can affect how tone is realized in that language.

Consider the following surface contrasts in Chumburung [ncu], a Kwa language spoken in Ghana.[6]

(8) Surface contrasts in Chumburung

$$\begin{bmatrix} - \end{bmatrix}$$ $$\begin{bmatrix} \diagdown \end{bmatrix}$$
   lɔ 'sore, wound'   wʊ 'chew'

Although there is definitely a surface contrast between the pitches in (8), cross-linguistically, contrasts like these do not necessarily translate into underlying contrasts between the two roots in question. This is because 'sore' is a noun and 'chew' is a verb. This might not initially seem like an important consideration when establishing tonal contrast. The fact is, however, that when pronounced in isolation, regardless of their underlying tones, Chumburung nouns with the syllable profile CV are never phonetically realized with anything other than a high level pitch, and verbs with the same syllable profile are never realized with anything other than a low falling pitch. (The term "syllable profile" refers to the number and types of syllables [e.g., CV, CVC, CVN, CVCV] that comprise a root, stem, or word (CVN [N=nasal coda]).[7] This notion is discussed in more detail in chapter 2.) As in many languages, this low falling pitch is the normal realization of a phrase-final low tone. In this particular example set, the roots of both words actually have underlying /H/ tone.[8] Differing constraints on the surface realizations of nouns and verbs in Chumburung when pronounced in isolation therefore render irrelevant any surface comparisons in pitch between them. So clearly, one of the factors that must be taken into account when determining whether two environments are comparable with respect to tone is the grammatical categories of the morphemes that are being compared.

Let us now consider the examples in (9) from Nawuri [naw], another Kwa language spoken in Ghana.

(9) Surface contrasts in Nawuri (personal field notes)

$$\begin{bmatrix} - & - \end{bmatrix}$$ $$\begin{bmatrix} - & \diagdown \end{bmatrix}$$
   ɔ-ka 'wife'   ɔ-d͡ʒaŋ 'thigh'
   C1-wife   C1-thigh

In-depth analysis shows that the underlying tone patterns of these two nouns are the same (viz. a prefix with /H/ followed by a simple stem with /L/). However, there is a surface contrast between the pitches of these words. This is because the stems have different syllable profiles: CV and CVC.

This difference is important because tones link to moras (Hyman 1992), the minimum units of phonological weight, and both nuclei and codas are moraic. For example, while CV stems have

---

[6]The Chumburung data that appear throughout this book were gathered over the years from 1982 to 2016 in the Chumburung village of Ekumdipe, N. R. Ghana. All of the data in chapters 5 and 6 were provided by Isaac Demuyakor, my friend and a mature native speaker of Chumburung who has lived his entire life in the village. Unfortunately, some of the remaining data were transcribed many years ago, and at times from sources I did not note at the time because I was living in the village and often wrote things down later. In order to ensure the validity of such data, I recently verified all of the Chumburung data in this book with Isaac in October 2016.

[7]My thanks to Steve Marlett for suggesting the term "syllable profile" to me.

[8]We discuss these Chumburung data in greater depth in chapter 2.

one mora, CVV and CVC stems each have two. In the case of the words in (9), the high tone of the prefix spreads rightward onto the first tone-bearing unit (hereafter TBU) of the stem. Since the stem of *ó-d͡ʒáŋ* has two tone-bearing units (nucleus and coda), the tones of the stem are realized phonetically as a contour pitch, falling from high to low. This is different from *ó-ká*, which has only one TBU in its CV stem, permitting only the phonetic realization of the high tone. While again the difference between CV and CVC might not seem a priori to be important, cross-linguistically, the presence vs. the absence of a syllable coda often plays a significant role in determining whether the final tone of an underlying sequence is realized phonetically.

The same can also be said with regard to whether the coda is sonorant or not. Look at the examples in (10).

(10) More surface contrasts in Chumburung

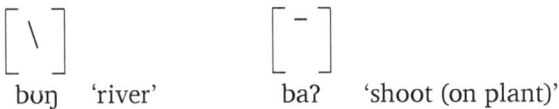

If a syllable ends in a sonorant coda, the second tone of a two-tone sequence is much more likely to be realized phonetically than if the coda is non-sonorant. Despite the obvious contrast in surface pitches in (10), there is no underlying contrast between the two patterns as both are /HL/.

So far we have seen the importance of controlling for grammatical category and syllable profile when establishing tonal contrasts. What additional factors must be taken into consideration, and how one goes about determining the contrasts, is discussed in detail in chapter 2. For now, what is important is that for any given language, the factors that can affect tone in that language must be the same for any pitch contrasts that are being compared. One consequence of this is that it is not necessary to discover "minimal pairs" in order to establish tonal contrast.[9] Tonal minimal pairs are pairs of words that occur in identical environments (usually isolation) and are phonetically identical except for their surface tone patterns (e.g., the Iquito minimal pair *máˈʃiku* 'raft' and *maˈʃíku* 'bird [species]' discussed in chapter 2). As nice as minimal pairs are, all that is really needed in order to establish contrast is for the morphemes being compared to be the same in all aspects that can affect tone.

We next examine a number of examples of contrast in order to demonstrate some of the ways in which contrast can be manifested. In (11), all factors that can affect tone in Chumburung are the same for both words.

(11) Chumburung falling pitches contrasted in isolation forms

The surface pitches in (11) clearly contrast when these words are spoken in isolation. Since the factors that can affect tone are the same in both cases, the difference can only be due to their having different underlying patterns. As will be shown in chapter 5, 'root' has the underlying pattern /HL/, and 'house' has the underlying pattern /L/.

The same can also be said of the Njyem [njy] forms in (12). Njyem is a Bantu A language spoken in eastern Cameroon and Congo (data from Cameroon, courtesy of Keith Beavon, personal communication).

---

[9] See also Snider 2014a for a critical discussion of tone and minimal pairs.

1.2 Tonal contrast

(12) Contrast in monomorphemic nouns in Njyem

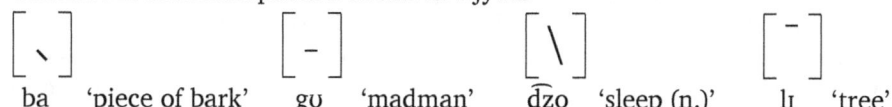

    ba 'piece of bark'   gʊ 'madman'   d͡zo 'sleep (n.)'   lɪ 'tree'

These are all morphologically simple nouns from class 7 (see section 2.1.6 for a discussion of noun and verb classes), which does not take a noun class prefix: all have the syllable profile CV, and all are pronounced in isolation. It is also the case that different consonant and vowel types do not influence tone in Njyem. Thus the environments are the same throughout, and we can conclude that the observable surface differences are due to underlying contrasts.

Tones that contrast underlyingly, however, do not necessarily contrast in all environments. Similar to segmental contrasts, tone contrasts can be neutralized in certain environments. Compare these two Chumburung utterances in which the tone patterns for 'house' and 'root', which contrast in (11), are neutralized when they follow the word 'weaver'.

(13) Neutralization in Chumburung

a. $\begin{bmatrix} - - \ \backslash \end{bmatrix}$ $\begin{bmatrix} \backslash \end{bmatrix}$

   ɔlʊpʊ lɔŋ 'weaver's house'   cf.   lɔŋ 'house'
   weaver house

b. $\begin{bmatrix} - - \ \backslash \end{bmatrix}$ $\begin{bmatrix} \backslash \end{bmatrix}$

   ɔlʊpʊ leŋ 'weaver's root'   cf.   leŋ 'root'
   weaver root

In example (13a), the final high tone of 'weaver' spreads to the following, underlyingly low-toned, syllable lɔŋ 'house', with the result that 'weaver's house' and 'weaver's root' have the same surface pattern. That is, the underlying tonal difference between 'house' and 'root' is neutralized due to phonological conditioning.

It is not only phonological environments, however, that can neutralize underlying tone contrasts. As discussed above, certain grammatical environments can also have neutralizing effects. In these next two Chumburung utterances, the surface pitches for 'go' and 'come' clearly contrast when they follow the first person singular imperfective subject prefix.

(14) Contrast established following 1S Imperfective Subject prefix

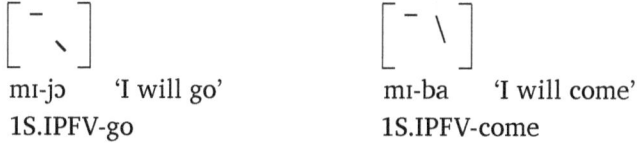

   mɪ-jɔ 'I will go'   mɪ-ba 'I will come'
   1S.IPFV-go   1S.IPFV-come

However, as seen in (15), these contrasts are neutralized in the imperative mood.

(15) Contrast neutralized in imperative mood

$\begin{bmatrix} \backslash \end{bmatrix}$ $\begin{bmatrix} \backslash \end{bmatrix}$

   jɔ 'Go!'   ba 'Come!'

In Chumburung, the imperative mood is the default form for verbs pronounced in isolation, and it imposes a low tone on the first TBU of the verb. This explains why, in the discussion following the examples in (8), verbs with the syllable profile CV are always pronounced with low falling pitch when said in isolation, and it helps to explain why surface pitch contrasts between roots from different word categories (e.g., verbs and nouns) do not necessarily translate into underlying phonological contrasts.

Most tonal contrasts manifest themselves in at least one environment on the host morphemes themselves (e.g., all of those discussed immediately above). In some cases, however, the contrast never manifests itself on the host morphemes, but it is rather displaced onto adjacent morphemes. Compare the words in (16), which are the same in all aspects that can affect tone in Chumburung.

(16) No surface contrast in isolation

    kɪdakaʔ 'box'   kɪsarɪʔ 'arm'

Regardless of which environment these words are spoken in, they always have identical surface pitches. Here are examples of these words in a second environment.

(17) No surface contrast in a second environment

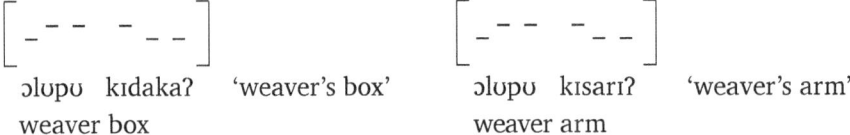

  ɔlʊpʊ kɪdakaʔ 'weaver's box'   ɔlʊpʊ kɪsarɪʔ 'weaver's arm'
  weaver box   weaver arm

Although the surface pitches of *kìdákáʔ* and *kìsáríʔ* are different in this second environment from what they were in the first environment, they are nevertheless still identical. So far, these words would appear to have identical underlying tonal patterns since their surface pitches are always identical. In this next data set, however, *kìdákáʔ* and *kìsáríʔ* have different effects on the tones that follow them, even though they again appear in identical environments and continue to have identical patterns.[10]

(18) Contrast established by effect on following tones

$$\begin{bmatrix} \_ \_ & \_ & \_ \_ \end{bmatrix}$$

  kɪdakaa ma nu fʊrɪ-ʔ 'a box won't hear an antelope'
  box NEG hear antelope-NEG

$$\begin{bmatrix} \_ \_ & \_ & \_ \_ \end{bmatrix}$$

  kɪsarɪɪ ma nu fʊrɪ-ʔ 'an arm won't hear an antelope'
  arm NEG hear antelope-NEG

Since the verb phrase 'won't hear an antelope' is underlyingly the same in each example, the fact that it has different surface realizations in these two utterances means that the

---

[10] When pronounced phrase finally, as in (16) and (17), 'box' and 'arm' end in glottal stops. In the utterances in (18), however, these 'lexical' glottal stops are not realized phonetically, and the final vowel of each word is long when the word is in phrase-medial position. Unrelated to the glottal stops of words like 'box' and 'arm', glottal stops also occur at the end of all negative phrases in Chumburung.

difference must be attributable to whatever differences exist between the underlying tone patterns of kìdáká? and kìsárí?. In this case, unlike kìdáká?, kìsárí? ends in a "floating" low tone that downsteps the high tones that follow it. The concepts of floating tones and downstep are discussed further below. Even though the surface pitches for kìdáká? and kìsárí? are identical in these phrases, they have different underlying tone patterns, and this difference manifests itself on a following high tone.

In summary, if the surface pitches of two morphemes differ from each other in even a single comparable environment, they must have different underlying tones. Also, if two morphemes have different tonal effects on adjacent morphemes, all other things being equal they must have different underlying tones, even if the surface pitches of these two morphemes are always the same. Tonal contrasts between morphemes can be neutralized in certain environments. Sometimes tonal contrast between two morphemes is neutralized: a) in certain phonological environments, b) in certain grammatical environments, or c) everywhere, with the differences only being realized on adjacent morphemes. In order for a language to be considered tonal, it must have morphemes whose pitches contrast (or displace the contrast onto adjacent morphemes) in at least one or more comparable environments.

1.3 Contrastive tone height

At this point in the discussion, we have talked in general terms about how to establish contrast between tone patterns, but we have yet to discuss contrast between different tone heights. Contrastive heights can manifest themselves either as level pitches (e.g., high vs. low) or as contour pitches (e.g., high falling vs. low falling). Since the principles for establishing contrastive height between level pitches are the same as for establishing it between contour pitches, we limit the discussion to that of level pitches, as this is slightly simpler.

If a language is tonal, it must have at least two contrastive pitch heights, one of which will be higher than the other. For the sake of convenience, we will call the higher one "high tone" (H) and the lower one "low tone" (L). Should there be a pitch whose frequency is between the frequencies of the high and low pitches and which contrasts with them phonologically, we will call it "mid tone" (M). Following the principles discussed above for establishing underlying contrast, for any two differing pitch heights to contrast phonologically, they must demonstrate that contrast in comparable environments. In the following example from Kako [kkj], a Bantu language spoken in Cameroon (personal field notes), the two pitches in 'ant', though different, do not demonstrate underlying height contrast because the heights do not contrast in the same environments (i.e., the high pitch is on the first syllable and the low pitch is on the second syllable).

(19) Phonological contrast in height not established in Kako

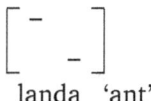

landa 'ant'

As far as this word is concerned, it could be the case that this is a non-tone language in which all syllables in an utterance are pronounced with high pitch except the final one, which is always pronounced with low pitch. It could also be the case that both syllables are underlyingly low, and there is a process of dissimilation whereby an underlying low tone is phonetically realized as high before a following low. In both these scenarios, there is no case for an underlying contrast because the difference between high and low would always be predictable, i.e., it would be induced by the environment. In order to "prove" that low tones contrast with high tones in Kako, we need to see examples like (20) in which both high and low pitch heights are realized in comparable environments (i.e., environments that are the same in all ways that are likely to affect tone, having made sure that the words are not embedded in clauses with different illocutionary force, such as statements or questions).

(20) Phonological contrast in height established in Kako

    kòmbɔ̀   'forest'   kòndɔ́   'skin'

In (20), the second syllable of *kòmbɔ̀* 'forest' demonstrates that Kako can have a low tone following a low tone. By the same token, the second syllable of *kòndɔ́* 'skin', shows us that Kako can also have a high tone following a low tone. In this case, we cannot attribute the lowness of the pitch on the second syllable of *kòmbɔ̀* or the highness of the pitch on the second syllable of *kòndɔ́* to anything other than a difference in the underlying height of each tone because the only other significant difference in the words, the coronal vs. labial place of articulation of the medial consonants, has never been demonstrated to affect tone in any language. So everything that can possibly influence how tones are realized in these two words is the same. Accordingly, we would be justified in claiming that this language has (at least) two contrastive tone heights, high (H) and low (L).

Let us now see what it would take to establish three contrastive levels in a given language. Consider these Chumburung examples.

(21) Non-contrastive phonetic mid height in Chumburung

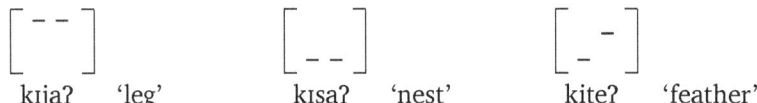

   kɪjaʔ   'leg'   kɪsaʔ   'nest'   kiteʔ   'feather'

Clearly, there are at least three phonetic levels in Chumburung: high, mid, and low. While the overall tonal make-up of each word is distinct (i.e., there are three contrastive tone patterns), evidence for contrast between all three heights is lacking. Contrast is clearly demonstrated between low and high in words like *kɪsaʔ* [_ _] and *kɪjaʔ* [¯ ¯] because the tonal environments are comparable. Contrast is also demonstrated between low and mid in words like *kɪsaʔ* [_ _] and *kiteʔ* [_ -] because, again, the tonal environments are comparable (i.e., the low in the second syllable of 'nest' contrasts with the mid in the second syllable of 'feather'). However, contrast is not demonstrated between high and mid by the second syllables of *kɪjaʔ* [¯ ¯] and *kiteʔ* [_ -] because the first syllables of each word bear different pitches, and this renders the two environments non-comparable. In order to establish three contrastive levels of pitch height in Chumburung, we would need to see examples of words in which low pitch is not only followed by low pitch (e.g., *kɪsaʔ* [_ _]) and by mid pitch (e.g., *kiteʔ* [_ -]), but also by high pitch. But such words do not exist in Chumburung. In the case of *kiteʔ* [_ -], the surface mid pitch is an underlying high tone that is downstepped[11] to the mid level following a low tone, which explains why the sequence of low pitch followed by high pitch does not exist in the language.

By way of contrast, the examples in (22) demonstrate a four-height distinction for level pitches in Bench [bcq], an Afro-Asiatic language spoken in southwestern Ethiopia.

---

[11] "Downstep" is a technical term, discussed further in chapter 2. When a high tone is downstepped, any high tone that immediately follows it is also realized at the lower pitch, and any other tones that immediately follow it are accordingly realized at lower pitches relative to the downstepped high.

1.4 The concept of tone patterns

(22) Four contrastive phonetic heights in Bench (personal field notes)

a. [⁻ ⁻]
   gor sam   'monkey's cabbage'
   monkey cabbage

b. [₋ ⁻]
   dor sam   'sheep's cabbage'
   sheep cabbage

c. [⁻ ⁻]
   ger sam   'hyena's cabbage'
   hyena cabbage

d. [⁻ ⁻]
   kir sam   'large bird of prey (species)'s cabbage'
   bird.of.prey.species cabbage

In these examples, there is a four-way contrast in pitch levels preceding the word for 'cabbage': low in the case of 'monkey', mid in the case of 'sheep', high in the case of 'hyena', and extra high in the case of a certain species of bird of prey. Further, all the factors that are likely to affect tone in this language are the same for these four words: they are from the same word category (nouns), they have the same syllable profile (CVS [S=sonorant coda]), and they occur in the same carrier phrase, or frame[12] ('___'s cabbage'). We therefore conclude that the surface contrasts in pitch height are due to underlying tone height differences and not due to any external factor that can influence tone.

1.4 The concept of tone patterns

When people discuss the subject of tone, one of the first things they often want to know is how many "tones" a language has. For many people, this means how many contrastive level and contour tones one finds on individual syllables. As interesting as that may be, it is more important for analytical purposes to know the number and nature of contrastive tone patterns on morphemes, since, as Hyman and Leben note in their definition of a tone language (see section 1.1), the pitch patterns of tone languages are always lexical. Throughout this book, these contrastive patterns are called tone patterns, regardless of whether the morphemes that sponsor the contrasts consist of whole words, single syllables, or whether they even have segmental content (i.e., whether they consist solely of floating tones).[13]

For many tone languages, the patterns consist of linear strings of anywhere from one to three tones that associate to TBUs in a particular manner (often language specific). This can be illustrated by looking at Mende [men], a Mande language spoken in Sierra Leone, with its five pattern inventory: /H/, /L/, /HL/, /LH/, and /LHL/ (see below). When a morpheme has more than one tone associated with it (e.g., /LH/ in *fande* [₋ ⁻] 'cotton'), these tones often

---

[12] Employment of the term "frame" as it is used in the present work dates back to at least Pike 1948.

[13] The notion that tone is best analyzed from the point of view of the "tone pattern," or melody, finds its roots in the seminal works of Leben 1971, 1973, 1978, and is supported more recently in Odden and Bickmore 2014 and other articles in that volume.

give evidence of being "cohesive." That is, they stay together and simply adapt their association patterns to the number of TBUs (in this case, syllables) available to them.

The following phenomena are better explained if one analyzes tone from the perspective of tone patterns: a) unity of underlying patterns though realized differently with different syllable profiles, b) stability of tone patterns regardless of segmental changes, and c) non-recognition by native speakers of individual tones in a pattern. We discuss each of these in turn.

1.4.1 Unity of underlying patterns though realized differently with different syllable profiles

Consider the following Mende data, adapted from Leben 1978:186.

(23) Five tones on Mende monomorphemic nouns

Tones	CV		CVCV		CVCVCV	
/H/	[¯] kɔ	'war'	[¯ ¯] pɛlɛ	'house'	[¯ ¯ ¯] hawama	'waistline'
/L/	[_] k͡pa	'debt'	[_ _] bɛlɛ	'trousers'	[_ _ _] k͡pakali	'tripod chair'
/F/	[\] m͡bu	'owl'	[¯ _] ngila	'dog'	[¯ _ _] felama	'junction'
/R/	[/] m͡ba	'rice'	[_ ¯] fande	'cotton'	[_ ¯ ¯] ndavula	'sling'
/R-F/	[/\] m͡ba	'companion'	[_ \] nyaha	'woman'	[_ ¯ _] nikili	'groundnut'

In the first data column, there are five contrastive pitch patterns associated with CV morphemes. A classic phonemic analysis of the data in the first column would yield five tones, or tonemes,[14] associated with any given single syllable: H (high), L (low), F (falling), R (rising), and R-F (rising-falling). Looking at the second data column, a classic phonemic analysis of *pɛ́lɛ́* 'house' would yield the tone /H/ followed by a second tone /H/ (i.e., /HH/). Similarly, *nyàhâ* 'woman' would be analyzed as /LF/, a low tone followed by a falling tone. Given this view of tone, in which tone is independently specified for each syllable, one should theoretically find 25 possible contrastive combinations of Mende's five tones on disyllabic forms (5 x 5), and 125 on trisyllabic forms (5 x 5 x 5). The language doesn't take advantage of all these possibilities, however. In fact, for any given syllable profile in the chart (CV, CVCV, or CVCVCV) one finds only five contrastive combinations,[15] with the five tones distributed in an, at best, perplexing manner.

---

[14] The term "toneme" refers to the tonal entity analogous to the segmental "phoneme."

[15] While these five patterns account for the vast majority of words in Mende, Leben also discusses several other patterns which, although rare, are also attested: H'H (Leben's apostrophe indicates downstep), H'H̄L, HLH, HLHL, HH̄L, and LLH. He assumes (1978:188) that "the preponderance of examples that conform to the patterns illustrated...is a result of the historical fact that Mende derives from a protosystem in which the principles...were maintained absolutely." Taking into account this historical perspective, Leben claims (personal communication) that the additional patterns found in these relatively few "aberrant" examples are most certainly concatenations of existing patterns brought together historically in morphologically complex forms.

1.4 The concept of tone patterns

On the other hand, from the perspective of tone patterns associated with morphemes, one can analyze Mende as a two-tone system that employs five contrastive tone patterns: /H/, /L/, /HL/, /LH/, and /LHL/. These five patterns, in turn, associate to TBUs in an insightful manner, as shown in (24).[16]

(24) Five patterns on Mende monomorphemic nouns

	CV	CVCV	CVCVCV
/H/	H │ kɔ 'war'	H ╱╲ pɛlɛ 'house'	H ╱│╲ hawama 'waistline'
/L/	L │ k͡pa 'debt'	L ╱╲ bɛlɛ 'trousers'	L ╱│╲ k͡pakali 'tripod chair'
/HL/	HL ╲╱ m͡bu 'owl'	HL │ │ ŋgila 'dog'	HL │╲ felama 'junction'
/LH/	LH ╲╱ m͡ba 'rice'	LH │ │ fande 'cotton'	LH │╲ ndavula 'sling'
/LHL/	LHL ╲│╱ m͡ba 'companion'	LHL │╲╱ nyaha 'woman'	LHL │ │ │ nikili 'groundnut'

As may be seen in the Mende data above, when the pattern has two tones (/LH/ or /HL/) and there are two or more TBUs available to accommodate the tones, one does not find contour pitches. Contour pitches only occur in Mende when there are not enough TBUs to accommodate all the tones of the pattern. With respect to the patterns /HL/ and /LH/, this is the case in m͡bû 'owl' and m͡bǎ 'rice', which each have two tones but only one TBU. Phonetically, this results in their being realized with high falling and low rising contour pitches, respectively. However, when the pattern in Mende has three tones (/LHL/), one finds contour pitches on all the words with this pattern except nìkílì 'groundnut', which has enough TBUs available so that each tone can be assigned its own TBU. When there are only two TBUs available, however, as in nyàhâ 'woman', the language permits the two rightmost tones to be linked to the rightmost TBU, which phonetically results in a high falling contour pitch on the final syllable. And finally, when there is only one TBU available to accommodate the three tones, as in m͡bã 'companion', only then does the language permit three tones to be linked to a single TBU, with the result that rising-falling contours are only permitted on roots with single syllables. In this respect, Mende is somewhat rare: most languages have constraints against associating multiple tones to single TBUs and typically permit this to happen only in certain circumstances.

---

[16] The representations in (24) demonstrate how the underlying tone patterns, represented within phonemic slashes, are associated in surface forms. Although the precise manner in which tone patterns link to TBUs was originally thought to be universally determined (e.g., Goldsmith 1976; Leben 1973, 1978), the cross-linguistic diversity found in linkage schemes suggests they are instead language-specific and need to be determined by the analyst.

The case for tone patterns based on the distribution of tones across different syllable profiles can be stronger in some languages than in others. In Mende, for example, the case is strong because the language allows up to three tones to be associated to single TBUs, and it also allows roots to be trisyllabic. This rare combination of factors makes Mende an ideal language to promote the case for tone patterns. However, most languages do not permit three tones to be associated to single TBUs, and this coupled with the fact that many languages do not have trisyllabic simple stems,[17] means that most tone languages do not demonstrate the same degree of distributional support for pattern cohesiveness as does Mende. This does not mean, however, that such languages would not profit from an analysis based on tone patterns. Indeed, even if Mende did not have trisyllabic roots, we would still prefer the analysis presented here since one would still need to explain why only 20% of the predicted 25 (5 x 5) possibilities occurs on disyllabic stems.

Njyem differs significantly from Mende in maximally having only disyllabic roots and in permitting no more than two tones to be associated to single TBUs. In this respect, it is more "normal" than Mende. The data in (25) are courtesy of Keith Beavon (personal communication).

(25) Contrastive tone patterns on Njyem Class 7 nouns

	CV	CVC	CVCV
/L/	[ˋ] ba 'piece of bark'	[ˋ] lɛr 'bat's wing'	[‾ˋ] baŋɔ 'dry season'
/H/	[‾] lɪ 'tree'	[‾] t͡ʃim 'cry (n.)'	[‾ ‾] baha 'overhanging rock'
/HL/	[\] d͡zo 'sleep (n.)'	[\] lam 'trap'	[‾ˋ] lima 'dream (n.)'
/LH/	[_] gʊ 'madman'	[_] d͡ʒim 'bad luck'	[_ _] dɪla 'burial'

In (25), one can see that even in the absence of trisyllabic roots, certain facts are easier to explain from the perspective of tone patterns assigned to morphemes than of individual tones assigned to TBUs. For example, while high falling pitches are present on CV and CVC profiles, they are entirely absent on the CVCV profile. This is easily explained, of course, when one recognizes that the high falling pitch is not found on disyllabic forms because disyllabic forms have enough syllables available to carry each individual tone (H or L). Monosyllabic forms, on the other hand, do not have enough syllables to support each tone of the /HL/ pattern. In this case, the problem is resolved by assigning both tones to the same syllable, resulting in a high falling pitch on these monosyllabic forms.

---

[17] Often, cases of purported trisyllabic (or longer) roots turn out, upon investigation, to be morphologically complex. The source of this complexity can be very obscure and is often buried deep in the history of the language. When this is the case, the complexity is often best determined on phonological grounds (e.g., certain phonological processes apply or do not apply across certain morphological boundaries) or on statistical grounds (e.g., a relative paucity of certain syllable profiles compared with more robust ones, suggests that the scarcer profiles are the result of morphological complexity). For further discussion of the use of statistical grounds to determine morphological complexity, see section 2.1.2.

1.4 The concept of tone patterns

As presented, the patterns /L/, /H/, and /HL/ are fairly transparent. The remaining pattern, /LH/, is less so, particularly since there is no evidence for a high tone anywhere in the isolation forms, even in words with the CVCV profile. This is due, however, to a process that spreads low tones rightward within words and delinks high tones, as shown in (26).

(26) Low tone spreading in Njyem

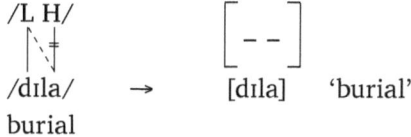
/dɪla/   →   [dɪla]   'burial'
burial

When roots with the pattern /LH/ occur in phrase-final position, the final H is not associated to the final TBU, but instead floats (i.e., it is not realized phonetically). One can think of floating tones as being similar to the *n* in the English word *hymn* (pronounced [hɪm] without the *n*). When one adds the suffix *-al* or *-ology* to it, however, the *n* is pronounced (viz. *hymnal, hymnology*). With regard to the /LH/ pattern of Njyem, the high tone is pronounced when it is followed by the demonstrative *jà:* 'the ___ (in question)', which, coincidentally, also has the underlying pattern /LH/.

(27) /LH/ pattern when followed by demonstrative *jà:*

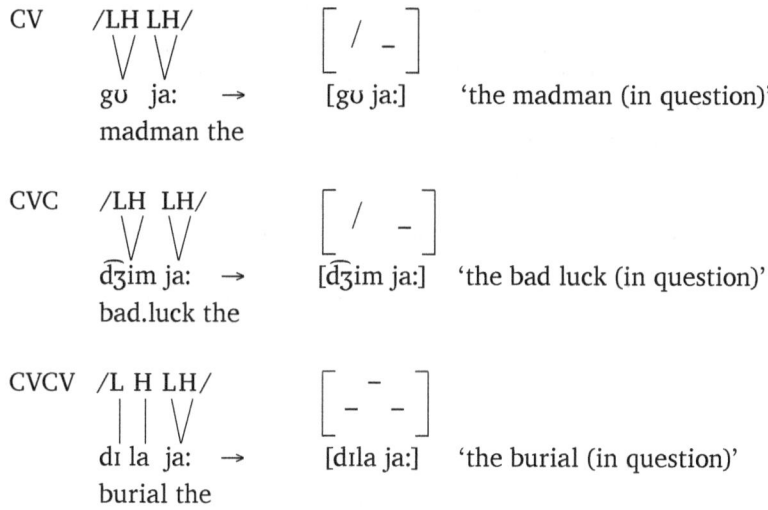

In (27), the high tone of the underlying /LH/ pattern is forced onto the final TBU of the word when it is followed by the low tone of *jà:*. This behaviour may be contrasted with what happens when the underlying /L/ pattern is followed by *jà:*.

(28) /L/ pattern when followed by demonstrative *jà:*

CV   /L LH/
     | \/
    ba ja: →   [ba ja:]   [− −]   'the piece of bark (in question)'
    piece.of.bark the

CVC /L LH/
     | \/
    lɛr ja: →   [lɛr ja:]   [− −]   'the bat's wing (in question)'
    bat's.wing the

CVCV /L LH/
     /\ \/
    baŋɔ ja: →   [baŋɔ ja:] [− − −] 'the dry season (in question)'
    dry.season the

When the pattern /L/ is followed by *jà:*, each TBU of the phrase is realized at the same level low pitch. These data support the assertion made above that the underlying pattern of the nouns in (27) is /LH/.

To conclude this discussion of Njyem, of the sixteen combinations of tones that are theoretically possible on CVCV roots (4 x 4), only four actually occur ([− ˇ], [⁻ ⁻], [⁻ ˇ], and [− −]), and these four readily correspond to the four found on CV and CVC roots. If one does not assume a morpheme pattern approach to tone analysis, distributional facts like these are difficult to explain. Distributional phenomena, however, are only one type of evidence for the existence of tone patterns. We turn now to other types of evidence.

1.4.2 Stability of tone patterns regardless of segmental changes

The fact that the tone patterns of individual morphemes tend to remain stable despite segmental changes also strongly supports the contention that individual tones belong to greater, independent patterns. Despite the addition or loss of segmental tone-bearing units, tone patterns typically remain intact and simply re-associate to different TBUs as needed.

Yip (2002:67) describes a "secret" language based on Thai [tha] whereby the rhymes of the first and second syllables of normal Thai words are interchanged.

(29) Tone stability in Thai secret language

Normal Thai		Secret Thai	
Tone linkage	Phonetic form	Tone linkage	Phonetic form
HL LH || || kluay hɔɔm	[\ /] [kluay hɔɔm] >	HL LH || || klɔɔm huay	[\ /] [klɔɔm huay] 'banana'
HL M || /\ tenram	[\ −] [tenram] >	HL M || /\ tamren	[\ −] [tamren] 'dance'

In these examples, the normal Thai tone pattern for *klúày hɔ̌ɔ́m* 'banana' is [HL LH]. Despite the swapping of the rhymes of the two syllables when creating the secret Thai version, the

1.4 The concept of tone patterns

tone pattern remains unchanged (viz. *klɔ́ɔ̀m hùáy*). The same situation holds for *téǹrām* (normal Thai) and *támrēn* (secret Thai) 'dance'.

A similar case is often found in the creation of contour pitches. Chen (2000:38) provides an example of this from Cantonese [yue].

(30) Tone stability in Cantonese resulting in contour pitch

```
    M H M              M H M
    / | \              \ | |
  /si yat si/    →    si  si         'give it a try'
  try one try          [  ̌   ̄ ]
```

In (30), despite the ellipsis of *yát*, its underlying high tone remains and "relocates" to the preceding syllable, where it joins with the underlying mid tone of *sī* to create a mid-high rising pitch.

A third case for tone pattern stability comes from the phenomenon of floating tones. Floating tones are often produced when a tone loses its segmental TBU. This can be due to tone spreading and delinking, or to synchronic or diachronic loss of a segmental TBU. The following is an example from Nawuri (personal field notes) of a floating low tone that results from the spreading of a preceding high tone and the consequent delinking of the original low from its TBU.

(31) Tone stability in Nawuri resulting in floating low tone

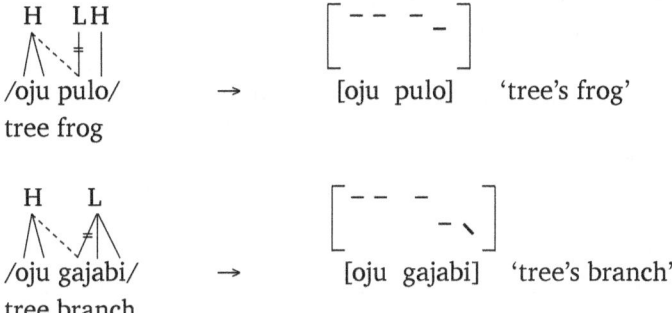

In the first example, the underlying high tone of *jú* has spread rightward and delinked the underlying low tone of *pù*. Rather than being deleted, the low tone remains floating, as evidenced by its lowering effect on the following high tone. Further support for this can be found in the second example, *ójú gájàbì*, in which the high tone of *jú* has spread rightward across the word boundary and delinked the low tone from the first TBU of *gàjàbì*. It is important to note in each example that the underlying pattern of the phrase itself remains unchanged; only the associations with TBUs have changed.

In each of the Thai, Cantonese, and Nawuri examples just discussed, despite changes to the association relationships between the tones and TBUs, both the underlying tones themselves and their underlying linear order remain intact because there is cohesion between the tones on an independent tier. Interestingly, it is precisely the cohesive, melodic nature of tone that historically gave rise to the notion that tones largely operate independently of segments, and it is this notion, in turn, that led to the development of the theory of Autosegmental Phonology. As the word "autosegmental" (autonomous segments) implies, this theory assumes a certain independence of tone from segments. Ironically, while most tone analysts employ autosegmental theory to good advantage, many nevertheless remain relatively ignorant of the insights that may be gained by analyzing tone from the morpheme pattern perspective. This results in many analyses being based on the tone contrasts of TBUs rather than the pattern contrasts of morphemes.

1.4.3 Non-recognition by native speakers of individual tones in a pattern

When native speakers of tone languages hear a long word or short phrase, they typically have no problem extracting the pitch from the segments, and they can typically hum or whistle the pattern of the utterance with little or no thought. On the other hand, it seems much harder for them to identify the pitch of a specific syllable in such an utterance. Even after speakers are made aware of the different pitch heights in their language, they are usually unable to discern which pitch is associated with which syllable or TBU. If pushed, they will normally count or tap out each syllable as it is whistled or hummed until they arrive at the correct one. By way of contrast, if one asks the same native speakers to identify a particular consonant in the chosen syllable, there is normally little or no hesitancy in identifying it. Why this difference? Why is it more difficult for native speakers to identify individual tones than to identify individual consonants or vowels? The reason is that it is the tone pattern of the morpheme that is relevant to the native speaker, not the individual pitches on syllables.

In cases where native speakers of languages give strong evidence of associating tone patterns with syllables (e.g. Quiaviní Zapotec [zab], an Eastern Otomanguean language of Mexico [Chávez-Peón 2010]), in reality many are still associating the patterns with morphemes because the morphemes themselves are mainly monosyllabic in these languages.

Taken together, the manner in which tones are distributed over morphemes, the stability of tones despite the addition or loss of segments, the maintenance of the linear order of tones despite significant segmental changes, and the fact that native speakers can more easily identify patterns than individual tones in utterances, all argue strongly for identifying contrastive patterns on morphemes as opposed to contrastive tones on TBUs.

Many tone languages have tone patterns of the type described above (i.e., linear strings of cohesive tones). In others, however, the patterns may consist of various combinations of single tone heights and/or contour tones of various sorts whose beginning and/or end points are not necessarily associated with particular contrastive heights. For example, Michaud (2004), Brunelle (2009), and Brunelle et al. (2010) claim that Northern Vietnamese [vie] has one level, relatively high pitch and five contour pitches that do not match well with standard heights like low, mid, and high. For other languages, the patterns might consist of a single tone height (high or low) that contrasts with its absence in various arrangements on different tone-bearing units. A case in point is Haya [hay], a Bantu language spoken in Tanzania (Hyman and Byarushengo 1984). Regardless of whether the tones of a language are similar to those of Mende, or Vietnamese, or Haya, a more insightful picture is likely to emerge if it is the contrastive morpheme pattern that is in focus, rather than the tones associated with TBUs.

The primary object of tone analysis in any language, therefore, is to discover the different underlying tone patterns that are potentially possible for each category of morphemes (e.g., verb roots, noun roots, subject markers) together with the different surface patterns with which they are realized in different contexts. A secondary goal is to explain the different surface realizations of these underlying patterns.

Recall that for any given category of morphemes, the complete set of contrastive patterns is unlikely to be revealed in any single context. While some contexts (e.g., isolation) may reveal some, or occasionally none, of the contrasts, others (e.g., preceding or following another word) may reveal additional contrasts. For any given category of morphemes, one must therefore gather information gleaned from as wide a range of morphosyntactic contexts as possible before one can establish the definitive set of underlying patterns.

Given this view of tone, the layman's question of how many tones a language has (i.e., how many different pitch realizations one finds associated with single TBUs) is little more than trivia. More important questions concern how many underlying patterns there are associated with morphemes, and how these patterns are phonetically realized on the different syllable profiles of the language.

1.5 Data collection

With the objectives just mentioned in mind, i.e., description and explanation, what kinds of data should be collected? One of the best ways to begin is to work with a word list. How long this list needs to be, of course, ultimately depends on how many different underlying tone patterns the language has and how many factors for which one needs to control in the analysis. For example, if all the morphemes in a particular language were assigned to one or other of only two underlying patterns, one wouldn't need as many words to discover those patterns as one would need if the pattern inventory were greater (e.g., five, as in Mende). Similarly, if all the syllable profiles in the language were the same (e.g., CV), and if the morphology of words was relatively simple (e.g., no prefixes or suffixes), the number of words needed would also be relatively small. Since one doesn't necessarily know in advance exactly how complicated any given tone system is going to be, a good beginning can usually be made with a word list of at least 1,000 words. This should allow for all of the patterns of the language to be revealed. Later, one will need to elicit the different morphemes that are discovered in different contexts (e.g., nouns should be examined in singular and plural forms, in subject and object positions, etc., and verbs should be examined in different tense/aspects, persons, nominalized forms, etc.).

1.5.1 Elicited vs. "natural" language data

Some linguists oppose the notion of using elicited data for phonological analysis on ideological grounds, preferring instead to analyze only data they have heard or recorded from natural speech situations. As admirable as this may sound, it is not only unnecessary, but it also has certain drawbacks. As has already been made clear, good phonological analysis depends on hearing a given morpheme in as many as possible of the phonological and grammatical environments in which it can occur. If linguists restrict themselves to analyzing only "natural" speech, there are likely to be serious holes in the paradigms constructed as some critical data may never occur in the linguist's hearing. Native speakers say words and phrases in isolation all the time in natural speech, and asking to have something said or repeated so that you can write it down does not necessarily destroy the naturalness of the pronunciation. By the same token, if linguists restrict themselves to analyzing only elicited data, they are likely to be unaware of certain words and constructions in the language that they would not think to elicit. Both methods of gathering data are therefore needed.

In order to elicit a sound in all of its possible phonological contexts, it may occasionally be necessary to put two words together that would normally not occur together in natural speech (e.g., 'hut's mushroom'). Is it acceptable to base one's phonological analysis on such semantically "odd" data? The answer is "yes," provided the construction is a) structurally well formed and b) productive; i.e., native speakers regularly use this construction to create novel forms.

The first criterion (construction is structurally well formed) may be demonstrated by the possessive construction in Chumburung. In this language, possession is normally indicated simply by placing two nouns in juxtaposition: the possessor in N1 position, and the thing possessed in N2 position. For instance, to say 'Afiya's box', one says 'Afiya' followed by 'box'. Indicating possession in kinship relationships, however, is done differently. To say 'Afiya's grandchild', one does not say 'Afiya grandchild' as might be expected, but instead, 'Afiya, her grandchild'. Other languages, like Abun [kgr] (Berry and Berry 1999), a language isolate spoken in northwestern Papua,[18] make similar distinctions with regard to the possession of alienable vs. inalienable body parts. For languages like these, it is not acceptable to ask a language consultant to say these two constructions the same way. So, while it would be wrong to elicit

---

[18] Although Abun was classified in Berry and Berry 1999 as West Papuan, it is now considered to be a language isolate (www.ethnologue.com/language/kgr).

Chumburung data in which 'Afiya's grandchild' consisted of two nouns placed in juxtaposition, it would not be wrong to elicit data like 'Afiya's box' and 'stone's box' in this manner. Although one might be hard pressed to ever hear utterances like 'stone's box' in natural speech, one can nevertheless envisage a world in which such a relationship is possible and then talk about it. Indeed, the folk stories of many societies are rife with examples of animals and even inanimate objects such as stones that take on human qualities. If utterances like 'stone's box' are syntactically well formed, native speakers can pronounce them just as easily and naturally as native speakers of English can pronounce their semantic equivalents in English.

The second criterion (construction is productive) may be demonstrated by compound forms in English. Although a compound word like *matchstick* is grammatical and conjures up the same meaning in the minds of all native speakers (i.e., a small stick with sulphur on the end used for igniting fires), compounding is not totally productive in English. For example, one cannot, in turn, create novel forms like **stonestick* that mean the same thing to all native speakers of English. By way of contrast, the possessive construction in English and many other languages is productive. One can make a possessor-possessee construction out of almost any two nouns. While forms like 'leopard's axe' and 'stone's beard' might be semantically odd, native speakers can at least generally agree on what they mean (i.e., noun 1 possesses noun 2/noun 1 is regularly associated with noun 2, etc.). No doubt there is a limit to how semantically weird elicited expressions can be, particularly when working with a language consultant for the first time, but patience and explanations as to what one is trying to accomplish go a long way towards overcoming these types of problems. So, as long as elicited data belong to constructions that are both structurally well formed and productive, they can be extremely helpful in phonological analysis.

1.5.2 Conventions for transcribing pitch data

Linguists have used a number of different conventions for transcribing pitch. These include: a) the "Chao" system, based on work by Chao (1930) and primarily favoured by Asianists, b) the "Pike" system, described in Pike 1948:96 and primarily favoured by early Mesoamericanists, although more recently it seems to be falling out of use, c) the diacritic system, primarily favoured by Africanists but used by others as well, and d) the "bar" system, often used by Africanists and employed considerably in this volume. I describe each in turn.

The Chao system appears in (32) and is illustrated in (33).

(32) Chao system (International Phonetic Association 2005)

˥	Extra high	˄	Rising
˦	High	˅	Falling
˧	Mid	ˈ	High rising
˨	Low	ˌ	Low rising
˩	Extra low	˄	Rising-falling

1.5 Data collection

(33) Chao system illustrated[19]

    ba˥ba˥˩   Extra high followed by Falling

A numeric version of the Chao system, preferred by some linguists, appears in (34).

(34) Numeric Chao system

55	Extra high	15	Rising
44	High	51	Falling
33	Mid	45	High rising
22	Low	23	Low rising
11	Extra low	353	Rising-falling

(35) Numeric Chao system illustrated

    ba^{55}ba^{51} Extra high followed by Falling

The Pike system is similar to the Chao numeric system, but the numbers are reversed, with the highest pitch designated 1 and the lowest pitch designated with whichever number corresponds to the number of pitch levels there are in the language. Level pitches are usually indicated by a single digit and contour pitches by two digits separated by a hyphen. These are illustrated in (36).

(36) Pike system illustrated

    ba^{1}ba$^{1-5}$ High level followed by Falling

The diacritic system, in (37), consists of several accent marks that appear as diacritics above vowels and tone-bearing consonants.

(37) Diacritic system (International Phonetic Association 2005)

ȅ	Extra high	ě	Rising
é	High	ê	Falling
ē	Mid	᷇e	High rising
è	Low	᷅e	Low rising
ȅ	Extra low	ê̌	Rising-falling
ꜜé	Downstepped high	ꜛé	Upstepped high

Finally, the reader is by now familiar with the bar system used extensively in the present work. This system employs level bars at various heights to represent corresponding level pitches, as in the Bimoba [bim] example in (38). Bimoba is a Gur language spoken in Ghana (data from personal field notes).

(38) Examples of bar system

    g͡batuk gori g͡batuk   'bushbaby[20] is looking at bushbaby'
    bushbaby look bushbaby

---

[19] In examples (33), (35), and (36), the segments *baba* have no meaning and are only used as dummy syllables to help demonstrate how the different tone-marking schemas are employed.

[20] Bushbabies, also called "galagos," are small nocturnal primates native to Africa.

In addition to level pitches, most if not all tone languages also employ contour pitches. Using the bar system, one represents a falling pitch with a bar that slopes downward from left to right (viz. [\]). Similarly, a rising pitch is represented with a bar that slopes upward from left to right (viz. [/]). In (39a), a rising pitch is illustrated with the first syllable, and in (39b), two types of falling pitches are illustrated. The first falls from a level that is lower than the preceding level pitch to a lower level still, and the second falls from the height of the preceding level pitch to a lower level.

(39) a. Representing a rising contour pitch in Bimoba

$$\begin{bmatrix} / & & \\ & - - & - - \end{bmatrix}$$

took gori g͡batuk   'colleague is looking at bushbaby'
colleague look bushbaby

b. Representing falling contour pitches in Chumburung

$$\begin{bmatrix} - & \\ & \diagdown \end{bmatrix} \qquad \begin{bmatrix} - & \\ & \diagdown \end{bmatrix}$$

mɪ jɔ   'I will go'   mɪ ba   'I will come'
1S.IPFV go   1S.IPFV come

While each system has its place, all are not applicable to every language in every situation. We first look at the International Phonetic Association's (IPA) 2005 endorsement of the tone diacritics in (37). There are two problems inherent in the diacritic notation. The first, as discussed at the beginning of this chapter, is that both pitch and tone are relative. This means that before one can definitively transcribe any given pitch, its status relative to other pitches in the utterance must be determined through analysis. This, of course, is very different from transcribing segments where an accurate transcription of one segment does not depend upon its relationship to other segments in the utterance.

The second (related) problem is the IPA principle that all sounds included in the International Phonetic Alphabet (also IPA, but distinguishable from the association by usage) must be contrastive in at least some language. The IPA is quite correct to recognize no more than five phonemically contrastive levels in any given language. However, one can, in principle, generate an infinite number of levels in many languages due to the register changing phenomena of downstep and upstep, although in practice one normally doesn't find more than eight or nine levels. The correct way to represent tones that have undergone downstep or upstep is to insert the down or up arrows that are included with the other diacritics. The problem is that without first analyzing the tone system, it is often not possible to know whether a particular level is phonologically contrastive or is the result of some register-changing phenomenon. This is because phonologically contrastive levels and phonologically generated levels often sound identical, as demonstrated in the following scenario.

The Chumburung word kɔtɔ 'crab' (cf. section 2.1.2) is pronounced with a level pitch on the first syllable and a lower level pitch on the second. How should it be transcribed? If we use the IPA diacritic system, the utterance as heard could, in principle, be transcribed in any of the following ways:

(40) Different possible representations of kɔtɔ 'crab' in Chumburung
 a) high tone followed by mid tone (kɔ́tɔ̄)
 b) high tone followed by downstepped high tone (kɔ́ˈtɔ́)
 c) high tone followed by low tone (kɔ́tɔ̀)
 d) mid tone followed by low tone (kɔ̄tɔ̀)
 e) low tone followed by downstepped low tone (kɔ̀ˈtɔ̀)

1.5 Data collection 25

At this point, if we wish to use the IPA diacritics, we have a "Catch-22" situation: We cannot properly transcribe Chumburung data without first analyzing the tone system, but we also cannot analyze the tone system without first properly transcribing the data. Clearly, this is not the best system to use when beginning tone analysis, despite its endorsement by the IPA. On the other hand, after the data have been analyzed, it is possible to accurately transcribe any phonetic tone data in the world, including *kɔtɔ*, which is properly transcribed *kɔ́'tɔ́*. The purpose of this discussion is not to denigrate the IPA system, but rather to help show that each transcription system has its strengths and weaknesses. In order to transcribe pitch in a manner that is most helpful for beginning tone analysis, one needs to recognize that transcribing pitch is inherently different from transcribing segments because pitch is relative. As a result, it is necessary to suspend the notion that every symbol used in pitch transcription must be contrastive in at least some language.

When beginning the analysis of a tone language, it is more helpful to use a system that allows one to state what one does know, without being forced to decide about what one doesn't or can't know. In the case of *kɔ́'tɔ́*, presented in (40), all one really knows initially is that both pitches are level and that the second one is lower than the first. There are three systems in common usage that allow one to indicate relative pitch like this: the Chao system, presented above and also endorsed by the IPA, the Pike system, and the bar system.

The Chao system, which grew out of work on Asian languages, allows one to represent up to five different level pitch heights. This system is therefore well-suited to transcribing data for Asian and other languages that do not have cumulative register-changing phenomena like downstep and upstep. By the same token, it does not have enough levels for languages with such register phenomena. The Pike system, not endorsed by the IPA, has no limits on the number of levels employed, and in this respect is not different from the bar system.

The present work makes extensive use of the bar system. As well as not being restricted by the number of level pitches it can represent, the bar system has the advantage of being relatively iconic, while still being able to represent pitch in all languages. One serious disadvantage of using it, however, is that it is difficult to properly represent single transcriptions without taking up two or more lines of text, as seen in the examples above. This can often be overcome to some degree by placing the pitch information in-line, like this: *kɔtɔ* [¯ ¯]; but this is not always ideal. In my own work, I primarily use the bar system during the initial stages of tone analysis. Then when writing, I tend to use it only when doing so helps demonstrate relative heights. The remainder of the time, I prefer to use diacritics, which are also applicable to all languages (once one has analyzed the data).

1.5.3 Transcribing pitch accurately

Transcribing pitch is one thing, but transcribing it accurately can be quite another. In order to transcribe pitch accurately, it is necessary to be able to "hear" pitch, that is, to be able to mentally extract it from the rest of the speech signal. This is admittedly difficult for beginning linguists and this difficulty has given rise to a number of common fallacies. For example, students sometimes say they are "tone deaf" and therefore unable to transcribe pitch accurately. While such students might be musically challenged, it is not the case that they do not hear pitch differences well enough to transcribe them accurately. Unless they are physically hearing-impaired, most people are fully capable of recognizing the subtle semantic nuances in their own language that are communicated through intonation patterns. They are normally also fully capable of producing those same subtle differences in their own speech. What they might lack, though, is the ability to isolate pitch differences from other elements of the speech signal. This is a problem that faces everyone to one extent or another, and it is something that most people can be trained to overcome.

Another common fallacy, at least amongst many language development workers, is the belief that native speakers of tone languages have an inherent ability to transcribe pitch accurately and can be relied on to provide accurate transcriptions. While native speakers of tone languages can usually accurately whistle or hum the patterns of spoken utterances, my own observations in this regard clearly suggest that they are no better at actually transcribing pitch (even in their own mother tongues) than are speakers of intonation languages like English. Everyone has to learn how to do it.

A final common fallacy is the belief that if one is having difficulty transcribing pitch accurately, one can overcome this by employing acoustic software such as Praat or Speech Analyzer. While novices who are unable to determine whether the pitch is going up or down could probably have such a question answered with instrumental help, in general, those who attempt to use it because they are not sure if they are hearing pitch correctly will usually not find it particularly helpful. This is because pitch traces typically reveal a lot of information that one normally does not consciously hear and that is irrelevant to the concerns of beginning analysts. Such beginners usually do not possess the skill and experience to know which information is likely to be relevant and which to ignore. My experience suggests that if someone is too inexperienced to hear pitch and transcribe it accurately, such a person is probably also too inexperienced to accurately interpret the output of acoustic software. Thus, learning to transcribe pitch accurately by ear should come before the use of acoustic instrumental analysis.

For any given pitch level, there is a range of phonetic heights that native speakers accept as being "the same." One therefore wants to transcribe all pitches the same that native speakers consider the same, and to transcribe differently all pitches that native speakers consider different. In order to ensure that this happens, Hyman (2014) encourages investigators to group together those words that they think have the same tone pattern and then ask the language consultant to repeat them one after the other. Any words that should be transcribed differently from the others will usually be pronounced differently, and those differences will be easier to discern when they are pronounced in contrast.

Hyper-correctivity (i.e., transcribing utterances as different that a native speaker judges the same) is therefore not helpful. And of course, at the other end of the spectrum, hypo-correctivity (i.e., transcribing utterances the same that a native speaker judges as different) is also not helpful. In the end, whether native speakers consider two pitches to be the same or different really depends on whether they contrast phonologically in the same environments, and this will come out as one works through the methodology advocated in chapter 2. Would-be tone analysts should therefore not let fears of making phonetic transcription errors keep them from tackling tone analysis. Everyone makes mistakes, and sooner or later these will be revealed.

One problem inherent with native speakers of English is the tendency to associate high pitch with stressed syllables, since high pitch is one of the acoustic correlates of stress in English. My personal experiences in this regard suggest that in any given language, the louder the stressed syllables are in relation to their non-stressed counterparts, the more difficult it is to distinguish high pitch from stress. This problem can largely be overcome by working on transcription exercises that include a mix of different known pitch levels associated with known stressed and unstressed syllables. For example, exercises designed to help students differentiate words like *báˈbá* from *báˈbà* can be very helpful in overcoming this problem.

When learning to transcribe pitch, many linguists find it helpful to have a language consultant whistle or hum the pitch of an utterance under investigation. This has the obvious advantage of abstracting pitch from segments and other elements of the speech signal (e.g., stressed syllables signalled by loudness), thereby making it easier to discern. It also has the advantage of helping to reveal which phonetic differences are relevant to native speakers and which are not. For example, if native speakers don't whistle certain contours that appear in instrumental

1.5 Data collection

pitch traces, it is probably also the case that they are not consciously aware of them and they are therefore irrelevant to the beginning analyst. Simply put, what native speakers whistle or hum is normally what beginning phonologists should transcribe. Many linguists, myself included, also find that whistling or humming the pitch patterns themselves helps them to abstract the pitch from spoken speech.

As helpful as whistled utterances can be, one pitfall to avoid concerns transcribing certain quick-falling contours heard in certain environments. Whistling a high level pitch followed by a much lower level pitch can be physically difficult for some people, and it sometimes results in an unintended falling transitory pitch between the two levels. If this proves to be a problem, having such utterances hummed might be more practical. Another problem that sometimes arises is that a language consultant may not be able to whistle for any one of a number of reasons. In some cultures, for example, women aren't allowed to whistle, while in other cultures, people aren't allowed to whistle in certain places (e.g., near religious shrines), and in still others, some people are just not in the habit of whistling and so do not know how to do it well enough to whistle accurately. Again, when whistling is not the best option, humming is often a good substitute.

Even when one is able to extract pitch from the rest of the speech signal, there are certain types of utterances that are still difficult to transcribe correctly. One is longer utterances. A technique that I have sometimes found helpful in such cases is to play the utterance, using an audio application that allows one to select and play all or any portion of the utterance. It can be very helpful to play only two syllables at a time, with a view to hearing what pitch differences, if any, exist between the two syllables played. After playing and comparing syllables 1 and 2, I then play and compare syllables 2 and 3, and then 3 and 4, and so on. Focussing on just two syllables at a time allows one to more easily hear the relative pitches, without being distracted by the remainder of the utterance. In addition, always overlapping the first syllable of each new couplet with the second syllable of the previous one helps to ensure that the pitch height of each syllable is compared in relation to that of the preceding syllable.

A second type of utterance that is difficult to transcribe correctly is one that consists of a single syllable, since there are no other syllables adjacent with which to compare its relative pitch height. For example, when hearing a single syllable (or even two or more) pronounced with a constant pitch, one sometimes doesn't know how high or low to transcribe the pitch. For situations like this, experienced linguists often employ a limited frame that is diagnostic. For example, in Chumburung, when I am trying to determine the height of, say, a level, single-pitch noun, I ask the native speaker to say the Chumburung translation of 'his/her ___'. In this case, I know that the word for 'his/her' is mì, always pronounced with a low pitch in phrase-initial position. If the word that follows is pronounced at the same low pitch level, I know it is a low pitch, and if it is pronounced with a higher pitch, I know that it is a high pitch.

Hearing and transcribing pitch accurately is something that everyone who investigates tone languages needs to be able to do. It is important, and it is possible.

From the earlier discussion of what constitutes contrast, it should be clear that in order to carry out tone analysis in a manner that properly reveals the underlying pattern and tone height contrasts in the language, it is important to ensure that the morphemes being compared are truly comparable. In view of this, chapter 2 provides a methodology for ensuring that the tonal contrasts one discovers occur in truly comparable grammatical and phonological environments.

There are two aspects to linguistic analysis—discovering linguistic patterns and explaining them—and both are important. The discovery and documentation of linguistic patterns and phenomena are, of course, prerequisite to their being explained. Due to limitations of space, the present work is limited primarily to teaching one how to discover the tonal contrasts in a language, together with the phonological alternations that tones undergo in different phonological and grammatical contexts.

2
Methodology for Phonological Analysis of Tone

In many respects, the contents of this chapter form the heart of this book. While theoretically the fundamentals of tone analysis are the same as those of segmental analysis, in practice they can seem to be quite different. One reason for this is, quite simply, that pitch is relative. While the phonetic correlates of any given segmental phone are confined to a fixed range of values, the phonetic correlates of any given tone are not so confined. For example, when one hears a segmental sound that is accurately transcribed as [b], the next time one hears that same sound, it should be transcribed in the same way. With respect to tone analysis, the case is often different. A syllable pronounced at 128 Hz might be accurately transcribed as low for one word, but as mid for another word. In this respect then, tone analysis is different from segmental analysis. Given this "slippery" nature of tone, it is important to employ a methodology that is not only rigorous, but that also takes into consideration the relative nature of pitch.

We begin with a brief summary of chapter 1. The object of tone analysis is two-fold: a) to discover the different underlying tone patterns (i.e., combinations of tones) that are potentially possible for any given morpheme, and b) to discover and explain the different ways in which those patterns link to TBUs and are realized phonetically in the various contexts in which they are found. This is best achieved by first observing contrasts in the pitch of different morphemes as they are pronounced in words that are spoken in isolation. Later, one needs to investigate any differences in pitch that emerge when those same morphemes are pronounced in different environments. In order to determine whether the underlying patterns of any two morphemes are the same or different, the morphemes need to: a) be comparable with respect to any factors that can affect tone, and b) be compared in identical phonological environments. In other words, all the factors that can influence how tones are realized phonetically must be the same for both morphemes (and for both environments) when they are compared. Accordingly, if any two morphemes are truly comparable in these respects, then any phonetic differences in pitch that emerge when they are compared will be due to differences in their underlying tone patterns and not due to any differences induced by their respective environments.

Compare the Chumburung examples in (1) and (2), repeated from chapter 1, which show two surface patterns that sound the same in isolation, but which are actually different underlyingly.

(1) Two patterns that sound the same but are different underlyingly

$$\begin{bmatrix} - \ - \ - \end{bmatrix}$$
kɪdaka? 'box'

$$\begin{bmatrix} - \ - \ - \end{bmatrix}$$
kɪsarɪ? 'arm'

(2) Contrast established by effect on following tones

$$\begin{bmatrix} - \ - \ - \ - \ - \ - \ - \end{bmatrix}$$
kɪdakaa ma nu fʊrɪ?   'a box won't hear an antelope'
box NEG hear antelope

$$\begin{bmatrix} - \ - \ - \ - \ - \ - \ - \end{bmatrix}$$
kɪsarɪɪ ma nu fʊrɪ?   'an arm won't hear an antelope'
arm NEG hear antelope

As described in chapter 1, it is only when these two words are compared in all relevant environments that the underlying contrast emerges. Next compare the Chumburung examples in (3) and (4), in which two surface patterns that sound different in isolation are actually the same underlyingly.

(3) Two patterns that sound different, but are underlyingly the same

$$\begin{bmatrix} - \ ^- \ \backslash \end{bmatrix}$$
kɪ-dabɔŋ 'cheek'
C3-cheek

$$\begin{bmatrix} - \ - \ - \end{bmatrix}$$
kɪ-sarɪ? 'arm'
C3-arm

(4) Lack of contrast in identical environments

$$\begin{bmatrix} - \ - \ - \ - \ - \ - \ - \end{bmatrix}$$
kɪdabɔŋ ma nu fʊrɪ?   'a cheek won't hear an antelope'
cheek NEG hear antelope

$$\begin{bmatrix} - \ - \ - \ - \ - \ - \ - \end{bmatrix}$$
kɪsarɪɪ ma nu fʊrɪ?   'an arm won't hear an antelope'
arm NEG hear antelope

The surface patterns of *kìdábɔ̂ŋ* 'cheek' and *kìsárí?* 'arm' do not sound the same in isolation, so the beginning analyst may be forgiven for concluding that their underlying patterns are different. But this would be premature. Despite the fact that the stem syllable profiles of both words appear to be the same (viz. CVCVC), one really cannot conclude from their isolation patterns that they have different underlying patterns: their syllable profiles differ in at least one important way that can affect how tone is realized phonetically—the final consonants of the two profiles are sonorant and non-sonorant, respectively. In actual fact, both words have identical underlying patterns, a fact that is supported by comparing the two utterances in (4): the prefixes of both words are low-toned, and the underlying patterns of both stems are /HL/.

When conducting tone analysis, it is therefore important that all of the factors that can affect tone phonologically be the same for all of the words being compared. When these factors are controlled for (i.e., kept the same), any tonal differences that the comparison reveals will be due to differences in the underlying tone patterns of the morphemes themselves and not due to any differences induced by non-tonal factors. By the same token, any factors that are known to only affect pitch phonetically and not phonologically (e.g., vowel height) can safely be ignored unless one is carrying out an acoustic phonetic study.

2.1 Setting up a database

In order to quickly retrieve comparable data for tone analysis, it is helpful to enter one's data into a linguistic database. A database that is set up with a view to analyzing tone should include all the fields of (5) and those that are necessary in (6), each of which can be used to filter out data that are not comparable.

(5) Database fields necessary for filtering data for tone analysis in all languages
   a) grammatical category (noun, verb, etc.);
   b) stem type (simple, complex, compound, borrowed, or ideophonic);
   c) syllable profile of stem (CV, CVC, CVN, etc.);
   d) surface tone patterns of the word in isolation and in different contexts. Each new context will require a separate field in the database; and
   e) underlying tone pattern. This field will only be filled in as the information is revealed throughout the analysis.

(6) Database fields necessary for some languages
   a) noun class of noun and/or verb class of verb (if the language family is known to have a morphological class system);
   b) consonant type(s) (if the language family is known to have consonant-tone interaction);
   c) phonation types of vowels (if phonation types of vowels are known to interact with tone in the language family);
   d) syllable stress pattern of word (if stress-tone interaction is known or suspected to occur in the language family).

We discuss each of these in turn, beginning with those fields that are necessary for analyzing tone in all languages.

2.1.1 Grammatical word category

Regardless of what aspect of a language one is analyzing, any linguistic database needs to be able to filter words according to grammatical category (e.g., nouns, verbs, adjectives). There are two reasons why this is important in tone analysis.

(7) Reasons to filter tone data according to grammatical category
   a. Words that belong to different grammatical categories often have different phonotactic constraints when they are pronounced in isolation.
   b. Words from different grammatical categories do not occur in identical environments.

We look at each of these, beginning with how words that belong to different grammatical categories can have different phonotactic constraints that compromise the integrity of surface tonal contrasts between them.

Consider these apparent minimal pairs in Chumburung.

(8) Nouns compared with verbs in Chumburung

Nouns		Verbs	
$\begin{bmatrix} - \end{bmatrix}$		$\begin{bmatrix} \diagdown \end{bmatrix}$	
k͡pa	'path'	k͡pa	'want'
ɲi	'mother'	ɲi	'know'
fe	'rope'	fe	'sell'

At first glance, the tone of each noun (high level pitch in isolation) appears to contrast minimally with the tone of the corresponding verb (low falling pitch in isolation). And indeed the last pair, *fe* [¯] 'rope' and *fe* [ˎ] 'sell' do contrast, although, perhaps contrary to expectations, 'rope' is underlyingly /L/ and 'sell' is underlyingly /H/, as may be seen in (9). There is no underlying tonal contrast, however, between the roots of k͡pa [¯] 'path' and k͡pa [ˎ] 'want', or between ɲi [¯] 'mother' and ɲi [ˎ] 'know', their points of contrast lying instead in their belonging to different grammatical categories.

(9) Actual underlying forms

UF	Nouns		UF	Verbs	
	$\begin{bmatrix} - \end{bmatrix}$			$\begin{bmatrix} \diagdown \end{bmatrix}$	
/H/	k͡pa	'path'	/H/	k͡pa	'want'
/L/	ɲi	'mother'	/L/	ɲi	'know'
/L/	fe	'rope'	/H/	fe	'sell'

Chumburung nouns with the syllable profile CV are always realized with a high level pitch when pronounced in isolation, regardless of their underlying patterns. This is due to two reasons: a) they are either underlyingly high toned and/or b) they have a noun class prefix that consists solely of a floating high tone that docks onto the stem. In a comparable manner, verbs with the same syllable profile are always realized with a low falling pitch in isolation, whatever their underlying patterns, because they are in the imperative mood. The imperative mood in Chumburung consists solely of a floating low prefix that docks onto the first syllable of a verb stem. Given that the underlying patterns of both monosyllabic nouns and monosyllabic verbs are neutralized in isolation, it is impossible to determine any tonal contrasts by comparing their surface forms in this environment. The point, of course, is that regardless of which language one is analyzing, words pronounced in "isolation" are never truly in isolation. Words are always pronounced in some grammatical context, and these contexts often differ from one grammatical category to another, even when no other words are present. In the case of CV verbs in Chumburung, their isolation environment is the imperative construction, an environment that is never comparable to that of nouns spoken in isolation.

This leads us to the second (related) reason why it is important not to mix grammatical categories when establishing tonal contrast: the additional environments one often needs to establish tonal contrast between words are also different when the words belong to different categories. For example, the words that can be found adjacent to nouns are often different from those adjacent to verbs, and there is the potential for floating tone morphemes in one or the other environment to compromise the comparability of the phonological environments.

In these next Chumburung examples, we will see that only by comparing nouns with nouns and verbs with verbs can any meaningful conclusions be drawn regarding their underlying tones. We first look at the nouns in (10), taken from (8) and (9).

2.1 Setting up a database

(10) Nouns in contrast in Chumburung

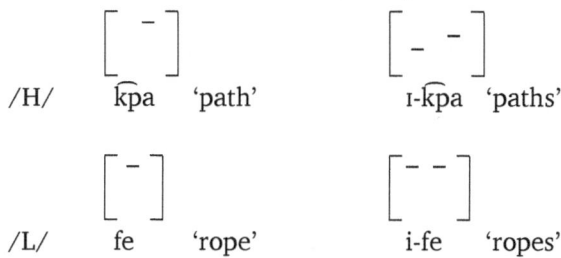

Although k͡pá and fé do not contrast tonally in isolation, they do contrast when they are pluralized.[1]

Next we compare two verbs, again taken from (8) and (9). Although k͡pà 'want' and ɲì 'know' do not contrast tonally in isolation (i.e., in their imperative forms), they do contrast in other environments including when they are nominalized with the *ki-/kɪ-* prefix, as in (11).

(11) Verbs in contrast

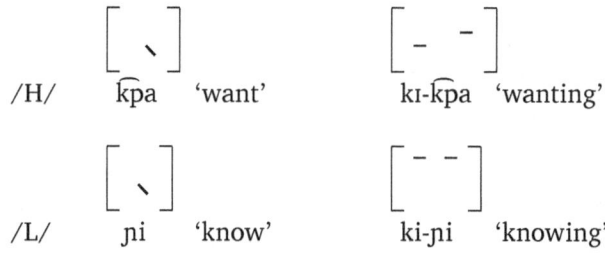

Since the verbs in (11) are comparable in every way that affects tone in Chumburung, the fact that the surface pitch patterns of the nominalized forms contrast must be attributed to the verbs themselves having different underlying tone patterns.

From the examples in (10) and (11), it should be obvious that there is little point in drawing conclusions about underlying tone patterns from any surface contrasts between CV nouns and CV verbs pronounced in isolation. Simply put, comparing the surface tone patterns of words from mixed grammatical categories is not a "best practice" because one cannot be sure that the phonological environments of such words are identical due to their having different grammatical environments. Recall from the discussion above in relation to examples (1) through (4) that only when the phonological environments are identical can two morphemes truly be compared.

For these reasons, when determining tonal contrast, one must avoid comparing words from different grammatical categories. Employing a database that allows one to filter words according to grammatical categories greatly facilitates the comparison of forms that are genuinely comparable.

2.1.2 Stem type

In practice, the term "root" is often confused with the term "stem." Since these two terms must be clearly distinguished and understood when doing tone analysis in many languages, the reader is referred to the following definitions from Crystal 2008.

---

[1] In these environments, the tone of the plural prefix *i-/ɪ-* (which allomorph is realized depends upon the ATR quality of the stem vowel) is realized as low when the stem tone is underlyingly high and as high when the stem tone is underlyingly low. In the case of *ɪ̀-k͡pá*, the surface low of the prefix downsteps the high of the stem to a phonetic mid pitch. In the case of *í-fé*, the high tone of the prefix spreads rightward onto the stem with the result that the surface pattern of the word is phonetically high-high.

root

> A root is the BASE FORM of a WORD which cannot be further analyzed without total loss of identity. Putting this another way, it is that part of the word left when all the AFFIXES are removed…(Crystal 2008:419; caps in original)

stem

> A term often used in LINGUISTICS as part of a classification of the kinds of ELEMENTS operating within the structure of a WORD. The stem may consist solely of a single ROOT MORPHEME (i.e. a 'simple' stem, as in *man*), or of two root morphemes (e.g. [sic] a 'compound' stem, as in *blackbird*), or of a root morpheme plus a DERIVATIONAL AFFIX (i.e. a 'complex' stem, as in *manly, unmanly, manliness*). All have in common the notion that it is to the stem that inflectional affixes are attached. (Crystal 2008:452; caps in original)

For the purposes of our discussion, we identify five types of stems that tone analysts should treat separately: a) simple stems that consist of a single root, b) complex stems that consist of a root plus one or more derivational affixes, c) compound stems that consist of two or more roots (compound stems are usually multi-syllabic), d) borrowed forms, and e) ideophonic[2] stems, which are often highly idiosyncratic. While we do not want to exclude any of these types from our analysis, we certainly do want to keep them separate from each other.

Although I do not discuss how to deal specifically with borrowed and ideophonic words, suffice it to say that one does not want to mix them with each other and with other kinds of words when doing tone analysis. Marking them differently in the database ensures that their unique characteristics do not compromise the tonal comparability of other words. While it is important during the beginning stages of tone analysis to avoid dealing with borrowed and ideophonic words, one should nevertheless analyze them later on, since doing so often reveals new things. Analyzing them can also shed light on problems that have remained unsolved to that point. Marking borrowed and ideophonic words differently in a database therefore not only keeps them out of the initial analysis, but it also makes them easier to retrieve for analysis later.

It is also important not to mix complex and compound stems with simple stems, since each morpheme brings with it its own tone pattern. Complex stems are normally not too difficult to identify because they have derivational affixation that is in common with other stems (e.g., the English suffix *-able* in *describe-able, treat-able*). Compound stems, on the other hand, can be more difficult to identify, and as the following scenario demonstrates, a failure to keep them separate from simple stems can result in faulty conclusions with regard to tone. The Chumburung nouns in (12) are all taken from the same noun class (no prefix) and all have the syllable profile CVCV. Superficially, there would therefore appear to be six contrastive patterns.

---

[2] Ideophones are words whose sounds are associated in some way with their meanings. For example, the English word *boom* is an ideophone whose single syllable is usually pronounced louder than normal with a fairly low tone. This word denotes a loud (reason why word is normally pronounced louder than other words), deep sounding (reason why word is pronounced with fairly low vowels and fairly low pitch) noise of fairly short duration (reason why word consists of only a single syllable).

2.1 Setting up a database

(12) Surface contrasts on CVCV nouns with no prefix

[LL] $\begin{bmatrix} - & \backslash \end{bmatrix}$ wad͡ʒa 'cloth'   [HL] $\begin{bmatrix} - \\ \backslash \end{bmatrix}$ sʊsʊ 'sky'

[HH] $\begin{bmatrix} - & - \end{bmatrix}$ dapʊ 'hawk'   [HM] $\begin{bmatrix} - & - \end{bmatrix}$ kɔtɔ 'crab'

[LM] $\begin{bmatrix} - & - \end{bmatrix}$ kɔtɪ 'monkey'   [HH-L] $\begin{bmatrix} - & \backslash \end{bmatrix}$ d͡ʒepu 'tongue'

There would also appear to be clear evidence for a mid tone, with patterns [HH], [HM], and [HL] apparently in contrast. There is a problem, however, because these data contain both simple and non-simple stems.

Unfortunately, it is not always clear which stems are simple and which are not, so the analyst needs to be open to the possibility that any stem that has two or more syllables is not simple, indeed that all such stems may be non-simple. Sometimes compound stems can be identified by recognizing at least one element of the compound (e.g., *blackberry*, cf. *black, berry*; *cranberry*, cf. *cran?, berry*). At other times, they can be discovered by conducting comparative research[3] with related languages. But in many cases, there is no morphological evidence (synchronic or diachronic) to single out compound stems, and few people, including native speakers, realize that such forms are in fact compounds. These are the troublesome ones for tone analysis.

There are two strategies, however, that have proven very helpful in identifying non-simple stems in cases like those just mentioned. The simpler and more immediately apparent strategy involves counting the numbers of words that conform to different phonological patterns (e.g., different tone patterns, different syllable profiles, different ways stems begin and/or end). In general, the more common the stem pattern, the more likely it is that the stem is simple, and vice versa, the less common the stem pattern, the less likely it is that the stem is simple. The second strategy involves studying the phonological interactions that take place between the different elements of known compound and complex stems and then comparing their outputs with the surface forms of morphologically "suspect" stems.

With regard to the different surface tone patterns in (12), let us look first at the numbers, drawn from statistics generated from my Chumburung database.

(13) Numbers of nouns from all noun classes with stem shape CVCV

Surface pattern	Total number	Known non-simple	Arguably simple
[LL]	40	9	31
[HH]	35	8	27
[LM]	20	4	16
[HL]	5	3	2
[HM]	2	1	1
[HH-L]	13	6	7
Total	115	31	84

---

[3] My thanks to Tania Pareja Ruíz for reminding me of this during a presentation I made in Mexico City at Centro de Investigaciones y Estudios Superiores en Antropología Social (CIESAS) in September 2015.

In my database, there are 115 nouns from all noun classes with the stem-shape CVCV.⁴ Of these, 31 are known to be compounds, leaving 84 whose stems are arguably simple. While the majority of these probably are simple, some of them may very well be compounds that are simply unrecognized as such. Looking at the figures for arguably simple stems in (13), the three figures below the line (2, 1, and 7) are significantly lower than the three above it (31, 27, and 16). The lower numbers suggest that the bottom three patterns are less natural than the top three, and this is a huge tip-off that the patterns below the line are the result of the concatenation of multiple morphemes.

It is also important to notice for each pattern the ratio between nouns known to have non-simple stems and the total number of nouns that have that pattern. Looking at the figures in (13), the non-simple/total number ratios are significantly higher for the patterns below the line (viz. [HL] 3/5, [HM] 1/2, [HH-L] 6/13) than they are for those above the line (viz. [LL] 9/40, [HH] 8/35, [LM] 4/20). The fact that morphological complexity is recognized more frequently in stems whose patterns appear below the line further suggests that all stems belonging to these patterns are morphologically complex. Ratios like these, of course, are only meaningful if the analyst is familiar enough with the language to be able to recognize one or more constituents of a reasonable number of non-simple stems, but they further demonstrate, nevertheless, the value of using the relative frequencies of phonotactic patterns to help identify morphological complexity.

The second strategy for identifying non-simple stems involves investigating phonotactic patterns relevant to known compound and complex stems. Understanding how different known tone patterns behave when they are adjoined to others in the same stem can be very enlightening. Unfortunately, properly demonstrating the patterns that are relevant to the compounds referred to in (13) requires more space than the present situation merits, so we will confine ourselves to simply noting that those tone patterns that appear below the line in (13) (i.e., the patterns of those stems identified through statistical means as being non-simple) match perfectly with patterns generated by known compounds.⁵

Such an awareness of tonal behaviour in known non-simple stems serves the tone analyst well, particularly when they are combined with insights gained by comparing the total numbers of words of differing phonological patterns. By taking care to separate simple stems from compound and complex ones in Chumburung, the analyst avoids the erroneous conclusion that there are three underlying tone heights in Chumburung (cf. the data in (12)), and correctly concludes that there are only two. These two then combine to form just three

---

⁴Since the tonal behaviour of all noun class prefixes in Chumburung is the same, I have grouped the classes together in order to better illustrate the value of using total numbers to identify compound forms.

⁵For those interested in seeing what this looks like, here are two examples, taken from the kI- noun class. In the first, the stem for 'upper grindstone' is tonally a /H+L/ compound that consists of the root /bú/ 'stone' followed by the root /d͡ʒì/ 'child/offspring'. In the second example, the stem for 'citizen' is a /HL+L/ compound that consists of the root /mâŋ/ 'ethnic area' followed by the same second root /d͡ʒì/ 'child/offspring'.
(a) /H+L/ (/bú/ + /d͡ʒì/), comparable to d͡ʒépû 'tongue'
   kì-bú-d͡ʒì 'upper grindstone'   cf. kì-bú 'stone'   cf. d͡ʒì-ɲán-sɛ́ 'son'
   C3-stone-child/offspring   C3-stone   child-male-relation
(b) /HL+L/ (/mâŋ/ + /d͡ʒì/) comparable to súsù 'sky'
   kì-máŋ-d͡ʒì 'citizen'   cf. mâŋ 'ethnic area'   cf. d͡ʒì-t͡ʃíí-sɛ́ 'daughter'
   C3-ethnic.area-child/offspring   child-female-relation

Evidence for the underlying root patterns may be seen in that /bú/ appears with a high pitch in kì-bú 'stone', /mâŋ/ appears with a high falling pitch in mâŋ 'ethnic area', and /d͡ʒì/ appears with a low pitch in the compound stems of d͡ʒì-ɲán-sɛ́ 'son' and d͡ʒì-t͡ʃíí-sɛ́ 'daughter'. Of course, recognizing one or more elements in a compound does not mean that all words with that same surface pitch pattern are necessarily compounds. However, knowing that the surface patterns of the words above can be attributed to prefixes followed respectively by the compound stem structures /H+L/ and /HL+L/ goes a long way towards explaining the scarcity of those patterns.

2.1 Setting up a database

contrastive surface patterns [LL], [LM], and [HH] in simple CVCV stems. This will become even clearer when doing the online Chumburung exercises associated with this book.

2.1.3 Syllable profile of stem

From the discussions of Mende and Njyem in chapter 1, it is clear that the syllable profile of the stem plays an important role in how any given tone pattern is realized phonetically. The Mende examples in (14), repeated from chapter 1, demonstrate that a single underlying pattern can have very different surface realizations, depending on how many syllables there are to "host" the pattern. In each case, the stem is simple.

(14) Tone and syllable profiles in Mende

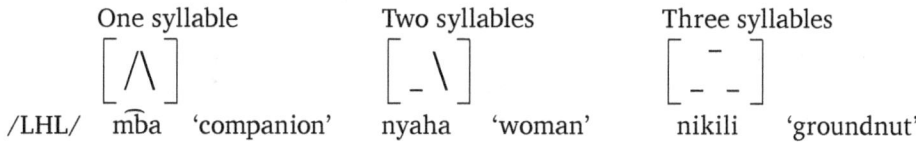

/LHL/ mba 'companion'   nyaha 'woman'   nikili 'groundnut'

In general, the more syllables there are to host a given pattern, the fewer the contours (or in the case of languages with unitary contours,[6] such as many languages in Asia, the less complex the contours).

When morphemes have more tones in their patterns than TBUs in their segmental structures, the extra tones of the patterns need to be accommodated somehow. This normally happens in one of three ways. First, as in the Mende data above, tonal contours are often created when two or more tones of differing heights are linked to single TBUs, as in the second syllable of (15).

(15) Contour creation in Mende

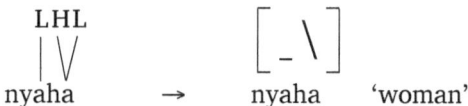

nyaha → nyaha 'woman'

Secondly, multiple tone heights are sometimes created, with two or more tones of differing heights being fused into single tones whose heights contrast phonetically with those of other single tones in the language, as in (16).

(16) Tone fusion in Chumburung

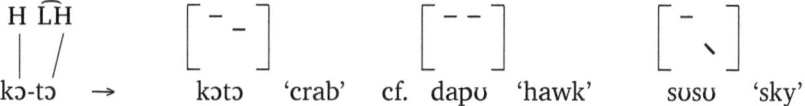

kɔ-tɔ → kɔtɔ 'crab'   cf. dapʊ 'hawk'   sʊsʊ 'sky'

And thirdly, tones that are not assigned to TBUs by one or other of the first two strategies are often simply left unassociated, or floating, as in (17).

(17) Floating high tone in Njyem

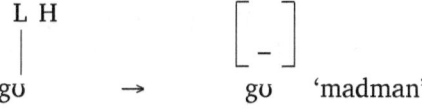

gʊ → gʊ 'madman'

---

[6] Unitary contours are contours that cannot be analyzed as consisting of two or more level tones realized on single TBUs.

When this happens, the floating tones usually don't manifest their presence phonetically unless they are in particular environments where they might dock onto the TBUs of adjacent morphemes, or they might cause downstep, etc. This may be seen in (18) where the floating high tone of *gù* docks back onto *gù* when it is followed by another word that begins with a low tone, thereby creating a low-to-high rising pitch on *gù*.

(18) High tone docking in Njyem

$$\begin{bmatrix} / & - \end{bmatrix}$$

[gʊ jaː]   'the madman (in question)'

It is not, however, only the number of syllables that can affect how an underlying tone pattern is realized phonetically. The number of moras in each syllable is also crucial. All moras are not necessarily tone-bearing in every environment, but it is nevertheless the case that all TBUs are moraic (Hyman 1992), so one must take into consideration the moraic constituency of each syllable. For languages and environments that give evidence of the syllable being the TBU, Hyman claims that in such cases it is the head mora of the syllable that is the TBU. Although moraic elements have apparently been documented in the complex onsets of at least some languages (Gordon 2005; Topintzi 2005, 2010; Nevins 2012), onsets generally play no role in syllable weight (Hyman 1984, 1985a), so the complexity of the syllable onset can usually be ignored when comparing different syllable profiles.

Accordingly, while it is important to distinguish the syllable shapes CV and CVV because they have one and two moras, respectively, the syllable shapes of CCV and CV can normally be lumped together because they both consist of one mora each. If evidence to the contrary should emerge, then of course, one would need to treat them separately.

While stress assignment can sometimes affect the moraic structure of syllables (see below), the fortis-lenis quality of coda consonants can also sometimes affect it. For example, Arellanes 2004, 2009, Chávez-Peón 2010, and Arellanes and Chávez-Peón (in preparation) describe lenis codas in different varieties of Zapotec, an Eastern Otomanguean language of Mexico, as triggering the addition of a mora to the nucleus of the syllable and fortis codas as triggering the addition of a mora to the coda. This may be seen in (19).

(19) Lenis and fortis codas in Quiaviní Zapotec

Lenis		Fortis	
láːd	'side'	látː	'tin can'
táːn	'Cayetana'	tásː	'cup'

There is further discussion below of Chávez-Peón's 2010 description of the interaction between tone and different vocalic phonation types in Quiaviní Zapotec. To sum up, all factors that affect moraic structure in a language need to be controlled for when establishing tonal contrast.

This is further illustrated by the following Chumburung data in which not only the number of moras in the stem but also the sonorancy of those moras that are codas plays a role in establishing tonal contrast. Underlyingly, monosyllabic stems with one mora may bear only one tone in Chumburung whereas monosyllabic stems with two moras may bear two underlying tones. This is demonstrated in (20) with stems that follow the C3 noun class prefix. Note that the underlying pattern /HL/ is found with CVN stems but not with CV stems.

2.1 Setting up a database

(20) Monomoraic vs. bimoraic syllables

Pattern	CV stem		CVN stem	
/H/	$\begin{bmatrix} - & - \end{bmatrix}$ kɪ-pa C3-hat	'hat'	$\begin{bmatrix} - & - \end{bmatrix}$ kɪ-laŋ C3-jug	'jug'
/HL/	NONE		$\begin{bmatrix} - & \backslash \end{bmatrix}$ kɪ-baŋ C3-paddle	'paddle'

For many languages, including Chumburung, whether the coda is sonorant or not also plays a significant role. In the examples in (21), even though both stems have the syllable profile CVC, and both have the same underlying patterns (viz., HL), the surface realizations of these patterns are different.

(21) Sonorant vs. non-sonorant codas

$\begin{bmatrix} - & \backslash \end{bmatrix}$ $\begin{bmatrix} - & - \end{bmatrix}$

kɪ-baŋ 'paddle'   ki-teʔ 'feather'
C3-paddle   C3-feather

In the case of *kɪ̀-báŋ̀*, since both stem moras are sonorant, the vocal folds vibrate continually as the pattern goes from H to L, with the result that a high falling pitch is phonetically realized over the duration of the syllable. For *kɪ̀-téʔ*, only the first mora of the stem is sonorant. Since the coda is non-sonorant, the L of the /HL/ pattern is not realized phonetically, with the result that only a high level pitch is phonetically realized over the duration of the syllable.

This does not mean, however, that there is no low tone associated with this syllable. In order to demonstrate the low tone's presence, consider first the phrases in (22), in which words that end in true high tones are brought into adjacency with following words that begin with high tones.

(22) Stems with /H/ pattern before /H/ pattern

$\begin{bmatrix} - & - & - \end{bmatrix}$ $\begin{bmatrix} - & - \end{bmatrix}$ $\begin{bmatrix} - \end{bmatrix}$

kɪlan sɔ 'jug's odour' cf. kɪ-laŋ 'jug' cf. sɔ 'odour'
jug odour   C3-jug

$\begin{bmatrix} - & - & - \end{bmatrix}$ $\begin{bmatrix} - & - \end{bmatrix}$

kɪbaa sɔ 'shoulder's odour' cf. kɪ-baʔ 'shoulder'
shoulder odour   C3-shoulder

In (22), when the two H tones are juxtaposed, they are both realized at the same phonetic pitch, as might be expected.[7] Now compare these phrases with those in (23), in which both of the /HL/ stems from (22) are brought into adjacency with *sɔ́*.

---

[7] In Chumburung, as in many African languages, nasal codas assimilate to the place of articulation of a following consonant. This explains the alternation between [n] and [ŋ] in the different realizations of (22) *kɪ̀-láŋ* 'jug' and (23) *kɪ̀-báŋ̀* 'paddle'. Also in Chumburung, when long vowels occur phrase

(23) Stems with /HL/ pattern before /H/ pattern

$$\begin{bmatrix} - & ^- & - \end{bmatrix}$$
kıbaŋ sɔ   'paddle's odour'   cf.
paddle odour

$$\begin{bmatrix} - & \backslash \end{bmatrix}$$
kɪ-baŋ   'paddle'
C3-paddle

$$\begin{bmatrix} - & ^- & - \end{bmatrix}$$
kitee sɔ   'feather's odour'   cf.
feather odour

$$\begin{bmatrix} - & - \end{bmatrix}$$
ki-teʔ   'feather'
C3-feather

In (23), when the words with /HL/ stem patterns precede sɔ́ (the final L of these words is floating in these examples), the high tone of sɔ́ is lowered due to the presence of the floating low tones. In the case of kìbán ꜝsɔ́, this is not surprising, given that kɪ̀-bâŋ ends in a high falling pitch in isolation. However, given that kì-téʔ ends in a high level pitch in isolation, the fact that sɔ́ is lowered when it follows kì-téʔ supports the conclusion that the underlying stem tone pattern of kì-téʔ is, in fact, /HL/. The reason why the underlying low tone of the stem is not realized phonetically when it is pronounced at the end of a phrase is due to the non-sonorant nature of the coda.

From the foregoing discussion, it should be clear that in addition to the number of syllables a stem has, there are two further factors that can influence how its underlying tone pattern is realized phonetically: a) the number of moras in each syllable, and b) whether or not the moras are sonorant. In short, anything that affects the number or sonorancy of the moras in a stem needs to be controlled for when establishing tonal contrast. As discussed in section 1.2, the present work refers to a stem's particular arrangement of these factors as its syllable profile. And of course, given that non-simple stems consist of multiple morphemes, the morphemic structure of the stem must be included in the description of the stem syllable profile. In order to keep the profiles of the different stem types separate in a database, while the syllable profile of a simple stem might be entered as CVCV, one way to distinguish a comparable complex stem in a database would be to enter it as CV]CV.

A database that allows one to filter words according to stem syllable profile (or word syllable profile, in languages where there is no difference between stems and words) greatly facilitates accurate tone analysis.

2.1.4 Surface tone patterns

So far, we have discussed how a database for tone analysis should include fields for grammatical category, stem type, and stem syllable profile. Controlling for these factors allows the analyst to compare the tone patterns of words that are comparable in each of these respects; if they still have different surface patterns, then they must have different underlying tone patterns. One therefore needs to enter into the database the phonetic, or surface, tone patterns of the words in isolation initially, and later in other environments.[8] In order to be able to filter and sort data according to surface tone patterns, all pitch pattern information needs to be entered into database fields that are distinct from those corresponding to the segmental information. Ideally, these surface patterns should be entered into the appropriate fields using the bar notation as advocated in chapter 1. This allows one to show pitch in a relative manner, as

---

finally, the final mora is realized as a glottal stop instead of as length. Elsewhere, however (i.e., phrase medially), the final mora of the long vowel is realized as vowel length.

[8] Recall from the discussion in chapter 1 that tone is better analyzed as patterns associated with morphemes than as tones associated with particular tone-bearing units.

2.1 Setting up a database

opposed to using, say, acute and grave accents to indicate surface pitch differences. That being said, since it is a database into which one is entering the data, in theory any schema that maintains the distinctiveness of each word's surface pattern will suffice. For example, one could label the patterns with codes like 1A, 2A, 1B, etc., with each code associated with a particular surface word pattern. In practice, though, an iconic system such as the bar notation advocated in this work is much more practical.

Although the isolation surface pattern of a word is important in tone analysis, one should resist the temptation to think that it is the underlying pattern. It should not be forgotten that the difference between two or more underlying patterns is often neutralized when words are spoken in isolation, meaning that their surface patterns will be identical. It is therefore important to elicit any given word in other contexts as well, and to enter the complete surface pattern transcription of each utterance in the appropriate field. (We return to this matter below.)

The number of contexts in which patterns need to be compared depends, of course, on the language; but as might be expected, the more contexts one chooses, the more likely one is to discover all of the underlying contrasts and to explain their different surface realizations. As discussed below, some of the different fields one might want to create for representing the surface patterns of nouns include: plural forms, possessive constructions, adjectival constructions, and nouns with demonstratives of various sorts, etc. For verbs, these can include nominalized verbs of various sorts, adverbial constructions, verb-object constructions, and the (usually many) different variations governed by the inflectional morphology, etc. (24) is an example of how one might enter these types of data for nouns in a database. Notice that it is the complete surface pattern of the utterance that is being entered in each case.

(24) Sample database entries for surface patterns of nouns

Gloss	Sing.	Sing. pattern	Pl.	Pl. pattern	'__'s antelope'	'__'s antelope' pattern
enemy	dʊŋ	[\ ]	adʊŋ	[⁻ \ ]	dʊŋ fʊrɪ	[⁻ ⁻ ⁻]
woman	ɔt͡ʃɪʔ	[⁻ ⁻]	at͡ʃɪʔ	[⁻ ⁻]	ɔt͡ʃɪɪ fʊrɪ	[⁻ ⁻ ⁻ ⁻]

For each unique phonological/grammatical context one enters, it is necessary to have two separate fields, one for segments and one for surface patterns. Including fields for both allows for greater flexibility when filtering, sorting, and comparing data; and it helps one find the right data at the right time, which greatly speeds up the analytical process.

2.1.5 Underlying tone pattern

When beginning tone analysis, the surface tone patterns are, of course, the only data available. However, as one proceeds through the analysis and determines the underlying patterns, it is advantageous to be able to add this information to the database. Accordingly, the database should be set up to include a field for entering underlying tone patterns.

We next discuss database fields that will not be needed for all languages; but if the family of the language under investigation is known to have any of the characteristics discussed below, the appropriate fields should be included in the database.

2.1.6 Noun and/or verb class

Not all languages have nouns and/or verbs that group into classes, but many do. In languages with verb classes, certain verbs might take, say, a particular set of affixes to indicate inflectional differences while other verbs might take a completely different or partially different set of affixes to communicate the same inflectional differences. For languages like these, the differences between the two sets of affixes is not attributable to phonological conditioning, but rather to genuine differences in grammatical forms.

Similarly, in languages with noun classes, nouns may be grouped according to different prefixes and/or suffixes to indicate such categories as singular, plural, and diminutive, as well as semantic categories such as animals, humans, and liquids, etc. Also, there is often agreement in such systems between the class of a noun and class markers affixed to its pronominal forms (e.g., associative markers, subject and object markers on verbs). If the language being analyzed employs a class system for either nouns or verbs or both, it is absolutely essential to analyze that system in order to reliably analyze tone in that language. And by the same token, it is also absolutely essential to analyze the tone system in order to correctly analyze the class system. Both must be done in symbiotic fashion.

Recall that when analyzing tone, underlying contrastive patterns are most clearly revealed when they contrast in identical environments. In languages with noun and/or verb classes, it is therefore important to compare only stems that belong to the same class. This is because stems from different classes often have different affixes attached to them or they have different agreement markers on adjacent words. In either case, "different classes" often means "different environments," and different environments render invalid any tonal comparisons that depend on them. Here is an example from Bamileke-Dschang [ybb], a Grassfields Bantu language spoken in Cameroon (data from Hyman and Tadadjeu 1976 and Hyman 1985b).

(25) Same patterns, different noun classes in Bamileke-Dschang

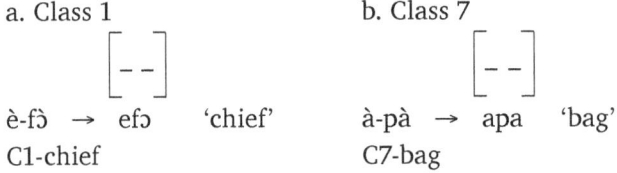

    è-fɔ̀ → efɔ   'chief'   à-pà → apa   'bag'
    C1-chief   C7-bag

The two words in (25) have identical tone surface patterns. Not only that but they do in fact have the same underlying patterns. However, as mentioned above, it is necessary to examine their behaviours in a full range of morphological and syntactic environments in order to ensure that their underlying patterns are indeed the same. One such environment, which proves to be revealing, is the possessive construction.

(26) Nouns compared in possessive construction

    a. Class 1

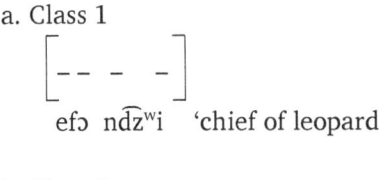

        efɔ ndz͡ʷi   'chief of leopard'

    b. Class 7

$$\begin{bmatrix} - - & - & - \\ & & - \end{bmatrix}$$

        apa ndz͡ʷi   'bag of leopard'

A cursory comparison of 'chief' and 'bag' in (26) suggests that there is something tonally different about these two nouns: in fact, we would be right to conclude that they should be kept apart. However, the difference is not to be found in the underlying patterns of the nouns, as the following data reveal.

(27) Associative construction in Bamileke-Dschang
   a. Class 1
   è-fɔ̀ è-ǹ-d͡zʷî → [èfɔ̀ ǹd͡zʷî] 'chief of leopard'
   C1-chief AM.C1-C9-leopard

   b. Class 7
   à-pà á-ǹ-d͡zʷî → [àpà ǹ⁺d͡zʷî] 'bag of leopard'
   C7-bag AM.C7-C9-leopard

As in most, if not all, Bantu languages, there is an associative marker (AM) between the "possessee" noun and the "possessor" noun that is concordant with the class of the head, or possessee, noun. A phrase translated as 'leopard's chief' therefore has the word order 'chief of leopard', with 'of' being the translation for the associative marker. It can be seen that the associative marker for Class 1 nouns, to which 'chief' belongs, is underlyingly low-toned (viz. /è-/), while that for Class 7 nouns, to which 'bag' belongs, is underlyingly high-toned (viz. /á-/), and it is this that makes it impossible to directly compare these words in possessive constructions.[9] This is a rather complex example, not least because the vowels of the associative markers are usually elided in normal speech, leaving only the interactions of their tones with other tones to signal their presence. However, the point should still be clear that in a noun class language, nouns should only be compared with other nouns from the same class.

While the general principle of not mixing morphological classes is important, it is not always easy in practice to distinguish the different classes, particularly when one is beginning tone analysis. There are two reasons for this. First, it is not uncommon for morphological class affixes to be segmentally identical and to differ only tonally. Secondly, morphological class affixes sometimes consist only of floating tones. This underlines the importance of analyzing tone as one seeks to properly distinguish the classes. Some examples of classes that are difficult to distinguish without adequate tone analysis appear in (28).

(28) Noun class affixes differentiated solely by tone

Mundani [mnf] (Parker 1989)		Mankon [nge] (Leroy 1980)		Akoose [bss] (Hedinger 2008)		Mada [mda] (Price 1994)	
C8 Genitive	é-	C1 Number	ì-	C9 Subject	è-	C1 Noun	Floating L
C9 Genitive	è-	C3 Number	í-	C10 Subject	é-	C2 Noun	Floating H

In Mundani, a Grassfields Bantu language spoken in Cameroon, the genetive prefix that agrees with Class 8 nouns is high-toned, while that for Class 9 nouns is low-toned. Since these two morphemes are identical segmentally, it is necessary to understand the tone system in order to properly identify the noun classes. In Mankon, another Grassfields Bantu language of Cameroon, the prefix on numbers that agree with Class 1 nouns is low-toned, while for Class 3 nouns it is high-toned. Again, since these two morphemes are segmentally identical, tone

---

[9] All underlying tones in 'chief of leopard' are low with the result that all four TBUs in this phrase are realized with low pitch. In 'bag of leopard', however, the final low-toned TBU is phonetically downstepped in relation to the low tones of the preceding three TBUs. For futher information, the interested reader is referred to chapter 7 of Snider 1999 for an analysis of how underlying tones are phonetically realized in the Bamileke-Dschang associative construction.

analysis is needed in order to distinguish the classes. A similar situation exists with respect to the Class 9 and 10 subject prefixes in Akoose. In the case of Mada, a Benue-Congo language spoken in Nigeria, the prefix for Class 1 nouns is a floating low tone, while that for Class 2 nouns is a floating high. That these nouns have any prefixes at all is only determined through careful tone analysis. In situations like these, it is essential to interleave tone analysis with morphological and syntactic analysis.

These, then, are the reasons why for those languages that have noun and/or verb classes, it is important to compare only words from the same class when determining contrastive patterns. Thus a database that allows one to filter words according to their different classes can greatly increase the accuracy of the tone analysis.

2.1.7 Consonant(s)

In some tone languages, the quality of the first root consonant (and occasionally other consonant positions) affects the surface tone patterns of words.[10] Sometimes consonants affect the surface pitch of the host words in isolation. At other times, they affect the surface pitch of the host words in other contexts, and at still other times they affect the surface pitch of words adjacent to the host words (Bradshaw 1999). Not only can consonants have a direct effect on tone patterns, but they can also block tone spreading.

In most languages with consonant-tone interaction, the consonants divide into two groups: one group, called "depressor" consonants, that consists mainly of voiced obstruents, and a second group, called "non-depressors," that consists of the remaining consonants (i.e., voiceless obstruents, implosives, and sonorants). While depressor consonants can have a lowering effect on tones and can also block high tone spreading, non-depressors have no effect on tone. For example, Beavon-Ham (2012) describes voiced obstruents in Saxwe [sxw], a Kwa language spoken in the southwest of Benin, as triggering a lowering of the tonal register as well as blocking the spreading of high tones. Then there are a few other languages with consonant-tone interaction in which voiceless obstruents and implosives block low tone spreading (see below). In such languages, the remaining consonants (i.e., voiced obstruents and sonorants), again have no effect on tone. While sonorant consonants typically play no role in consonant-tone interactions (i.e., they are typically neutral), sonorant induced interaction is nevertheless not entirely unknown,[11] and such behaviour should not take one entirely by surprise.

Pearce (2007) describes Kera [ker], a Chadic language spoken in Chad as having three phonemic tones: H, M, L. Disyllabic nouns may have any combination of these except ML and LM. Thus, on disyllabic nouns one finds the surface melodies: HH, HM, HL, MH, MM, LH, and LL. There is a clear relationship, however, between the voicing of the noun's first consonant and its tone pattern, and this has led linguists to group Kera nouns according to the first consonant, as in (29).

(29) Kera consonant-tone interaction
   a. never before a TBU with high tone: b, d, j, g, v, z ('depressor consonants' in Ebert 1979, Pearce 1999)
   b. never before a TBU with low tone: p, t, c, k, f, s ('raiser consonants' in Pearce 1999)
   c. with all three tones: m, n, ŋ, l, r, ɓ, ɗ, h, ʔ ('neutral consonants' in Pearce 1999)

Pearce (personal communication) speculates that historically, consonant voicing was contrastive and there were four underlying tone patterns: H, L, LH, HL, with raiser consonants

---

[10] The reverse situation, i.e., tone affecting consonants, also occurs, but it is much rarer.

[11] For example, in Moloko [mlw], a Chadic language of northern Cameroon, while most *h*'s are neutral and have no effect on tone, certain *h*'s act as depressor consonants (personal field notes). One can speculate that such depressor sonorants were voiced obstruents, historically.

2.1 Setting up a database

causing underlying L tones to be realised as M. However, it seems that this analysis can no longer be supported because of the way the voicing and tone relationship is changing. A synchronic analysis today posits three level underlying tones, with consonant voicing now dependent on the tone (and also on the dialect). Pearce believes that the development of three tones in Kera arose through consonant-tone interaction, with voiceless obstruents 'raising' low tones and voiced obstruents 'lowering' high tones. In the examples in (30), initial syllables with low tone begin with either voiced obstruents or neutral consonants (see right hand column) while initial syllables with high and mid tones begin with either voiceless obstruents or neutral consonants (see left hand column).

(30) Disyllabic nouns in Kera

H and M			H and L		
[H]	túrtí	'boat'			
[H]	mə́yán	'river'			
[M]	pāatāl	'needle'	[L]	dàygà	'jar'
[M]	māanɨ	'co-wife'	[L]	hɔ̀ynà	'type of spirit'
[MH]	tāatá	'big jar'	[LH]	gùugúr	'chicken'
[MH]	māahúr	'flute'	[LH]	hùɗúm	'hole'
[HM]	kúntī	'flour'	[HL]	táabùl	'table'
[HM]	máalāŋ	'bird of prey'	[HL]	mánhɔ̀r	'ten'

The following examples come from Bolanci [bol], a West Chadic language spoken in northern Nigeria. Citing Lukas 1969, Schuh 1978:226 describes high tone spreading in this language as being blocked by "a non-prenasalized voiced obstruent."

(31) High tone spreading in Bolanci

a. /kǔm sàawùrà/ → [kǔm sáawùrà] 'ear of a falcon'
b. /kǔm nzìmòkì/ → [kǔm nzímòkì] 'ear of an eagle'
c. /kǔm zòngé/ → [kǔm zòngé] 'ear of a hyena'

In (31), the high tone of the LH rising pattern on *kǔm* 'ear' spreads rightward to the first syllable of the following word when the following consonant is a voiceless obstruent as in (31a), or a prenasalized consonant as in (31b). In (31c), however, the first syllable of the following word begins with [z], a non-prenasalized voiced obstruent that blocks high tone spreading. The first syllable of *zòngé* is therefore phonetically realized with a low pitch.

Citing Schuh 1971, Schuh 1978:226 also describes Ngizim [ngi], another West Chadic language spoken in northern Nigeria, as permitting low tone spread unless the following syllable "begins in a voiceless or glottalized [implosive] obstruent."

(32) Low tone spreading in Ngizim

a. /à gáfí/ → [à gàfí] 'catch!'
b. /à ráwí/ → [à ràwí] 'run!'
c. /à ɗálmí/ → [à ɗálmí] 'repair!'
d. /à káčí/ → [à káčí] 'return!'

In (32a,b), low tone spreading clearly occurs when the following consonant is respectively, a voiced obstruent and a sonorant. It is also clear, however, in (32c,d), that low tone spreading is blocked when the following consonant is either an implosive or a voiceless obstruent.

Consonant-tone interaction does not take place in most tone languages, but if it is known to occur in languages related to the language under investigation, it is important to include a field in the database that indicates the quality of the first obstruent of the root (or other obstruents if necessary). Later, when the nature of the interaction becomes clearer, one can group the sonorants accordingly. For example, if voiced obstruents are either lowering tones or blocking high tone spreading, and voiceless obstruents and sonorants are not, then one would want to group sonorants together with voiceless obstruents. As stated above, one doesn't necessarily know when beginning the analysis exactly which consonants belong to which group, but as this information becomes known, it can be added if the field is in the database.

2.1.8 Phonation type of vowels

In certain tone languages, mainly in Southeast Asia and Mesoamerica, the phonation type of vowels affects the surface tone patterns. Phonation types are typically referred to in the literature as modal (normal) voice, breathy voice, creaky voice, and glottalized voice. Chávez-Peón 2010:104 describes these as follows:

> Phonation types refer to the manner in which vocal folds vibrate. Modal voice is the standard vibration type. The vocal folds are adducted along their full length and with a suitable degree of tension to allow vibration in a rhythmic manner, opening and closing at regular intervals of time. Breathy voice or murmur is where the folds are held partly apart while the vibration continues, and creaky voice or laryngealization is where the folds are held stiffly and vibration is partially inhibited. The different ways the vocal cords vibrate, or do not vibrate at all, create a variety of phonation types (Ladefoged, 1971; Catford, 1977; Laver, 1980). As suggested by Ladefoged (1971; see also Catford, 1964), these various glottal states may be represented in the form of a phonation continuum, "[...] defined in terms of the aperture between the arytenoid cartilages, ranging from voiceless (furthest apart), through breathy voiced, to regular, modal voicing, and then through creaky voice to glottal closure (closest together)." (Gordon and Ladefoged 2001:384)

Quoting Maddieson and Hess 1986, Yip 2002:31 describes Jingpho [kac], a Tibeto-Burman language spoken in Myanmar, as having a phonological contrast between breathy and plain vowels, with the breathy vowels having a lowering effect on pitch. Historically, the breathy vowels have resulted from the historical loss of voicing in syllable onsets. Since voicing in syllable onsets is well known to lower pitch (see immediately preceding section), it is not surprising that vowels with phonation types that result from a historical loss of onset voicing would also lower pitch.

Chávez-Peón 2010 describes the vowels of Quiaviní Zapotec as having a four-way phonation contrast between modal, breathy, creaky, and glottalized voices (see also Munro and Lopez 1999). These may be seen in (33), where all four contrast on underlyingly low-toned nouns with CV syllable profiles.

(33) Quiaviní Zapotec phonation type contrasts

	Modal	/be/ ˩	→	[bè:]	'mesquite bean'
	Breathy	/be̤/ ˩	→	[bè̤:]	'mold (growth)'
	Creaky	/bḛ/ ˩	→	[bḛ̀:]	'notch made in sheep's ear'
	Glottalized	/baʔ/ ˩	→	[bàʔà]	'eyeball'

2.1 Setting up a database

Chávez-Peón also describes consonants in the language as being either fortis or lenis. When a syllable coda consists of a lenis consonant, or when the syllable is open, the nucleus is realized with phonetic length. However, when the coda consists of a fortis consonant, it is the coda that is realized with phonetic length. Since the fortis-lenis distinction in Quiaviní Zapotec affects the stem syllable profiles in this manner, and since syllable profiles play a major role in how different tone patterns are realized phonetically, the fortis-lenis distinction is controlled for in the codas of the examples below.

Chávez-Peón goes on to describe most native roots in this language as being monosyllabic and as having a four-way tone contrast between low, high, rising, and falling tones on root vowels pronounced with modal voice, as shown in example (34).[12]

(34) Four-way tone contrast on modal vowels in Quiaviní Zapotec

High	/daɲ/ ˥	→	[dáːɲ]	'injury'
Low	/daɲ/ ˩	→	[dàːɲ]	'mountain'
Rising	/ʒilj/ ˬ	→	[ʒǐːlʲ]	'saddle'
Falling	/ʒilj/ ˯	→	[ʒîːlʲ]	'sheep'

All codas in (34) consist of lenis consonants with the result that all vowels are realized with phonetic length.[13]

For each of the three other (i.e., non-modal) phonation types, the tone possibilities are more restricted. These are listed in (35).

(35) Quiaviní Zapotec tone contrast possibilities with different phonation types

	High	Low	Falling	Rising
Modal	√	√	√	√
Breathy	X	√	√	X
Creaky	√	√	√	X
Glottalized	√	√	√	X

Here are examples of contrasts with each of the remaining three phonation types.

(36) Two-way tone contrast on breathy vowels in Quiaviní Zapotec

| Low | /gjet̤/ ˩ | → | [gʲèt̤ː] | 'squash' |
| Falling | /nje̤s/ ˯ | → | [nʲêːs̤] | 'water' |

Both codas in (36) consist of fortis consonants, with the result that the final consonants are realized with phonetic length.

(37) Three-way tone contrast on creaky vowels in Quiaviní Zapotec

High	/r-gib̰j/ ˥	→	[rgíḭ́ɸʲ]	'(he) washes'
Low	/r-gid̰j/ ˩	→	[rgìḭ̀θʲ]	'(he) sticks on'
Falling	/r-dib̰j/ ˯	→	[rdîḭɸʲ]	'(he) ties to'

In these examples, all codas consist of a lenis consonant followed by a glide, with the result that the vowel nuclei are realized with phonetic length. It is also the case that the first mora of

---

[12] But see Munro and Lopez 1999 for an alternative analysis.
[13] Sonorant consonants are lenis in this language.

the vowel is realized with modal voice and the second with creaky voice. Non-Sonorant lenis coda consonants are always realized as fricatives in coda position, either voiced or voiceless.

(38) Three-way tone contrast on glottalized vowels in Quiaviní Zapotec

High	/ɾ-gaʔ/ ˥	→	[ɾgáʔᵃ̥]	'(it) gets green again'
Low	/ɾ-gaʔ/ ˩	→	[ɾgàʔà]	'(it) gets caught'
Falling	/ɾ-gaʔ/ ˥˩	→	[ɾgáʔà]	'(it) pours'

The verbs in (37) and (38) are all in habitual aspect (ɾ- prefix) with 3S subject implied. Glottalized vowels are normally realized as "rearticulated" (i.e., VʔV). When the vowel has high tone, however, it is realized as "checked" (i.e., realized with a final glottal stop followed by a voiceless "echo vowel").[14]

From the foregoing discussion, it is clear that if the phonation type of vowels is suspected to affect tone in a language, a database field dedicated to differentiating vocalic phonation type is essential in order to ensure the validity of all tone pattern contrasts.

2.1.9 Syllable stress pattern

A number of languages have mixed tone-stress systems in which stressed syllables play a role in determining the surface realization of underlying tone patterns. Such languages are also sometimes called pitch-accent languages (cf. Van der Hulst and Smith 1988). Consider Iquito, a Zaparoan language spoken in northern Peru, which has just such a system. Michael (2011a:11) describes it as follows:

> It is useful to distinguish two kinds of tones in Iquito: lexical tones and metrical tones. Lexical tones are insensitive to metrical structure and to the presence of other lexical tones, while metrical tones are both sensitive to the metrical structure of words and affected by the presence of lexical tones in the word. I will argue that, as the names suggest, lexical tones are associated with specific moras in a morpheme as part of the morpheme's lexical entry, while metrical tones are not, but rather are assigned to the syllable bearing primary stress in precisely those cases in which the prosodic word contains no lexical tones.

He goes on to describe the tones of Iquito, whether lexically or metrically assigned, as being privative, consisting of single high tones that contrast with their absence. The placement of lexical highs is unpredictable and therefore contrastive, as may be seen in the examples of (39).

(39) Lexical tone in Iquito (Michael 2011a:10–11)

| má'ʃiku | 'raft' | ma'ʃíku | 'bird (species)' |
| 'túuku | 'tumpline' | 'tuúku | 'ear' |

The placement of metrical highs, on the other hand, is totally predictable. If, as is usually the case, no high tone is assigned to a prosodic word by the lexicon, the syllable that bears primary stress is then assigned a metrical high tone. In Iquito, primary stress is assigned to

---

[14] For more information on the interaction between tone and phonation types in Mesoamerican languages, see also Silverman 1997, Herrera 2000, Blankenship 2002, DiCanio 2008, Arellanes 2009, and Hernández (in preparation).

the head of the rightmost bimoraic trochee.[15] When an affix is added, the stress shifts in such a manner that the primary stress assignment constraint is always satisfied, as may be seen in the examples in (40). Parsing of trochees in Iquito is right to left, and in these examples, the trochees are placed within parentheses. When there are three syllables in a word, the leftmost syllable in the word forms a degenerate foot,[16] as may be seen in (40b).

(40) Metrical tone in Iquito (Michael 2011b:3)

    a. (ˈkú.ʃi)   'pot'
    b. (ˌku) (ˈʃí.ka)   'pots'
    c. (ˌku.ʃi) (ˈhá.ta) 'with (a) pot'

The high tone assigned to the first syllable of 'pot' in (40a) is clearly metrical because it shifts with the stress in (40b) and (40c) when affixes are added. In this respect, it is very different from lexical high tones, which do not shift when affixes are added. In (41), the 1S POSS prefix *kí-* is underlyingly high and always remains high, regardless of whether it is stressed or, as seen in (41c), whether it is even part of a prosodic foot.[17]

(41) Unshifted lexical tones in Iquito (Michael 2011b:3)

    a. (ˌkí) (ˈku.ʃi)   'my pot'
    b. (ˌkí.ku) (ˈʃi.ka)   'my pots'
    c. kí (ˌku.ʃi) (ˈhá.ta) 'with my pot'

In (41c), *kí-* is not part of the prosodic word and so the first syllable of ˈ*há.ta* receives a metrical high tone. Regardless of the fact that Iquito has metrically assigned tones, the fact that it also has lexically specified tones indicates that it is a tone language, following Hyman and Leben's (to appear) definition of a tone language (see section 1.1).

It should be clear that if a language is suspected of having a mixed tone-stress system (i.e., of being a pitch-accent language), it is important to include a field in the database dedicated to stress assignment location, and then to identify the tone patterns that are in contrast for each stress assignment location.

2.2 Procedure for tone analysis

Tone analysis can be thought of as a detective game, the goal of which is to discover the underlying tonal contrasts that are possible with respect to comparable morphemes of any given grammatical category. Example (42) demonstrates a three-way contrast among Chumburung data that are comparable (i.e., class 3 nouns, simple stems, CVC syllable profiles, all with non-sonorant codas).

---

[15] A trochee is a metrical foot that consists of a stressed syllable followed by an unstressed syllable. For an excellent introduction to the field of metrical phonology, see Goldsmith 1990.

[16] A degenerate foot is a foot that consists of only one syllable.

[17] Prosodic words maximally consist of two feet, so if there is a five-syllable utterance, the left-most syllable will be unparsed, or extrametrical.

(42) Isolation environment reveals three-way contrast

Pattern 1	Pattern 2	Pattern 3
[− −]	[⁻ ⁻]	[⁻ −]
kɪ-maʔ 'rubber'	kɪ-jaʔ 'leg'	kɪ-bɪʔ 'mountain'
kɪ-saʔ 'nest'	ki-jiʔ 'tree'	ki-teʔ 'feather'

However, as is obvious by now, not all tonal contrasts are necessarily revealed in a single environment (e.g., isolation). One also needs to identify any further contrasts that reveal themselves only in other environments. In fact, the more environments in which one observes any given comparable set of morphemes the better. More environments, as demonstrated in (43), translates into more possibilities for additional contrasts to reveal themselves.

(43) Second environment reveals four-way contrast

Pattern 1

[− −]	[− − ⁻ ⁻]
kɪ-maʔ 'rubber'	kɪ-maa kɪ-tɔ 'rubber's thing'
kɪ-saʔ 'nest'	kɪ-saa kɪ-tɔ 'nest's thing'

Pattern 2

[⁻ ⁻]	[⁻ ⁻ ⁻ ⁻]
kɪ-jaʔ 'leg'	kɪ-jaa kɪ-tɔ 'leg's thing'
ki-jiʔ 'tree'	ki-jii ki-tɔ 'tree's thing'

Pattern 3a

[⁻ −]	[⁻ − ⁻ ⁻]
kɪ-bɪʔ 'mountain'	kɪ-bɪɪ kɪ-tɔ 'mountain's thing'

Pattern 3b

[− ⁻]	[− ⁻ ⁻ ⁻]
ki-teʔ 'feather'	ki-tee ki-tɔ 'feather's thing'

We see that words with isolation Pattern 3 in (42) subdivide into two patterns in (43) when they are compared in the same non-isolation environment, and this now results in a four-way contrast.

As important as it is to identify the contrastive patterns in different environments, it is also important to identify the individual tones that constitute each pattern. In other words, it is not enough to say that there is an underlying four-way pattern contrast among the comparable morphemes of (42). One also wants to know the tonal makeup of the underlying patterns, and what constraints apply to them in different contexts. Again, the more environments in which one observes any given pattern, the more potential clues one has when analyzing its underlying makeup. At this point, it is helpful to have a general understanding of the tonal phenomena common to the language family under investigation. The remainder of this section outlines an order of investigation that flows from simple to complex.

2.2.1 Which words to analyze first

Since the grammatical categories that have the most members in all languages are nouns and verbs, one should begin with whichever has the simpler morphology, as this will keep unknown elements to a minimum. Those categories that have more complex morphologies can be investigated later once one has a better grasp of the phonological phenomena that are present in the language. When the underlying pattern of, say, a given noun root is not known, identifying it is much easier if there are no accompanying affixes, each of which would, of course, contribute its own tone pattern to the mix. It may be, however, that the words with the simplest morphology nevertheless do consist of more than one morpheme. Regardless, it is important to keep the morphology of that first group of words as simple as possible, whether they be nouns or verbs. That being said, nouns tend to be morphologically simpler than verbs, cross-linguistically, and if that is the case, they should be analyzed first. Another reason to begin with nouns is that the semantic notions most frequently associated with verbal morphology (e.g., number, tense, aspect, mood, subject, object) are often more difficult to elicit accurately and to distinguish from each other than are the notions most frequently associated with nominal morphology (e.g., number, case, class).[18]

Once one has decided which grammatical category has the simplest overall morphology, if there is a sub-group within that category that has a simpler morphology than the rest (e.g., a class with no affixes), then this is where one should begin, assuming there is at least a reasonable number of words in this sub-group. One should, however, be on the lookout for floating tone affixes (affixes that consist solely of tone[s]), which will not necessarily be apparent when the words are spoken in isolation. Other sub-groups that could potentially exhibit strange tonal behaviour would be nouns that refer to body parts (e.g., head, arm, leg) and/or kinship relationships (e.g., son, wife, father). The morphology of such nouns is sometimes different from that of other nouns, and if so, mixing the two groups can compromise the comparison of tone patterns.

If, as discussed in section 2.1.6, the language under investigation has noun and/or verb classes, all other things being equal one should begin with the class that has the most members, because this class is most likely to reveal more of the possible underlying patterns. Working with the largest class therefore minimizes the possibility of being surprised later by additional patterns and new phenomena. Later, of course, one will want to investigate all noun classes.

There may be times when the largest class of words does not have the simplest morphology, in which case these guiding principles are at odds with each other. My general advice in this regard is to first try analyzing the group with the simpler morphology, assuming that it is not overly small, without investing too much time in it. If the analysis appears to be productive, then continue with it. However, if what emerges is not relatively transparent, then I'd suggest dropping it in favour of beginning with the largest group that has the next simplest morphology.

Following the general principle of beginning with simple structures, the first group of words for investigation should be those that have simple (single root) stems, and therefore single tone patterns. Since the underlying patterns of the stems are unknown (i.e., they are the object of the analysis) it is easier to begin with stems that have one unknown pattern, as opposed to stems that have two or more unknown patterns (e.g., one for each root of a compound stem). Furthermore, the fact that part of any given pattern can consist of a floating tone makes it even more important to begin the analysis with single patterns at a time. Often one does not know the status of stems until one has been working in the language for a longer period of time. Some stems, however, are easily recognizable as compounds or reduplications, and in such cases, one should avoid including them in the original groupings. Later, one should begin

---

[18] I am grateful to David Weber for bringing this point to my attention.

analyzing complex stems with derivational morphology, since this is regular, followed later, perhaps, by reduplicated stems, compounds, and finally, borrowed words.

Given the very important role that syllable profiles play in determining how tone patterns are realized, it is important that the first words to be analyzed have stem profiles that are the most likely to reveal the underlying patterns. Determining the underlying patterns of morphemes is much easier if one can hear all the tones of the pattern, and this is more likely to happen with the profile that has the greatest number of sonorant TBUs. This being the case, simple stems with two TBUs (e.g., CVCV or CVN) are more likely to reveal their underlying patterns than are simple stems with one TBU (e.g., CV). Similarly, a stem that ends in a sonorant coda is more likely to reveal its underlying pattern than is one that ends in a non-sonorant coda. For these reasons, it is best to begin with stems with more than one mora, and then to proceed with shorter ones.

There are times, however, when the longer stem may not be the best initial choice. For example, when faced with a simple CVCVC stem in which the final C is non-sonorant, and a simple CVCV stem, I would recommend beginning with the CVCV stem over the CVCVC one. Although CVCVC is longer, there is a greater chance of the final non-sonorant consonant "hiding" the final tone of the pattern.

Even following these guidelines, one can still be left with several competing syllable profiles that meet the above criteria. For example, stems with profiles CVCV, CVS (where S is any sonorant coda), and CVV each consist of two sonorant moras. In such a case, I would suggest NOT beginning with CVCV stems because disyllabic stems of theoretically unknown simplicity have greater chances of being compound or complex than do comparable monosyllabic stems. This then leaves the choice between CVS and CVV stems: when V-initial suffixes are adjoined to such stems, syllables are more clearly delineated with CVS stems than with CVV stems. Beginning with CVS syllable profiles therefore removes the possibility of any tonal ambiguity that might arise when vowel nuclei are brought into adjacency (i.e., in deciding which tone belongs with which TBU).

If the family of the language under investigation is known to have consonant-tone interaction, one should begin with words that have only "neutral" consonants, thereby avoiding consonants that potentially have a raising or lowering effect. Words with consonants that do not influence tone provide better opportunities to discover patterns that contrast, since "depressor" or "raiser" consonants have the potential to neutralize some or all of the tone contrasts. The same can be said of languages in which the phonation qualities of vowels influence tone. In such cases, begin with non-influencing (i.e., modal) vowels. Although vowels affected by phonation qualities don't necessarily neutralize contrasts, the potential is certainly there for this to happen.

Finally, if there are known to be mixed tone-stress systems in related languages, begin by looking for contrastive pitch patterns within the most representative word-stress pattern, before moving on to less prolific patterns. If tone patterns indeed contrast lexically in a language, the contrasts are more likely to be revealed in a larger group than in a smaller group.

This suggested order for comparing groupings of words spoken in isolation is summarized in (44).

(44) Ranking of criteria for deciding which words to analyze first
    a) grammatical category: least complex > most complex
    b) noun/verb class: largest class > smallest class (if relevant)
    c) stem type: simple > complex > compound > borrowed
    d) syllable profile: most TBUs > fewest TBUs; sonorant codas > non-sonorant codas
    e) consonants: non-depressor/non-raiser > depressor/raiser (if relevant)
    f) phonation type of vowels: modal > breathy, creaky, glottalized (if relevant)
    g) syllable stress pattern: most prolific pattern > least prolific pattern (if relevant)

Taking the time and trouble to control for the factors just discussed and to work in the suggested order will better allow one to discover the patterns that the language employs and to move to the next stage of the analysis with fewer "unknowns."

2.2.2 Order of investigation

Once the isolation patterns of the "first" group (or groups) of words have been identified, it is useful to examine these words in other phonological and grammatical contexts before moving on to other groups. Analyzing as completely as possible this (hopefully most transparent) group of words before moving on offers two main advantages. First, it provides one with maximal insight into the tonal patterns and processes of the language at an early stage in the analysis. Secondly, it provides feedback on the usefulness of the procedure to this point, which, in turn, enables one to revise, if necessary, the order of investigation and the chosen phonological and grammatical environments. Armed with these initial insights, one can then move on to analyzing the remaining groups of words.

Words are the smallest element of the phonological hierarchy that a native speaker can pronounce independently of other constituents. That being said, one needs to be aware of all the factors that affect how the underlying patterns of morphemes are phonetically realized. First, words spoken in isolation often consist of more than one morpheme (e.g., a root and often one or more inflectional or derivational affixes, multiple roots in the case of compound stems). If this is the case, there is the potential for interaction between the tone patterns of root(s) and affix(es), and individual morphemes can be realized with several different phonetic forms, depending on the contexts in which they are found.[19] In addition, a word spoken in isolation is not only a phonological word, but it is also a phonological phrase and, as such, it is subject to phrasal phenomena. For example, in some African languages there is a process of pre-pausal tone lowering that renders low all phrase-final high tones (e.g., Kikuyu, Clements and Ford 1977). Analyzing words spoken in isolation therefore does not necessarily reveal the underlying patterns of all morphemes. Nonetheless, it is certainly an excellent place to begin because isolation environments ensure that external factors affecting tone are kept to a minimum. This, in turn, reduces the possibility that underlying patterns will be realized in a manner different from what would otherwise be expected.

Once one has analyzed words spoken in isolation, it is important to expand the number of morphological environments. There is usually a great deal to be learned by examining: a) the plural forms of nouns, b) various nominalized forms of verbs, and c) different conjugations of verbs including their imperative and infinitival forms (if one or the other of these isn't the normal isolation form). This allows the analyst to observe the tonal behaviour of roots in different contexts without introducing the complications that can arise from adding words to the phrase.

Finally, one should elicit the words in different phrasal environments as new phonological environments may reveal additional tonal behaviour. With the knowledge gained to this point, it may be necessary to revise the order of investigation somewhat. For example, words that initially seemed to have simple tone patterns when spoken in isolation might reveal themselves to have more complex patterns. In such a case, it is the genuinely simpler patterns that should provide the starting point. As discussed above, as one progresses in the analysis, one should always be prepared to revise one's original hypotheses and/or order of investigation as necessary.

---

[19] With regard to tone, such alternations are sometimes referred to in especially older literature as "tone sandhi." When tone sandhi takes place within words (i.e., when the environment that triggers the change is across a morpheme boundary), it is sometimes called "internal sandhi" and when it takes place across word boundaries, it is sometimes called "external sandhi."

We next discuss, in turn, the different environments recommended for phonological investigation: words spoken in isolation, words spoken in other morphological environments, and words spoken in other phrasal environments.

2.3 Words spoken in isolation

With regard to the methodology presented to this point, the analyst should have entered into a database a reasonably large number of words in their isolation forms. Further, one needs to be able to filter these entries in order to select words that are alike in all the ways that can affect tone patterns (i.e., according to grammatical category, class, syllable profile, etc.). One should then identify the first group of words to be analyzed following the principles outlined above and sort this group into sub-groups according to their surface patterns. If the analyst has been rigorous when entering these data into the database, one can conclude that any differences in the surface patterns of these words will be due to differences in the underlying patterns of their roots. Such rigour has the potential to reveal early on many underlying contrasts (i.e., patterns). Examination of further groups of words (e.g., other noun/verb classes) may reveal additional patterns.

Once the data are organized along the lines described above, it is helpful to assemble a chart like the one in (45), that shows verb data from Ashe [ahs], a Benue-Congo language spoken in Nigeria.[20] Counts of each pattern, which also appear in the chart, help the analyst distinguish productive forms from less productive ones.

---

[20] These data were provided by Gideon Madaki during a tone analysis workshop I conducted in Jos, Nigeria in 2012, and are used here with his kind permission.

2.3 *Words spoken in isolation*   55

(45) Contrastive pitch patterns of imperative verbs in Ashe

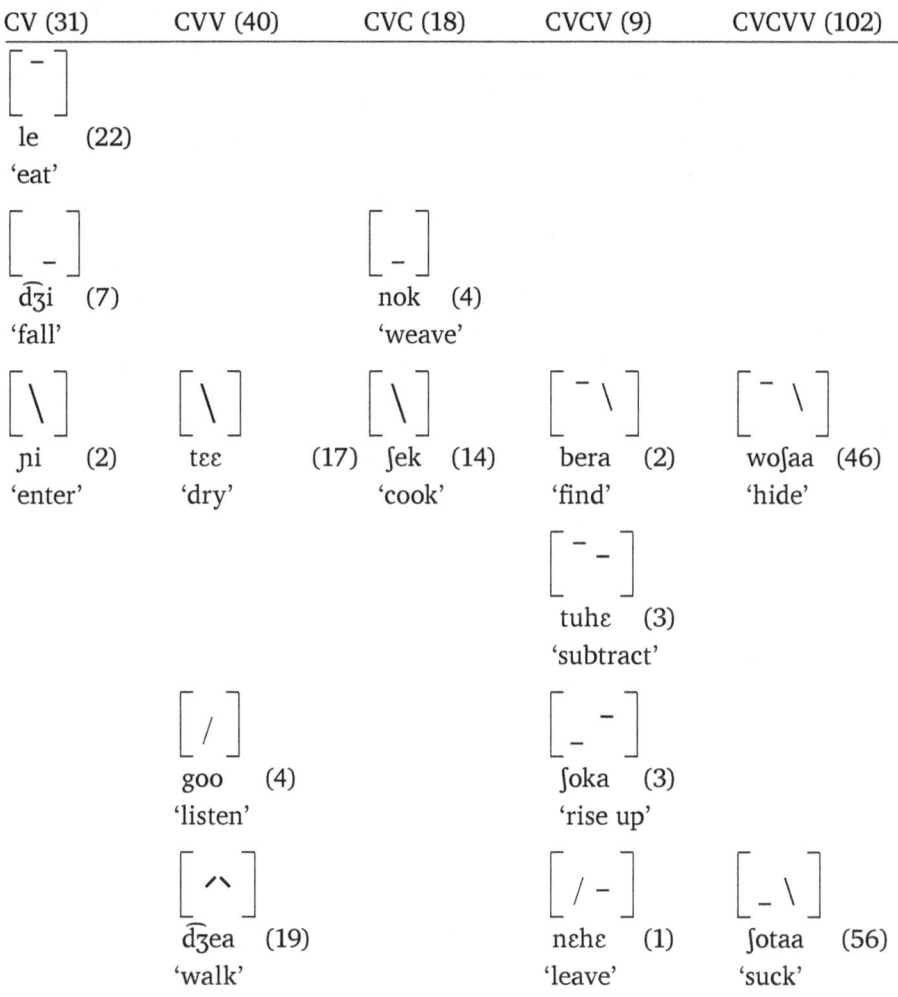

This chart, with preliminary findings only, consists entirely of verbs spoken in isolation in the imperative mood. Initially, all verbs were thought to have simple stems, although the low numbers and the complexity of some of the patterns definitely suggest otherwise. A chart like this is very helpful because, to the extent that the verbs in each column have simple stems, each column reveals true tonal contrasts.

Recall that the goal of tone analysis is to discover the different underlying tonal contrasts of the morphemes in a language and then to identify the underlying patterns of these contrasts by carefully examining their tonal behaviour in different contexts. When undertaking such analysis, it is therefore important to begin constructing hypotheses—as the facts become known—concerning the tonal makeup of the underlying patterns. These hypotheses will subsequently be built upon and revised as further facts become known. The analyst should now assign tentative underlying patterns to the first group of contrastive surface patterns, bearing in mind that at this point, these assignments are based solely on the observation of the patterns in a single (i.e., isolation) context.

In following this procedure, it is not as important to assign underlying patterns that resemble the surface patterns as it is to assign patterns that reflect the actual contrasts in the language. If a language has a tone system, then a priori it must contrast high and low tones, and we expect to find at least the patterns /L/ and /H/ in contrast. Thus if we find a category of morphemes (e.g., nouns) that tonally splits into two groups, and if the contrasts are clearly not due to any of the external factors that can affect tone, then regardless of how those patterns are realized in their various surface forms, we can reasonably ascribe to them the underlying patterns /L/ and /H/. This might not always be the case, but it will be more often than not. Returning to the data in (45), one of the most striking aspects is the CVCVV column. These data, which clearly account for the majority of verbs in the data (110 out of a total of 189) have only two contrastive patterns. The underlying patterns are not at all obvious from examining their isolation surface forms, but the fact that there are only two patterns strongly suggests that one is /H/ and the other is /L/, or perhaps toneless.

Given, however, that most tone languages have morphemes that consist of two or more moras (TBUs), and given that the patterns /LH/ and /HL/ are extremely common cross-linguistically, one can expect bimoraic roots to bear at least the underlying patterns /L/, /H/, /LH/, and /HL/. In general, if a particular set of words divides into only four (or fewer) tone groups, it is entirely reasonable to hypothesize (at least initially) that they represent the four patterns mentioned above (or a subset of them), regardless of how they are realized in their surface forms. For example, for reasons of economy one would not expect to find underlying mid tones on disyllabic roots that have only four or fewer contrastive patterns, even if some of those patterns included surface mid tones.

2.4 Words spoken in other morphological environments

Once one has established—by examining words in isolation—as many underlying tonal contrasts as possible for any given category of morphemes (e.g., verb roots), it is now helpful to investigate the pitches of those same morphemes in related words spoken in isolation (e.g., help: helping, helper, etc.). If verbs have been elicited in isolation as infinitives, the analyst could further elicit them in imperative and nominalized forms, as well as with different subject markers, object markers, and tense/aspect markers, etc. For nouns, if most isolation forms are, say, singulars, other forms could include plurals, nouns with different demonstrative affixes, nouns with a locative affix, etc. What is possible will of course depend on the morphology of the language.

When eliciting word lists, I typically ask for the plural forms of nouns at the same time as their singular forms. I also elicit verbs in at least one environment additional to the isolation one during the first pass. Not only is this more efficient time-wise, but I have found that the extra time spent on each word also pays off in other ways: the morphology of each word immediately becomes more apparent than it otherwise would, and this can stimulate productive discussion. In addition, this practice helps to better establish the word's identity (for both the analyst and the language consultant) so there is less likelihood of anyone later confusing it with other (similar) words.

Paradigmatic data like these are most easily compared when they are systematically organized in charts such as the one in (46), constructed for verbs with simple CVC stems in Akoose, a Bantu A language of Cameroon (data from Robert Hedinger, personal communication). In this chart, each column contrasts the surface patterns of underlyingly high and low verb roots for that column's morphological context, and each row contrasts the surface patterns of a number of different grammatical forms for a given verb.

2.4 *Words spoken in other morphological environments*

(46) Akoose verb paradigm of CVC roots

	Imperative '___!'	Infinitive 'to ___'	Inf. Purpose 'to ___'	3S Hortative 'he should ___'	Neutral 'he ___s'	Gloss
/H/	[⁻] wɔg	[⁻ ⁻] awɔg	[⁻ ⁻] awɔg	[⁻ \] awɔg	[⁻ ⁻] awɔg	'wash'
/L/	[´] wub	[⁻ \] awub	[⁻ \] awub	[⁻ \] awub	[⁻ \] awub	'pull out'

In order to examine this same information from, say, CV and CVV roots, one would construct separate (new) paradigms. One could also construct a paradigm for Akoose verbs along the lines of (47).

(47) Akoose verb paradigm of infinitives with simple stem

	CV	Gloss	CVV	Gloss	CVC	Gloss
/H/	[⁻ ⁻] abɛ	'to be'	[⁻ \] asii	'to iron'	[⁻ ⁻] awɔg	'to wash'
/L/	[⁻ \] abɛ	'to give'	[⁻ \] asuu	'to pass air'	[⁻ \] awub	'to pull out'

Other charts would allow one to examine these same verbs in their imperative and other grammatical forms. Alternatively, one could be creative and put all of this information into a larger, complex paradigm, as in (48).

(48) Akoose verb paradigm

	Imperative '___!'	Infinitive 'to ___'	Inf. Purpose 'to ___'	3S Hortative 'he should ___'	Neutral 'he ___s'	Gloss
CV						
/H/	[‾] bɛ	[‾ ‾] abɛ	[‾ ‾] abɛ	[‾ \ ] abɛ	[‾ ‾] abɛ	'be'
/L/	[╱] bɛ	[‾ ╲] abɛ	[‾ ╲] abɛ	[‾ ╲] abɛ	[‾ ╲] abɛ	'give'
CVV						
/H/	[‾] sii	[‾ \ ] asii	[‾ ╲] asii	[‾ \ ] asii	[‾ ‾] asii	'iron (v)'
/L/	[╱] suu	[‾ ╲] asuu	[‾ ╲] asuu	[‾ ╲] asuu	[‾ ╲] asuu	'pass air'
CVC						
/H/	[‾] wɔg	[‾ ‾] awɔg	[‾ ‾] awɔg	[‾ \ ] awɔg	[‾ ‾] awɔg	'wash'
/L/	[╱] wub	[‾ ╲] awub	[‾ ╲] awub	[‾ ╲] awub	[‾ ╲] awub	'pull out'

In paradigms such as these, one can focus either on what is common to any row or on what is common to any column. Viewing data from these two perspectives almost invariably brings to the fore any random errors made in transcription. This is because data with errors will usually not fit in with the analysis of at least one or the other of the two axes. The main advantage, however, of viewing data in morphological paradigms like these is that one is able to analyze the data in a controlled manner: each new environment contributes only a single new element without involving additional words in the phrase.

2.5 Words spoken in other phrasal environments

As important as it is to expand the morphological environments of morphemes beyond that of their isolation forms, it is perhaps even more important to expand their phrasal environments. While morphological environments for any given morpheme can sometimes be quite limited, phrasal environments usually have much fewer restrictions. This is particularly true of nouns. While verb roots can often be placed into a variety of different morphological contexts, the potential for additional morphological contexts for noun roots is usually more restricted; in some cases, the only option is to elicit plural forms, which often do not provide enough information to determine underlying forms. Multi-word phrasal environments, on the other hand, usually provide a greater range of phonological contexts into which morphemes can be placed, and hence, more opportunities to observe their tonal behaviour. As is the case for morphemes in different morphological environments (above), the construction of paradigmatic charts also provides an excellent way to display morphemes in different phrasal environments.

In order to construct a chart of paradigmatic phrasal data, it is helpful to use substitutionary frames. The idea is to provide a "known" tonal environment (i.e., a frame) that includes a "slot" into which words with unknown patterns can be placed. The frame, or carrier phrase, is a grammatical/ phonological environment that remains constant, whatever the word in the slot. A simple frame could be something like 'house of __' or 'big __'. Paradigms constructed from frames like these are helpful in two ways. First, they permit the analyst to observe the tonal behaviour of a group of comparable words in the slot of a single phrasal environment. Second, they permit the analyst to observe the tonal behaviour of a single word in multiple phrasal environments, assuming one is employing more than one frame. As is the case when examining morphological environments, one needs to place careful limits on any unknown patterns in the frame so that if possible, the only unknown patterns belong to the morphemes that go into the slots.

Ideally, one wants to begin with the four phrasal environments given in (49).

(49) Four ideal tone environments for analyzing tone in phrases:
　　a) word with known (or suspected) underlying pattern H placed immediately to the *right* of the word whose pattern is under investigation
　　b) word with known (or suspected) underlying pattern L placed immediately to the *right* of the word whose pattern is under investigation
　　c) word with known (or suspected) underlying pattern H placed immediately to the *left* of the word whose pattern is under investigation
　　d) word with known (or suspected) underlying pattern L placed immediately to the *left* of the word whose pattern is under investigation

There may be other frames to be investigated subsequently, but one should begin with at least these environments because they reveal how any given pattern influences and is influenced by the two "foundational" patterns /H/ and /L/ on both edges. In many cases, these four environments will reveal most, if not all, of the possible tonal alternations that any given underlying pattern can undergo. When choosing frame words, it is helpful to choose words that meet the word choice ranking criteria of section 2.2, in order to reduce the risk of any of them having floating tones. So, all other things being equal, a bimoraic frame word with all sonorant moras is preferable to a monomoraic one because there is a better chance that its surface tones correspond to its underlying tones. Also, if any tone spreading occurs from the word under investigation (i.e., the slot word) to a frame word, the longer the frame word is, the easier it is to discover the domain of the spreading process (i.e., how far the spreading goes).

If at all possible, frames should avoid bringing two vowels into juxtaposition across grammatical boundaries. Such environments often result in one or other of the vowels being elided, which, of course, results in the loss of a TBU. To avoid these kinds of situations, Hyman (2014:540) recommends using forms that "are framed by consonants." This can be accomplished by ensuring that for any given two-word sequence, either the first word of the sequence ends in a consonant, or the second word begins with a consonant.

Unfortunately, just as expanding the morphological environments is limited by morphological constraints, so too expanding the phrasal environments is limited by syntactic constraints. This means that it might not always be possible to place any given word into all of the environments suggested above. But whatever the environment, it is always helpful to limit the number of words in the complete phrase to the minimum allowed by the syntax. This keeps to a minimum the number of any unknown tone patterns, and it also reduces the possibility of inserting additional tone phenomena into the mix.

The importance of restricting the environments to grammatically acceptable constructions cannot be emphasized enough. When words are put into phrasal environments, one must not simply place one word adjacent to another. Rather, the construction must be a bona fide grammatical construction that can occur naturally in the language. It must also allow for the creation of novel forms (see the discussion in section 1.5.1 regarding "elicited" vs. "natural" language data).

Some constructions that lend themselves to expanding the phrasal environments of nouns and verbs in a controlled manner appear in (50) and (51).

(50) Examples of noun phrases conducive to expanding the phrasal environment
  a) noun with something it can possess
  b) noun with something that can possess it
  c) noun with an adjective
  d) noun with a quantifier
  e) noun with a determiner

Hyman (2014:542) also suggests using a frame like 'the place of ____' because "place" can fit semantically with almost any noun.

(51) Examples of verb phrases conducive to expanding the phrasal environment
  a) verb with an object
  b) verb with an adverbial element
  c) verb with a locative element
  d) verb with a temporal element

The environments suggested in (50) and (51) are intended as examples, and what is used in practice will, of course, be language specific. The important thing is to compare patterns in as many tonally different phrasal environments as possible.

After determining which frames to use, the analyst will then elicit the first phrasal frame with the first of the words to be analyzed in the slot. Once that phrase is transcribed, the analyst and language consultant will repeat this procedure until the first frame has been pronounced with all the words in the slot. They will then repeat this whole procedure with the second frame and continue until all of the frames have been employed. Once one has transcribed the surface forms for each of the elicited phrases, it is important to chart this data in a format that makes patterns and differences easy to see. This is best accomplished by constructing a phrasal paradigm and placing the data in a table.

Phrasal paradigms are very similar to morphological paradigms. In both cases, the focus is on analyzing the underlying patterns and the tonal behaviour of roots in different environments. The data in (52) demonstrate a noun phrase paradigm for Laarim [loh], a Nilo-Saharan language spoken in the Eastern Equatorial province of Sudan (data courtesy of Timothy Stirtz and Lopeok Clement, personal communication).

2.5 *Words spoken in other phrasal environments* 61

(52) Laarim noun phrase paradigm

Isolation	Frame 1: H before ícín ńgáá ____ 'woman sees ____'	Frame 2: L before ícín màà ____ 'lion sees ____'	Frame 3: H after ____ tőrőrà ícìtò '____ in ditch'	Frame 4: L after ____ ńgìlòmá ícìtò '____ in cave'
/H/				
vatik 'stick'	icin ngaa vatik 'woman sees stick'	icin maa vati 'lion sees stick'	vatik tõrõra icito 'stick in ditch'	vatik ngiloma icito 'stick in cave'
/L/				
lũwat 'fence'	icin ngaa lũwat 'woman sees fence'	icin maa lũwat 'lion sees fence'	lũwat tõrõra icito 'fence in ditch'	lũwat ngiloma icito 'fence in cave'
/HL/				
tdõlõk 'shrew'	icin ngaa tdõlõ 'woman sees shrew'	icin maa tdõlõk 'lion sees shrew'	tdõlõk tõrõra icito 'shrew in ditch'	tdõlõk ngiloma icito 'shrew in cave'
/LH/				
lĩbath 'cloth'	icin ngaa lĩbath 'woman sees cloth'	icin maa lĩbath 'lion sees cloth'	lĩbath tõrõra icito 'cloth in ditch'	lĩbath ngiloma icito 'cloth in cave'

If one wishes to focus on analyzing a particular unknown underlying pattern, that is, the pattern of one of the "slot" words, one would begin with its form as spoken in isolation and then work from left to right in the table. In so doing, the different alternations (or lack thereof) are revealed as the word in question appears in the different frames and contexts. One would also want to examine how that underlying pattern affects the underlying patterns of the different phrases in the frames. Another way to begin would be to focus on a particular frame (e.g., Frame 1) and work from top to bottom, with a view to determining how the different word patterns affect the frame word, and of course how the frame word affects the different patterns.

The methodology put forward in this chapter is largely atheoretical, as are the contrastive patterns this methodology reveals. To the extent that one works with data that are truly comparable, careful descriptions of the contrasts and phenomena that emerge will prove useful to generations of linguists, whatever their theoretical persuasions happen to be.

3

Phonetics of Pitch

Linguists analyze pitch acoustically for various reasons. Sometimes, it is with a view to developing or improving linguistic models that generate tone and/or intonation patterns for spoken language. At other times, it is to contribute to the development of synthesized speech and/or speech recognition software. Often, however, field linguists analyze pitch acoustically in order to confirm the accuracy of their pitch transcriptions, which are typically based solely on auditory impressions. For instance, if it is claimed that the pattern [_ -] contrasts with the pattern [_ ¯], then it is important to be able to objectively verify that difference. Similarly, if one claims that the level of the first and last pitches of the pattern [- ¯ ¯ -] are the same, then again it is important to be able to confirm (or disprove) this since these transcriptions serve as inputs to phonological analyses, and such analyses, of course, can only be as accurate as the data upon which they are based. Moreover, since these analyses, in turn, often serve to inform the development of linguistic theory, the importance of ensuring quality pitch transcriptions cannot be emphasized enough. The purpose of this chapter is therefore to help linguists who are otherwise relatively capable of transcribing pitch to confirm the accuracy of their transcriptions.[1]

But first, what is pitch, and what is its relationship to fundamental frequency (abbreviated F_0)? While pitch is a perceptual term that denotes tone as it is "heard," F_0 is an acoustic term that denotes "the lowest frequency component in a complex sound wave" (Crystal 2008:203–204). Pitch is often measured in units known as mels, while F_0, which correlates directly with the rate at which the vocal folds vibrate, is measured in units known as hertz (abbreviated Hz and discussed further below). Pitch is often closely associated with F_0. For example, if one increases the F_0 of an utterance, it will generally be perceived as an increase in pitch. Similarly, if one decreases the F_0 of an utterance, it will generally be perceived as a decrease in pitch. It is important to realize, however, that a fixed change in F_0 does not always lead to the same change in pitch. For example, if a sound produced at 200 Hz is followed by a second sound produced at 250 Hz (a difference of 50 Hz), the second sound will be significantly higher in pitch than the first. However, if the first sound is produced at 2000 Hz and the second at 2050 Hz (again a difference of 50 Hz), the perceived difference between the two pitches will not be nearly as great as it was in the first comparison. This is because the

---

[1] Novice linguists who attempt to use acoustic analysis software because they are unable to "hear tone" will most likely not find acoustic analysis software particularly helpful. This has been covered in some detail in section 1.5.3.

relationship between pitch and F_0 is not linear but rather logarithmic. Given these differences, when reference is made throughout this book to perceived tone (i.e., tone as it is heard), the term pitch is used, and when reference is made to the acoustic properties of tone, the term fundamental frequency is used.

In his *Field Manual of Acoustic Phonetics,* Baart (2010:1) outlines three traditional domains of phonetic study: articulatory phonetics, the study of "how speech sounds are produced by a speaker"; auditory phonetics, the study of "how speech sounds are perceived by a listener"; and acoustic phonetics, the study of "the properties of the sound waves that are associated with speech sounds." This chapter focusses on the first and third of those domains insofar as they relate to the analysis of pitch.

We begin by taking a brief look at how pitch is produced physiologically. We then spend the remainder of the chapter examining the properties of sound waves associated with different pitch levels.

3.1 The articulation of pitch

The primary physiological structures responsible for the production of sounds in human speech are the vocal folds of the larynx, or voice-box. And it is the rate, or frequency, at which these folds vibrate that is primarily responsible for the perceived height of the pitch of any utterance: the faster they vibrate, the higher the perceived pitch. Stevens (1998) describes the vocal folds as consisting of two parallel bands of cordlike tissue, each with a thickness of 2 to 3 mm and a length of 1.0 to 1.5 cm in adults. These bands, in turn, are described by Hirose (1997:126), basing his conclusions on earlier work by Hirano (1974), as primarily consisting of an outer "cover," which includes "the epithelium and the superficial layer of the lamina propria," and an inner "body," which includes the vocalis muscle.

The anterior ends of the vocal folds are joined, close together, to the inner, lower, front surface of the thyroid cartilage and stretch back to where their posterior ends are attached to the two arytenoid cartilages (see figure 1).

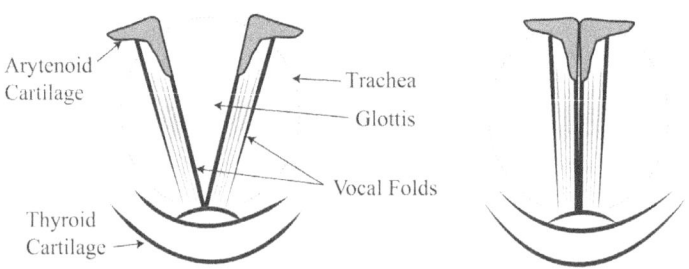

Figure 1. The vocal folds. (The left drawing shows the folds in abducted position while the right one shows them in adducted position.)

By rotating the two arytenoid cartilages, the vocal folds may be brought apart in the abducted, or open position, with the result that air flows freely through the glottis, the opening between the vocal folds, or they may be brought tightly together in the adducted, or closed position, with the result that the air stream is totally blocked.[2] When air is forced out of the lungs and the folds are brought loosely together, a situation is created that enables the vocal folds to vibrate. When this happens, the subglottal air pressure (i.e., pressure below the

---

[2] For more in-depth descriptions of laryngeal anatomy and behaviour, the interested reader is referred to Ohala 1978; Denes and Pinson 1993; Hirose 1997; Stevens 1998; and Gick, Wilson, and Derrick 2013.

larynx) increases behind the closed glottis until it overcomes the tension that keeps the vocal folds together. At this point, the vocal folds are pushed apart. Air rushing through the now (albeit only slightly) open glottis gives rise to the Bernoulli effect,[3] which results in an immediate decrease in air pressure between the vocal folds. This decrease in air pressure, together with the elasticity of the vocal folds, causes the folds to snap back together again, which, in turn, creates the conditions for the cycle to repeat itself. The cyclic openings and closings of the glottis result in cyclic increases and decreases in air pressure, which are otherwise known as "sound waves." Sound waves, in turn, travel through the atmosphere and strike the ear drum causing it to vibrate at the same rate of vibration as that of the vocal folds that produce the sound waves. The auditory region of the brain interprets these vibrations as sound: the greater the rate of vibration, the higher the pitch, and the lesser the rate of vibration, the lower the pitch.

While this description explains how vocal sounds are produced, it does not account for how pitch changes are effected. An early study by Halle and Stevens (1971) suggests that pitch change in human voice is controlled by a single mechanism, namely vocal fold tension, with there being three particular states involved: stiff, slack, and neither stiff nor slack. This, in turn, gives rise to three contrastive tone levels: high, mid, and low. More recently, however, Duanmu (2000) credits Zemlin (1981) as identifying two mechanisms for effecting pitch change that operate independently of each other: a) contraction of the cricothyroid muscles and b) contraction of the vocalis muscles.[4]

As may be seen in figure 1, the vocal folds are attached to two types of cartilages, the thyroid cartilage and the arytenoid cartilages. Contraction of the cricothyroid muscles tilts the front of the thyroid cartilage downward and forward, thereby increasing the distance between it and the arytenoid cartilages. This movement elongates the vocal folds, which, according to Hirose (1997), decreases their thickness and increases the stiffness of both the cover and the body of the folds. The longer the vocal folds, the thinner and stiffer they will be and, all else being equal, the faster the folds will vibrate. By way of contrast, the shorter the vocal folds, the thicker and slacker they will be and the slower they will vibrate. In this respect, their behaviour is very similar to that of a guitar string as it is tightened and loosened.

The second mechanism for changing pitch is contraction of the vocalis muscles, located deep within the body of the vocal folds themselves. According to Hirose, contraction of these muscles increases the isometric tension of the body of the folds, which increases the stiffness of the body independently of that attributable to any contraction of the cricothyroid muscles. The greater the isometric tension of the vocalis muscles, the greater the stiffness of the vocal fold body and, all else being equal, the faster the vocal folds will vibrate; i.e., the greater the F_0. By way of contrast, the lesser the isometric tension of the vocalis muscles, the lesser the stiffness of the body of the vocal folds and the slower the folds will vibrate. These conclusions are summed up in (1).

---

[3] The Bernoulli effect is an observation in the field of hydrodynamics that as the velocity of a fluid or gas increases, the pressure it exerts decreases. This effect is notably responsible for providing "lift" to airplane wings, for the "sucking" of leaves behind a passing car in autumn, and for the "pull" one feels towards a large vehicle when it passes on the highway.

[4] See also Hallé et al. 1990 and Hallé 1994.

(1) Articulatory, acoustic, and auditory correlates of independent laryngeal mechanisms

	Contraction of cricothyroid muscles	Contraction of vocalis muscles
Articulatory result	increased length of vocal folds	increased isometric tension of vocalis muscles
which, in turn, results in	decreased thickness and increased stiffness of both cover and body of vocal folds	increased stiffness of body of vocal folds
Acoustic result	increased F_0	increased F_0
Auditory result	higher pitch	higher pitch

3.2 The acoustics of pitch

Baart (2010:16–22) categorizes speech sounds into four groups: a) silence (i.e., the silent part of plosive consonants and speech pauses), b) plosion (i.e., the "sudden flow of air due to the build-up and subsequent release of a pressure difference," such as is found in "plosives, clicks, ejectives, and implosives"), c) friction (i.e., "turbulence due to air that is forced through a narrow constriction," such as is found in fricatives), and d) voice (i.e., "repetitive opening and closing of the vocal folds," such as is found in vowels and other sonorant sounds). He goes on to equate these four speech sound groups with the four wave types of (2).

(2) Speech sound groups and wave types

Wave type	Sound group	Wave characteristics
silence	silence	absence of fluctuations
burst	plosion	momentary event of short duration (15–20 ms)
random wave	friction	sustained sound but no regular, recurring pattern
periodic wave	voicing	patterns that regularly repeat themselves

Examples of the four wave types appear in figure 2.

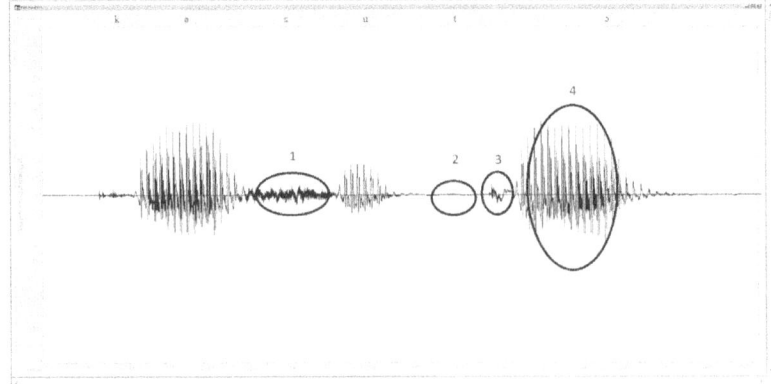

1. random wave
2. silence
3. burst
4. periodic wave

Figure 2. Wave types found in Chumburung word $k^h\acute{ɔ}sút^h\acute{ɔ}$ 'forehead'.

3.2 The acoustics of pitch

In this utterance, 1) a random wave is found in the production of the voiceless fricative [s]; 2) silence is found in three places: the lead-up to the burst of the initial plosive [kʰ], the lead-up to the burst of the plosive [tʰ], and following the periodic wave of the vowel [ɔ]; 3) bursts are found at the plosions of the plosives [kʰ] and [tʰ]; and 4) periodic waves are found at the productions of the vowels [ə], [u], and [ɔ]. Since pitch in human language is regularly associated with sonorant sounds, the remainder of this chapter deals with investigations of sounds that have periodic waves, i.e., wave patterns that regularly repeat themselves.

Smooth, perfect, simple waves are called sine waves, and the greater the amplitude of the wave (i.e., the greater the distance between the wave's peaks and valleys), the louder the perceived sound. A cycle is one complete repetition of a wave (1 cycle per second = 1 Hz), and the faster the cycle repeats itself, the higher the perceived pitch.

Figure 3 shows two sine waves produced with the same amplitudes at different frequencies: the first, Wave a, is produced at 500 cycles per second (viz. 500 Hz), and the second, Wave b, at 300 cycles per second (viz. 300 Hz).

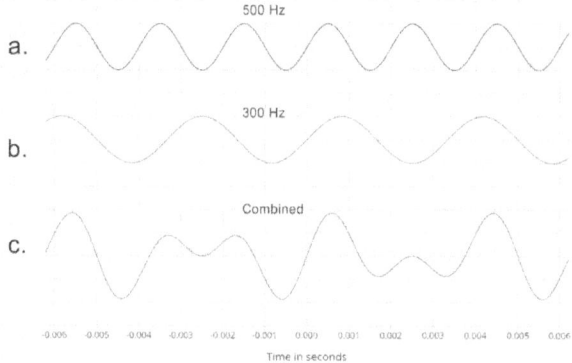

Figure 3. Two sine waves with cycle periods of 500 Hz and 300 Hz, respectively.[a]

[a] Modified from "Wave Interference Beat Frequency Demonstration", https://academo.org/demos/wave-interference-beat-frequency/, used courtesy of Edward Ball.

When the two sine waves of figure 3 are produced simultaneously, however, they produce the complex wave c. The two tuning forks responsible for the sine waves affect the resultant air pressure in such a manner that "when both forks are working together to increase the pressure...the resultant pressure is above that produced by either alone; similarly when both forks are working together to decrease the pressure, the resulting pressure is less than that which would result from the action of either fork alone; but when the two forks are working against each other, one trying to increase the pressure while the other is trying to decrease it,...the resultant pressure is somewhere between the two" (Ladefoged 1962:27).

The periodic waves of human sonorant sounds are complex, composed of many simple component waves produced simultaneously. Of the component waves in the complex wave of a sonorant sound, the frequency of the slowest wave is the fundamental frequency (F_0), and it is this frequency with which we are primarily concerned in this chapter. As explained above, F_0 is an acoustic term that refers to the frequency of air pressure fluctuations, and in natural speech, this frequency corresponds to the frequency of the opening and closing of the vocal folds (e.g., if the vocal folds open and close 100 times per second, the F_0 will be 100 Hz).

Figure 4 shows an expanded part of the complex wave of the Chumburung vowel ɔ.

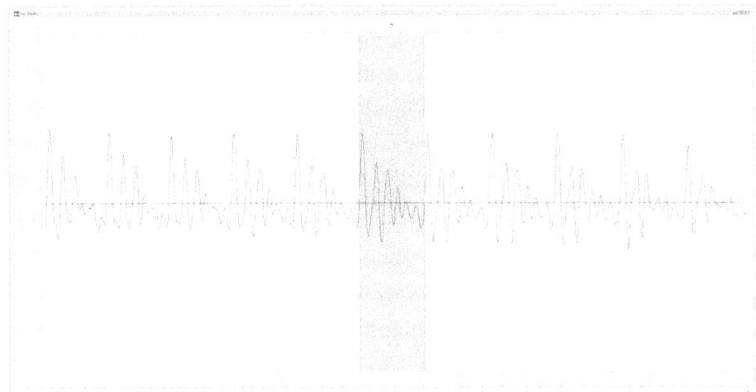

Figure 4. Complex wave from Chumburung vowel ɔ.

In figure 4, the highlighted portion is one cycle of the complex wave, which corresponds to one opening and closing of the vocal folds.

Since it is important for those who analyze pitch to be able to isolate and measure F_0, speech analysis software packages typically provide "pitch traces" of utterances, together with readouts of the F_0 and other relevant information at places selected by the analyst.

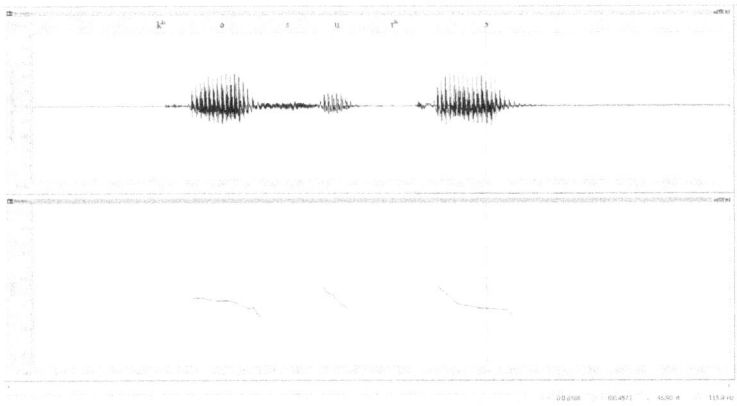

Figure 5. Wave form and pitch trace.

In figure 5, both the wave form and the pitch trace of the Chumburung word $k^h\acute{ɔ}s\acute{u}t^h\acute{ɔ}$ 'forehead' are shown using the Speech Analyzer software. Although perhaps too small to be seen properly in the above graphic, Speech Analyzer provides an F_0 reading of 115.9 Hz in the lower right-hand corner of the display for the point in the utterance at which the cursor crosses the pitch trace.

3.3 Acoustic analysis

As mentioned in the introduction to this chapter, linguists sometimes have different purposes for analyzing pitch acoustically, and depending on the purpose, there are different ways to go about the task. For example, in an effort to establish algorithms that generate tone and intonation patterns that parallel spoken speech as closely as possible, phoneticians sometimes take multiple measurements of F_0 at close, regular intervals of complete utterances. However, since the purpose of the present work is to help linguists confirm the accuracy of their phonetic transcriptions, what follows assumes that only one measurement is needed for level pitches and two for contour pitches (i.e., the beginning and end points of the contours).

3.3 Acoustic analysis

While most speech analysis software packages make it relatively easy to identify the F_0 at any given point in an utterance, in practice knowing where to take those measurements is usually more difficult. This is because TBUs are pronounced over the course of time, and the F_0 is seldom constant over the duration of any given TBU.

There are several reasons for this. Often, there are consonants on one or both sides of any given vowel nucleus, and consonants, especially obstruents, are known to significantly affect the trace. Another reason is that the surface tones of any utterance are often not all the same, and it is not unusual for sequences of unlike tones to be associated with single TBUs, resulting in contour pitches. Whatever the reasons, for any given measurement, multiple factors must normally be taken into consideration in order to determine exactly where to take the measurement. Occasionally, some of these factors are at odds with others, and when this happens, the analyst must decide which factors are more pertinent. This makes interpreting pitch traces almost as much of an art as a science. Although determining where to measure F_0 is seldom completely straightforward, there are nevertheless a number of general principles which, if followed, can greatly facilitate obtaining accurate F_0 measurements for level pitches. At the same time, one needs to bear in mind that while adhering to these principles is helpful when carrying out acoustic analyses of pitch, other principles come into play when one is analyzing other aspects of sound (e.g., duration of consonants and vowels).

3.3.1 Avoid measurements to the left of a TBU's mid-point

Ideally, for any given TBU, the analyst wants to measure the F_0 at the place where the speaker produces the intended pitch (i.e., at the target of the tone). Typically, this target is reached later, rather than earlier, in the course of a TBU's pronunciation, in order to allow a speaker adequate time to adjust the laryngeal apparatus to the precise tension required to produce the intended pitch. This "delay" also allows the listener the time needed to "tune in" to the intended pitch. So all things being equal, one normally wants to measure the F_0 somewhere between the mid-point and the right edge of the TBU (or as close to the mid-point as possible if there are valid reasons why the measurement must be taken to the left of the mid-point).

3.3.2 Measure at points in flat stretches

During the course of a TBU's pronunciation, when the intended pitch is reached, it is often held constant slightly longer than other pitches in the TBU. When this happens, one sees a relatively flat stretch, or "shelf" in the pitch trace, and it is here that one normally wants to measure the F_0. Here are two examples taken from the Chumburung word *dápú* 'hawk'.

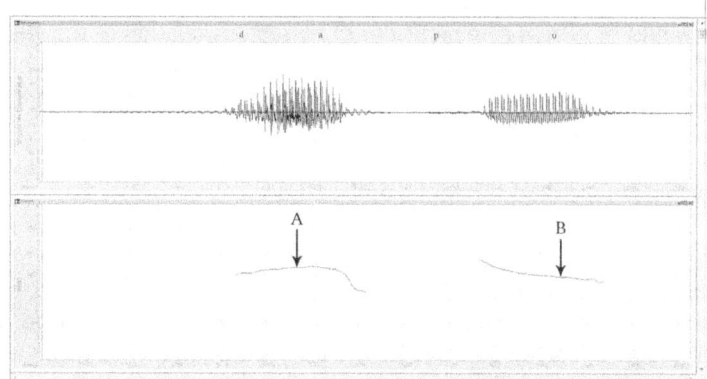

Figure 6. Measurements taken in "flat" stretches in trace.

In figure 6, the pitch traces of both TBUs change throughout the duration of their pronunciation except for the short flat stretches, marked by the arrows for point A, which is near the mid-point of the TBU (147.2 Hz), and point B (139.4 Hz), which is well to the right of the TBU's mid-point.

3.3.3 Avoid measuring perturbations caused by obstruents

As mentioned above, consonants (especially obstruents) are well known to perturb pitch traces. In particular, voiced obstruents tend to produce a "dip" in an otherwise level trace, accompanied on occasion by a break in the trace. Sonorant consonants such as nasals and l's also sometimes produce dips in the trace. Voiceless obstruents always produce a break in the trace. The end of the trace before the break (i.e., immediately before the obstruent) will often rise slightly and then fall sharply in relation to the unperturbed level. Immediately after the break, the trace will typically begin quite high and then fall to the unperturbed level. In such cases, one always wants to avoid measuring the F_0 anywhere near these perturbations. Normally, there will be no conflict between avoiding measuring the effects of consonants and measuring the flat stretches in a trace (cf. section 3.3.2). In those rare cases, however, where such conflicts do arise, it is better to avoid measuring the perturbations caused by obstruents.

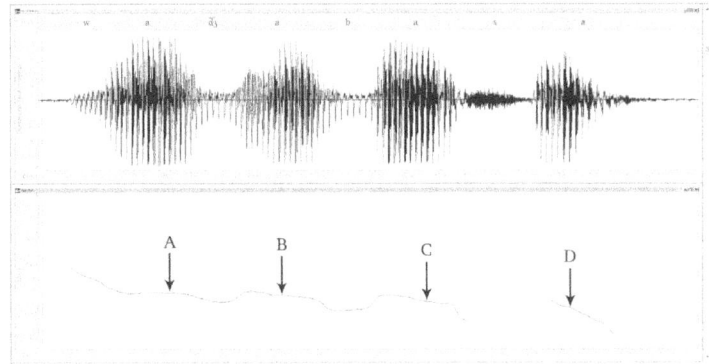

Figure 7. Perturbations caused by obstruents.

In figure 7, although the phonological tones of the Chumburung phrase, wàdʒ̀à bàsà 'cloth's needle', are all level and low, the pitch trace is anything but level; the voiced obstruents d͡ʒ and b produce noticeable dips in the trace, and the voiceless obstruent s produces a significant break in the trace for the duration of the voicelessness. Notice the slight rise up and then sharp fall down that occurs immediately before the s. Then immediately after the s, the trace is significantly higher than it otherwise would be. These same effects can be seen in relation to the voiceless obstruents s and t^h in figure 5, above. The measurements for the four TBUs in figure 7 are as follows: A-116.4 Hz (measured at flat spot), B-113.6 Hz (measured at energy peak, see section 3.3.6), C-109.1 Hz (measured at flat spot), and D-104.9 Hz (measured at energy peak).

3.3.4 Measure at points marked by peaks and valleys

When sequences of differing tones result in well-defined peaks and valleys in the pitch trace, measure the F_0 at these points regardless of where they occur in relation to the segments, avoiding, of course, any perturbations produced by obstruents (see section 3.3.3). In many respects, the principles involved in measuring the peaks and valleys of utterances apply equally well to measuring the beginning and end points of contour pitches.[5]

---

[5] With regard to measuring the beginning and end points of contour pitches, one problem beginning field linguists sometimes have is to identify which contours in a pitch trace should be measured, and

3.3 Acoustic analysis

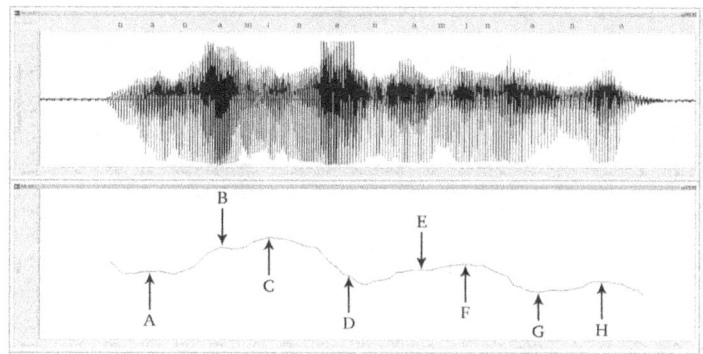

Figure 8. Peaks and valleys.

In figure 8, the alternating sequences of surface low and high tones in the Chumburung phrase *nàná mí nàná mí nàná* 'grandfather's grandfather's grandfather' produce clearly defined peaks and valleys in the pitch trace. These are indicated in the figure by the arrows that are placed below the trace. The two arrows placed above the pitch trace indicate points of measurement for TBUs that are simply transitional (see section 3.3.5).

With respect to point A, the measurement (128.6 Hz) is taken in the flat stretch (see section 3.3.2) that occurs immediately before the slight dip caused by the following sonorant *n* (see 3.3.3). With respect to point C, the measurement (158.0 Hz) is taken at the very highest point on this peak. With respect to point D, the measurement (125.6 Hz) is taken at the little ledge just to the left of the lowest point in this valley. Measuring here instead of at the actual lowest point avoids the perturbation dip produced by the sonorant consonant *n*. The measurement for point F (135.3 Hz) is again taken at the highest point on the peak. The measurement for point G (111.5 Hz), is taken at the lowest part of the valley since, unlike point D, the lowest point does not coincide with the consonant *n*. For point H (120.4 Hz), the measurement is taken in the flat stretch that occurs at the highest point on the peak.

3.3.5 Recognize TBUs that are only transitional

When a given phonological tone is associated with multiple TBUs, the target of the tone is not necessarily located on the first TBU. For example, if the tone sequence LH is linked to three TBUs such that the L is linked to the first TBU and the H to the remaining two, the target of the H (i.e., the highest point on this part of the trace) might actually be located on the second of the two high-toned TBUs. In such a case, it is the F_0 measurements of the first and third TBUs that should inform the analysis, not that of the second, which in effect is only a transitional point located between the targets of the L and H tones.

Again referring to figure 8, above, the two points marked by arrows placed above the pitch trace are examples of transitional TBUs. In the case of point B, it is located just to the left of the perturbation dip produced by the sonorant *n*. As a transitional point along the path between the targets of the low and high tones, it has a measurement of 150 Hz, which is between that of the low tone, point A (128.6 Hz), and that of the high tone, point C (158.0 Hz). In the case of point E (130.1 Hz), it is again located between the targets of the preceding low tone, point D (125.6 Hz), and the following high tone, point F (135.3 Hz), and it is measured in the flat stretch that occurs before the rise to point F.

---

which should be ignored. In other words, which contours are relevant for phonological analysis? My experience suggests that listening carefully to a native speaker whistle or hum an utterance can be very helpful in this regard. Those contours that a native speaker produces while whistling or humming an utterance are typically those that linguists should transcribe and analyze acoustically.

3.3.6 Measure at points of syllable energy peaks

There may be times when the pitch of a particular TBU is not constant, resulting in no flat stretches in the trace to indicate where one should take the F_0 measurement. In addition, it may also be the case that there is no obvious peak or valley in the pitch trace to indicate the tone's target. In such cases, as a last resort one should measure the F_0 at the location of the syllable's energy peak (the place at which the amplitude of the wave form is the greatest) provided the energy peak is to the right of the mid-point of the TBU, or as close to the mid-point as possible if the energy peak happens to be to the left of the mid-point.

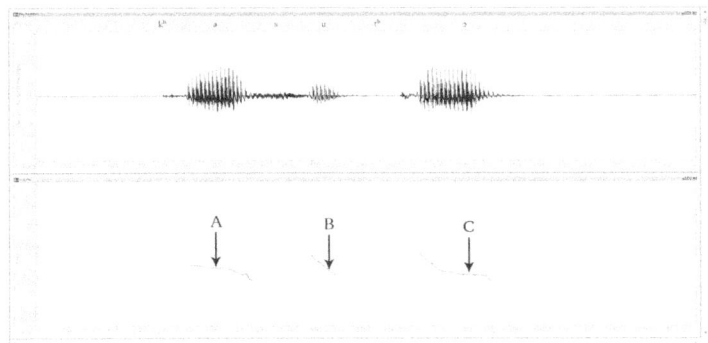

Figure 9. Measurement at energy peak.

In figure 9, even though the phonological tones for all TBUs of $k^h\acute{\partial}s\acute{u}t^h\acute{\partial}$ 'forehead' are high, the perturbations to the trace caused by the consonants on either side of point B are such that it is not immediately clear where one should take the appropriate F_0 measurement for point B (122.0 Hz). In this case, the location of the syllable's energy peak offers the best place to measure it; this also happens to be well to the right of the mid-point of the TBU. Measurements for points A (122.1 Hz) and C (115.9 Hz) were taken at appropriate flat stretches in the trace.

3.3.7 Allow for declination

Declination is the general downward drift in F_0 that occurs throughout the duration of an utterance, even when the phonological tones of the utterance are all the same. Or, as Connell and Ladd (1990:2) state so eloquently, it is the "gradual modification (over the course of a phrase or utterance) of the phonetic backdrop against which the phonologically specified local F_0 targets are scaled—a tilting of the graph paper, to use Pierrehumbert's vivid metaphor (Pierrehumbert 1980:63)." If one doesn't take into account the effect of declination, one could wrongly conclude that two pitch levels measured at different points in the utterance are phonologically different. An example of this may be seen in figure 10, repeated from figure 7.

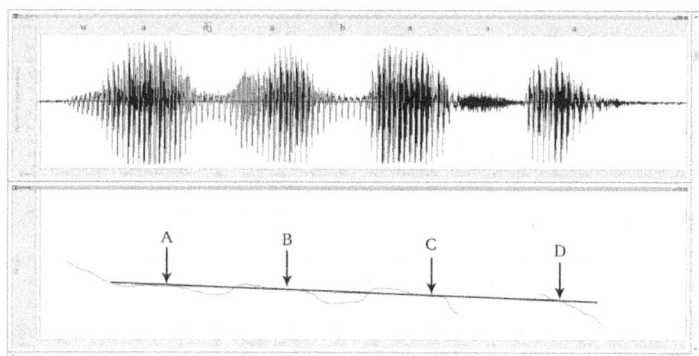

Figure 10. Declination.

Phonologically, the tones in the Chumburung phrase *wàdʒà bàsà* 'cloth's needle' are all low, but due to declination (idealized by the solid line), the F_0 of the four TBUs steadily descends.

3.4 Acoustic studies

In general, acoustic studies of pitch address specific research questions. In setting up such a study, it is important to ensure that regardless of which aspect of the tone system is being investigated, all variables that can affect the surface realizations of tones are the same for whatever words or phrases are being compared. In this respect, setting up an acoustic study is similar to setting up a phonological study to determine tonal contrast. For example, just as one does not establish tonal contrast by comparing the tone patterns of words that have different syllable profiles (cf. chapter 2), so also one should not try to compare the acoustic measurements of words that have different syllable profiles (e.g., CV vs. CVC, vs. CVN) since the same phonological tone will normally have significantly different measurements when it is realized on different syllable profiles. In addition, unless one is studying the effects of consonants on tone, Bruce Connell (personal communication) recommends that for reasons discussed above, the ideal test sentence is one that contains no obstruents but only sonorant consonants; to the extent that including obstruents is unavoidable, voiced obstruents are preferred over voiceless ones. Connell also recommends that vowel height be controlled for as much as possible. Although the influence of vowel height is not known to interact phonologically with tone in any language, studies such as Connell 2002 make clear that low vowels typically have a lower intrinsic F_0 than do high vowels, so vowel height needs to be taken into consideration as much as possible when constructing acoustic studies of pitch.

At one point, I conducted an acoustic study to answer some questions about downstep in Bimoba, a Gur language spoken in Ghana (Snider 1998). One of these questions was: "Is the degree of downstep in Bimoba that is attributable to a nonfloating low tone (automatic downstep) the same as that which is attributable to a floating low tone (non-automatic downstep)?" In order to answer this question, I constructed the two sentences in (3) and randomly recorded ten tokens (i.e., ten repetitions) of each one as spoken by a single male native speaker of Bimoba. More speakers (at least three, with a mixture of male and female voices) would have been better, but unfortunately no other speakers were available when the opportunity to conduct the study presented itself.

(3) Sentences employed in Bimoba acoustic study

a. Automatic downstep
/gbátúk gòt gbátúk/ → gbatuk got gbatuk   'bushbaby looked at bushbaby'

b. Non-automatic downstep
/gbátúk ŋmít ˋ gbátúk/ → gbatuk ŋmit gbatuk   'bushbaby cut bushbaby'

The sentences themselves were constructed carefully in order to make them as comparable as possible, yet different enough to answer the question. For example, both sentences consisted of the same number of syllables in order to equalize the effects of declination. Then the words in both sentences were kept identical as much as possible in order to minimize the effects of any consonant-tone interactions. And finally, the second and fourth TBUs in each sentence were chosen for measurement comparisons, again in order to ensure that declination didn't affect the measurements of the two sentences differently.

From auditory impressions only, it was impossible to judge whether the two kinds of downstep resulted in the same degree of lowering. So, following the principles for measurement discussed above, I recorded the measurements in (4) and (5), using CECIL, the speech analysis software that later evolved into Speech Analyzer. I then entered the hertz values for each TBU into a spreadsheet, which also calculated the average measurement for each TBU.

(4) Measurements (Hz) for automatic downstep (Sentence 1)

	A	B	C	D	E
1.1	158.3	158.1	95.8	111.3	111.9
1.2	150.3	146.8	106.0	112.8	110.9
1.3	159.9	151.7	96.2	113.2	111.6
1.4	183.5	179.6	114.8	125.2	125.4
1.5	148.2	140.3	92.8	107.5	111.4
1.6	137.2	136.7	102.5	104.3	103.7
1.7	154.6	149.5	104.0	120.4	123.9
1.8	162.9	150.5	104.4	120.2	114.8
1.9	161.0	143.4	102.7	112.4	115.8
1.10	151.8	147.8	94.2	110.6	106.8
AVG	156.77	150.44	101.34	113.79	113.62
	gbá	túk	gòt	ꜜgbá	túk

3.4 *Acoustic studies* 75

(5) Measurements (Hz) for non-automatic downstep (Sentence 2)

	A	B	C	D	E
2.1	158.1	159.4	158.3	118.4	117.0
2.2	144.3	145.6	147.3	108.7	108.9
2.3	147.1	146.7	146.6	113.3	113.2
2.4	152.5	152.6	149.5	110.0	111.0
2.5	146.5	139.9	144.4	106.7	108.8
2.6	143.8	145.3	141.7	111.0	109.6
2.7	159.3	160.8	157.5	118.1	119.1
2.8	168.3	162.2	159.3	119.9	120.6
2.9	157.9	151.7	161.3	112.2	115.6
2.10	148.2	150.6	146.1	111.5	112.5
AVG	152.60	151.48	151.20	112.98	113.63
	gbá	túk	ŋmít	⁺gbá	túk

Finally, I plotted the average measurements for each TBU on a graph, again using a spreadsheet.

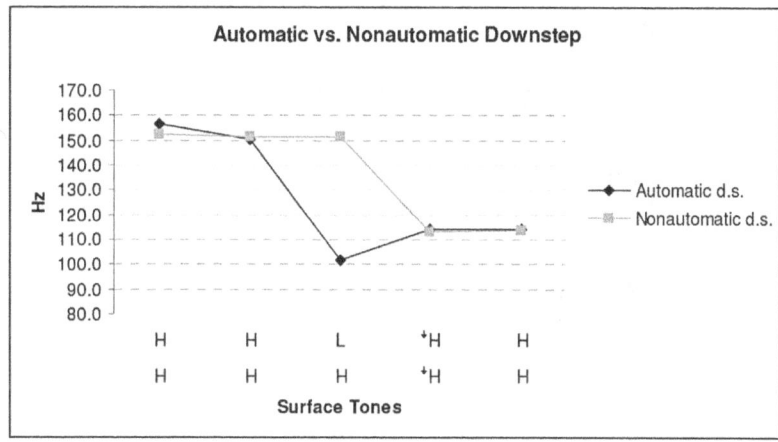

Figure 11. Automatic vs. non-automatic downstep.

In figure 11, one can see that the degree of lowering attributable to automatic downstep looks to be almost the same as that attributable to non-automatic downstep, and this is further supported by comparing the averages in (6) and (7).

(6) Difference in hertz between syllables B and D in automatic downstep (Sentence 1)

	B	D	B-D
1.1	158.1	111.3	46.8
1.2	146.8	112.8	34.0
1.3	151.7	113.2	38.5
1.4	179.6	125.2	54.4
1.5	140.3	107.5	32.8
1.6	136.7	104.3	32.4
1.7	149.5	120.4	29.1
1.8	150.5	120.2	30.3
1.9	143.4	112.4	31.0
1.10	147.8	110.6	37.2
AVG	150.44	113.79	36.65

(7) Difference in hertz between syllables B and D in non-automatic downstep (Sentence 2)

	B	D	B-D
2.1	159.4	118.4	41.0
2.2	145.6	108.7	36.9
2.3	146.7	113.3	33.4
2.4	152.6	110.0	42.6
2.5	139.9	106.7	33.2
2.6	145.3	111.0	34.3
2.7	160.8	118.1	42.7
2.8	162.2	119.9	42.3
2.9	151.7	112.2	39.5
2.10	150.6	111.5	39.1
AVG	151.48	112.98	38.50

From the data in (6) and (7), one can see that the degree of lowering attributable to automatic downstep (average lowering of 36.65 Hz) is virtually the same as that attributable to non-automatic downstep (average lowering of 38.50 Hz). These averages, however, are not exactly the same.

This raises the question of how different two averages need to be before one should consider their difference to be significant.[6] While the size of the difference between two averages is part of the answer, of course, other important factors include the sample size (the larger the sample size, the more reliable the average) and the homogeneity of the samples (the closer the individual numbers in each sample are to the average, the more reliable the average).

Fortunately, we do not need to rely on our intuition here because statisticians have developed a number of different tests for statistical significance that take the pertinent factors into

---

[6] It is beyond the scope of the present work to teach a course in statistics. There are, however, many textbooks that assume this task, and the interested reader is encouraged to investigate them. In particular, Larson and Farber 2005 is highly recommended by those who teach introductory courses in statistics. Although later (and presumably better) editions of this book have appeared, this third edition is easily accessible and relatively inexpensive.

account. One of the easiest statistical tests to obtain and to use for the present purposes is the *t*-test, which is included in most statistical analysis software packages. The *t*-test determines the probability that the difference between two averages is not significant. For most practical purposes, statisticians assume a probability value (*p*-value) of 0.05 or less to be a suitable indicator of statistical significance. A *p*-value of 0.05 (or less) means that there is a 5% (or less) probability that the difference between two averages is not significant. Let us return to the question raised above regarding whether the lowering of high tones attributable to automatic downstep in Bimoba (average of 36.65 Hz) should be considered to be different from that of non-automatic downstep (average of 38.50 Hz). A *t*-test for these averages returns a *p*-value of 0.52, which is well above the 0.05 upper threshold for statistical significance. From this we can safely conclude that the difference between automatic and non-automatic downstep in Bimoba is not statistically significant.

4
Tone and Orthography

One of the most controversial subjects associated with any language development project is that of orthography. There are various factors to consider in this regard, and there are often several different options with respect to any given factor. This means that there is seldom universal agreement on orthography issues. Often there are socio-political questions at stake, e.g., should the orthography be different from that of the majority language, or should it resemble it, and if so, to what degree? This is just one area where disagreements can arise. The point is that what is considered ideal by a linguist is not necessarily considered ideal by everyone else. For this reason, orthography developers need to allow multiple domains to inform the orthographies they develop. Such domains should include, but not be limited to: the social situation (e.g., what aspects do users of the orthography wish to see included), the political situation (e.g., what restrictions, if any, does the government place on orthographies), the psychology of reading (e.g., how dense should tone marking be), and, of course, the linguistic structures of the language.

Sometimes linguists find themselves working in situations where they have minimal input into orthographic decisions. At times, their contribution is limited to guiding members of language communities in participatory-type workshops, the goal of which is to produce practical orthographies that local members of the community have produced together and agreed upon, but which are not necessarily well-informed linguistically. The question therefore arises whether an orthography actually needs to be linguistically ideal in order to be successful. This question, of course, is easily answered when one considers the English and the traditional Chinese [zho] orthographies. Both of these are less than ideal from a linguistic, especially a phonological, standpoint, but both orthographies have nevertheless served their societies well. So clearly, a linguistically ideal orthography is not absolutely essential to an orthography's success.

Why should this be so? The answer lies, at least partly, in the fact that languages have a considerable degree of redundancy built into their linguistic structures, so this leaves plenty of room for compromise. Consider a communication situation in which two people can't properly hear each other speaking, either because they are physically too far apart or because there is too much ambient noise. In order to compensate for situations like this, languages have redundancy built into virtually every aspect of them so that there are very few contrasts within the communication act that are totally dependent upon single linguistic features. For example, phonological redundancy is created when processes spread features from one segment to other segments. When this happens, if listeners miss a certain feature during the pronunciation of one segment, they can often still pick it up later when they hear the other segments.

Morphological redundancy is also pervasive. In many languages, pronouns and modifiers are redundantly marked with affixes that are concordant with the genders or classes of the nouns they modify. In such cases, listeners that miss part of the information for, say, the subject of the sentence, can still pick it up later when they hear the pronoun that modifies it. Languages also have built-in syntactic redundancy, as may be seen in the French [fra] negation, *Je ne sais pas* (1S NEG know NEG 'I don't know'). Although the first negative marker, *ne,* is often dropped in spoken French, both negative markers are included when the speaker feels the need to ensure there is no confusion. Finally, discourse structures can also generate redundancy by means of repetitious devices such as tail-head linkage. For example, a speaker might conclude one sentence with "…after that I went to a restaurant" and then begin the next sentence with "The reason why I went to the restaurant…." The functional value of linguistic redundancy is that listeners can often miss much of the speech signal, including, at times, whole words, and still understand perfectly what is being said, often without being aware of having missed any information.

Much of the redundancy that is built into spoken language compensates for less than ideal oral communication situations (e.g., speaking across long distances or overcoming loud ambient noise). However, when the communication situation is not oral but rather visual (viz. eye contact with words on paper), the reader does not need all of the redundancy that is built into the spoken language, especially the lower-level redundancy that is built into the sound system (discussed in further detail below). Moreover, other (new) factors now come into play such as print size, number of and location of tone marks, etc. There can therefore be a reasonable difference between a sound-based representation that encodes everything a speaker says and a visual representation that encodes what a reader needs to see in order to easily understand what the writer intends to communicate. This difference provides a significant "cushion" that allows for compromise when one is advocating for a linguistically-based orthography. So what is the bottom line when it comes to compromising linguistic input into orthography development? Ultimately, the bottom line rests with whether or not a proposed orthography works. And in order to know this, one must test an orthography (see discussions further below).

While it is true that the English and ancient Chinese orthographies are not as well-informed linguistically as might be desired, the fact that they work so well is as much a testament to the high value their societies place on literacy and training people to read as to anything else. Sadly, the societies for which many first-time orthographies are being developed today often do not value mother tongue literacy as highly as do the speakers of English and Chinese. For this reason, those engaged in language development should enthusiastically embrace all efforts to develop orthographies within the context of participatory workshops in order to capitalize on the desire for literacy that such events can generate within the language community. And again, because many such societies are not as motivated for literacy as are the English and Chinese ones, those developing orthographies for these societies should also make every effort to include insights from the field of linguistics. This chapter is therefore devoted to helping orthography developers make linguistically informed decisions with regard to tone.

4.1 Functional load

Given the degree of redundancy built into linguistic structures (see above), it is possible to have a successful orthography that does not represent all of the phonological contrasts in the language. Nevertheless, there is a limit to what can be left out. Even if there are only a few minimal tone pairs in the language, the functional load of tone might nevertheless be heavy enough to warrant representing tone orthographically, especially for beginning readers. The

4.1 Functional load

functional load of tone is the degree to which native speakers of tone languages rely on tone distinctions to convey differences in meaning. Accordingly, when developing an orthography for such a language, one of the things that must be determined as best as possible is the functional load of tone.

Within the context of orthography development, it is helpful to make a distinction between the functional load borne by: a) lexical tone and b) what is often called grammatical tone. When the term lexical tone is used, it tends to refer mainly to tonal differences that are associated with the roots of words (e.g., Chumburung *kì-bá?* 'shoulder' vs. *kì-sà?* 'nest') and to a lesser extent to those associated with affixes. When the term grammatical tone is used, it tends to refer either to the tone differences of segmentally identical grammatical affixes (e.g., Chumburung *mí-ká* 'my wife' vs. *mì-ká* 'his wife') or to the tone differences of segmentally identical grammatical constructions that are effected by floating tone affixes (e.g., Kenyang *bá-pá* 'they spat' vs. *bá-ꜜpá* 'they are spitting'). Strictly speaking, all tones (whether floating or otherwise) are lexical in the sense that every morpheme has an underlying tone pattern that has the potential to interact with its environment.[1] However, given the currency of the term grammatical tone, the present work employs this term in the manner in which it is commonly used.

So, by these popular definitions, differences such as those in (1) and (2) are lexical.

(1) Lexical tone in Cantonese (Yip 2002:175)

    si: 55   'poem'
    si: 33   'affair, undertaking'
    si: 24   'market, city'
    si: 53   'silk'

(2) Lexical tone in Bamileke-Dschang (Bird 1999:12)

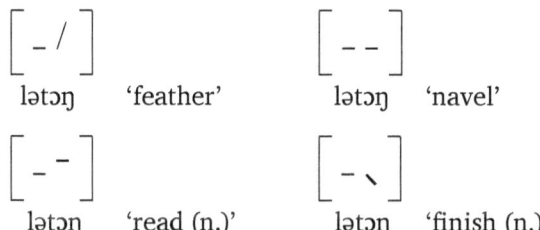

lətɔŋ 'feather'   lətɔŋ 'navel'

lətɔŋ 'read (n.)'   lətɔŋ 'finish (n.)'

Although the examples of lexical tone contrasts in (1) and (2) demonstrate contrastive tone patterns associated with words that have identical segments, we saw in chapter 1 that minimal pairs are not actually required. Lexical tone exists whenever a language assigns (in an unpredictable manner) tone patterns to morphemes, especially the roots of nouns and verbs. These next examples from Chumburung equally illustrate lexical tone contrasts, even though none form minimal pairs.

(3) Lexical tone in Chumburung (personal field notes)

Isolation Pattern 1	Isolation Pattern 2
kì-k͡píní 'plan (n.)'	kì-d͡ʒàfú 'fish scale'
kì-párá 'loan (n.)'	kù-kùt͡ʃé 'oyster'

Since all of the nouns in (3) are the same with respect to factors that are known to influence tone (see previous chapters), this means that the two isolation patterns are unpredictable and therefore contrastive. So languages with tone contrasts that occur only in analogous environments are also described as having lexical tone.

---

[1] I am grateful to Thilo Schadeberg for first drawing this to my attention.

Grammatical tone, as the term is commonly employed, tends to refer to grammatical distinctions indicated solely by tone. This may be seen in the examples in (4) and (5).

(4) Grammatical tone in Alur [alz] (Kutsch Lojenga 2014:53)

à-mákù	'I have taken'
à-má⁺kú	'I habitually take'
á-màkù	'I will take'
á-⁺má⁺kú	'I am taking'

(5) Grammatical tone in Kenyang (personal field notes)

bă-tè	'you (pl.) are standing'
bă-tê	'you (pl.) stood'
bă-⁺té	'you (pl.) have stood'
bă-pá	'you (pl.) spat'
bá-pá	'they spat'

The Kenyang examples in (5) are typical of what is commonly called grammatical tone because the grammatical differences are indicated solely by tone, and the tonal differences indicate only grammatical differences. By way of contrast, the tone difference in the examples in (6), which helps to distinguish the 3S form from the 3P form, would not normally be attributed to grammatical tone because in addition to the tone difference, there is a segmental difference. Indeed, in most linguists' parlance, this would be considered a further example of a lexical tone contrast.

(6) Kenyang (Cameroon, personal field notes)

3S	à-pá	'he/she spat'
3P	bá-pá	'they spat'

So how does one go about determining the functional load of tone? We discuss three methods that orthography developers can use: a) compare the number of minimal tone pairs/triplets, etc., with the total number of words being compared, b) compare native speakers' ability to read with and without tone being marked in the orthography, and c) compare the number of tonal contrasts per morpheme with the number of other devices per morpheme the language uses to create lexical contrast. We discuss these in order.

One of the easiest and most obvious places to begin is to simply scan a list of words and count how many minimal tone pairs/triplets, etc., there are. In principle, the more purely tonal contrasts there are (in relation to the number of total items being scanned), the heavier the functional load. This method is one way of assessing functional load, but it is only one. For the most part, the failure of an orthography to differentiate between members of minimal pairs in which the contrasting members belong to different word categories (e.g., nouns vs. verbs) or different semantic categories (e.g., species of animals vs. bodies of water) does not pose serious problems for its readers. Similarly, if one or the other member of a minimal pair collocates with certain other words (e.g., it is part of an idiomatic expression), or it is a high frequency word, or it is distinguishable from the other word(s) by word order constraints, again, failing to distinguish the minimal pair is normally not problematic. So simply identifying minimal pairs/triplets, etc. without taking into account other factors that affect the functional load of tone is not adequate.

4.1 Functional load

Imagine a situation in which there are very few or no minimal tone pairs. Should this automatically be taken as an indication that tone does not need to be represented orthographically? Not necessarily. In a critical review of Powlison's (1968) "attempt to define functional load in terms of an orthographic rank of phonemes," Gudschinsky (1970:21) points out that Powlison's work overlooks "the psycholinguistic element in the functional load of a phoneme." Discussing Terena [ter], an Arawakan tone language of Brazil, and Huautla [mau], a Mazatec tone language of Mexico, Gudschinsky demonstrates that due to psycholinguistic factors, "tone carries a much heavier functional load than any mechanical scale would have predicted" (Gudschinsky 1970:22). Regardless of the number of minimal tone contrasts lexically, if the ratio between the number of contrastive tone patterns and the number of other contrastive phonological elements (see below) is high enough,[2] lexical tone representation in the orthography could still be called for. Ultimately, extensive testing of alternative orthographies needs to be carried out with native speakers before drawing any firm conclusions regarding the functional load of tone.

This brings us to the second way to determine the functional load of tone, and hence the degree to which tone can be under-represented in an orthography: test the reading of different types of texts that are totally unmarked for tone, in order to see where the difficulties, if any, lie. This involves testing native speakers who have been taught how to read consonants and vowels reasonably well, either in their mother tongue or in some language of wider communication. The testing should include reading comprehension, as well as fluency and accuracy in oral reading. The latter can be accomplished by carrying out classic miscue analysis, of the type that is used when researching children's reading difficulties (see Goodman and Goodman 1994). This would involve recording readers as they read out loud and later noting and quantifying where in the texts and in what types of situations any difficulties occurred. When testing in this way, one should bear in mind that not all mistakes are necessarily attributable to problems with the orthography. In some cases, they could be due to other factors such as unknown words, skill level, or dialect variation, etc.

The third and final way we discuss in order to determine the functional load of tone in a language is to compare tonal contrasts with the extent to which other aspects of the language contribute to lexical and grammatical contrast. In addition to employing tone pattern contrasts, tone languages also employ contrastive vowels, consonants, and syllable profiles in order to create lexical and grammatical contrast. If any device that is used to create lexical contrast in a language should have fewer members compared to the other devices, the burden of creating lexical contrasts increases, in principle, for each of the other categories. For example, morphemes in non-tone languages like English and French typically have a much richer inventory of syllable profiles than do morphemes in tone languages like Chinese and Chumburung. In principle, and all other things being equal, tone in languages whose roots have a rich variety of syllable profiles (e.g., CV, CCV, CVC, CCVC, CVCV, and CVCVC) will have a lighter functional load than it will in languages whose roots have, say, only CV syllables. Similarly, tone in languages with more syllables or TBUs per morpheme will generally have a lighter functional load than will tone in languages with fewer syllables or TBUs per morpheme. And finally, all things continuing to be equal, tone in languages with a greater number of underlying vowel contrasts will in principle have a lighter functional load than it does in languages with a smaller number of underlying vowel contrasts.

These notions mesh nicely with Kutsch Lojenga's (2014) conclusions, drawn from her typology of African tone systems. Kutsch Lojenga divides African tone languages into two groups: "languages with 'stable' tone, in which tones are not changed by their tonal environment; and languages with 'movable' tone, in which various tonal processes operate, so that tones may

---

[2] How best to quantify these types of contrasts has yet to be determined, but see Clements' 2003 work on quantifying the functional load of phonological features for an indication of what this research might look like.

change based on the tonal context" (2014:59). These two types of languages, in turn, tend to have the characteristics set out in (7).

(7) Typology of African languages (Kutsch Lojenga 2014:62)

Languages with "stable" tone	Languages with "movable" tone
• more contrastive tone levels	• fewer contrastive tone levels
• shorter words	• longer words
• heavy functional load of tone in the lexicon as well as in the grammar	• much lighter functional load of tone in the lexicon, but often an equally heavy functional load of tone in the grammar

When determining the functional load of tone for any given word category, it is therefore important to consider: a) the number of different syllable profiles there are associated with morphemes in that category, b) the ratio of TBUs to morphemes, c) how many potentially different vowel and consonant contrasts are possible for any given morpheme (taking into consideration the phonotactic constraints of the language), and of course, d) how many contrastive tone patterns there are.

Regardless of how one goes about determining the functional load of tone in a given language, the important thing is that it be determined prior to developing the orthography, and especially prior to deciding that tone does not need to be represented.

4.2 Failure of writing surface representations

While most orthography developers agree that writing segments phonetically (i.e., representing the surface level) is not ideal (see also Pike 1947), in practice it seems to be a different matter for tone, as it is not uncommon to see orthographies that represent surface tones. Often, this is accomplished by representing the surface tones of words as they are pronounced in isolation. Let us now consider whether an orthography that represents the surface forms for tones works any better than does one that represents the surface forms for segments.

Surface tone marking involves simply marking the surface pitch of utterances as they are pronounced by native speakers. Apart from working out the phonetic details of the tone system, it does not involve any serious phonological or grammatical analysis. As one orthography developer told me, "There are too many problems in reading if we do not write tone. However, since the tone system of this language is too difficult for us to analyze, the only thing we can really do is write the surface tones."

Since the surface level of representation functions well in spoken speech, one might wonder why it cannot also function well for orthographic purposes. The problem is that native speakers are not fully aware of all surface sounds, and this applies as much to tone as to consonants and vowels. While the high degree of phonological redundancy that is encoded at the surface level is helpful in oral situations, as explained above, it can cause serious problems when employed orthographically.

The most serious of these is that surface writing can result in single words that have multiple spellings in different phonological contexts. Since surface writing forces writers to sound out everything before they actually write it, having multiple spellings for single words is not only frustrating, but it also slows down the writing process because native speakers are not aware of all the sounds they make when they speak. By the same token, surface writing also forces readers to sound out everything they read before they are able to understand what is written. While beginning readers can sometimes find this helpful, in many instances it is not helpful at all because beginning readers usually can't read fast enough for all surface representations to make sense to them, especially when the representations involve phonological processes that occur across word boundaries. Similarly, even though experienced readers often can read fast enough for the surface representations to make sense, forcing them to sound out everything is not helpful because they typically read by sight (Katz and Frost 1992, Nida 1954, Venezky 1970, Voorhoeve 1962). Such readers do not need to sound out a word in order to know what it means because the sight of the word immediately conjures up the correct meaning in their minds.

One less problematic variation of surface marking is to represent the pattern of each word as it is spoken in isolation. One advantage of this is that each word has a single, consistent visual representation. Since it is advantageous for orthographies to maintain constant word-images (see below), that makes this form of word representation much more useful than its phrase-representation counterpart. On the other hand, Bird (1999) points out the following problems with "marking the isolation tone of a word."[3]

> (a) A word may have more than one isolation form, and these can be tonally distinct; or lexical contrasts may be lost in isolation forms...
> (b) The isolation form may carry phrase-level prosodic information, such as boundary tones, to make it into a well-formed free-standing utterance (Pierrehumbert & Beckman 1988); yet this irrelevant phrasal information may still need to be represented, since linguistically naïve readers may not be able to distinguish lexical and phrasal tones.
> (c) The isolation tone may not be distinctive (contra Voorhoeve). For example, suppose we have two monosyllabic words which are segmentally identical, where one word had high tone and the other has downstepped high. These words cannot be distinguished in isolation, and therefore they will be orthographically identical. The same problem arises for words having lexical floating tones which are only detected in context. (Bird 1999:18)

The problems associated with carrying out proper linguistic tone analysis notwithstanding, representing surface tone orthographically is not really any more of an option than is representing surface consonants and vowels. Both should be avoided because there are better options. These options do, however, require careful linguistic analysis. This next section investigates several of those strategies, including zero marking of tone.

4.3 Critiques of some strategies for marking tone

This section presents a critique of three strategies that attempt to keep orthographies as simple as possible by either not representing tone at all or by diacritically distinguishing only those words and grammatical functions that would otherwise be confused. The three strategies critiqued are: zero marking, distinguishing only minimal pairs, and diacritically marking grammatical functions that are distinguished solely by tone. The intention is to describe situations in which employment of these strategies might work, but also in which they can be less than ideal. We discuss each in turn.

4.3.1 Zero marking

The orthographic strategy for dealing with tone that (at least historically) appears to have been most frequently employed is that of zero marking. An orthography with zero tone marking

---

[3] When Bird says that some words may have more than one isolation form, he is referring to situations in certain languages in which some words (e.g., verbs) may have two or more forms that can be pronounced as single words (e.g., imperative form, infinitival form).

simply does not represent tone or the functions it encodes in any way. Rather, it provides only segmental information, together with the usual suprasegmental information (usually non-tonal) that is conveyed through punctuation. It is also, perhaps, the strategy that has received the harshest criticism.

Critics of this strategy often blame its use on lingual-centric attitudes associated with mother-tongue speakers of non-tone languages (see Welmers 1973 and also Cahill 2001 for discussions on this topic). While it is true that many of those responsible for toneless orthographies are indeed of this group, others are national mother tongue speakers of tone languages. In these latter cases, however, the reluctance to countenance tone marks may be due to the fact that these researchers are literate in one or more non-tone languages (e.g., English, French, Spanish [spa], Arabic [ara]). In this regard, I have had experience in one country in which government policy for a period of time prohibited the representation of tone so that orthographies of indigenous languages would more closely resemble that of the national language.

There are a number of reasons why zero tone marking is attractive to orthography developers. Of all the strategies for representing tone, zero marking not only presents the least difficulty for writers, but it is also the easiest strategy to teach both readers and writers. However, another (less noble) reason for its prevalence is that many people who develop orthographies for tone languages are relatively ignorant of how to analyze tone. And even those who are less ignorant in this regard do not necessarily understand the implications of their analysis for orthography development; hence the reason for this chapter.

While one may debate the various reasons why many tone language orthographies lack tone marking, a more fundamental question is whether tone needs to be represented in tone languages at all. In this respect, critics of zero tone marking find ample fodder for their positions in a number of anecdotal references in the literature. For example, Gudschinsky 1970 relates the following:

> An intelligent, educated native speaker of a tone language of West Africa was asked to read a page from a primer in his own language. He remained staring at the page without speaking for so long that the people around him became embarrassed. Finally they said, "Never mind. It's quite all right if you don't want to read it." The African replied, "Oh no, no. I'll be ready in a minute. It's just that I haven't figured out yet what it is supposed to say, so I don't know what tone to read it with." (Gudschinsky 1970:23)

In a second story, Gudschinsky continues,

> It was, in fact, a speaker of a closely related West African language who stated that in his language it is not possible in silent reading to understand more than 75 per cent of the New Testament, and that in public reading probably not more than 50 per cent is understood. Native speakers of that language use the English diglot in order to understand what is said in their own language. (Gudschinsky 1970:24)

Then in a third story, Gudschinsky says,

> Another illustration involved a native speaker of a Bantu language of Rhodesia. He was asked, "Does the fact that the tone in your language is not written make any problems when people read it?" He replied immediately, "No, not at all. Everyone learns to read and has no problem." He was then asked, "But don't people sometimes have to read things twice? Once to know what it says and once to read it correctly?" With a look of shocked surprise, he said, "Oh! Is that why we read our language back and forth and back and forth, but that we read English straight along. We can read English in

about half the time it takes to read our own language, but I never knew before why." (Gudschinsky 1970:24)

These and other stories do indeed point to a need to represent tone somehow in the orthographies of some, if not many, tone languages. That being said, I have observed good comprehension and fluent oral reading in a number of tone languages whose orthographies do not mark tone. In the end, the decision of whether to represent tone or not in an orthography needs to rest with the results of extensive testing.

Orthography testing of tone, however, can be tricky. For example, if the tone marking strategy employed in a test is inadequate, or if the people being tested are not taught to interpret tone marks well, those being tested may have trained themselves to simply ignore the tone marking. In such cases, it would be inadvisable to compare the results of reading-tests that pit tone-marked texts against zero-marked texts because readers wouldn't be looking at the tone marking in either test. If researchers are not aware of this potential problem, a lack of statistical difference between the two tests could lead to the erroneous conclusion that tone doesn't need to be marked in the orthography.

Rather than comparing texts that are marked for tone with ones that are not, a better strategy would be to simply note in texts that are unmarked for tone where, in particular, any reading difficulties lie, if indeed there are difficulties. If, after testing various literary genres, zero marking is not found to cause problems, then tone can be left unmarked. But unfortunately, there often are problems, and these must not be ignored. Good solutions do exist.

4.3.2 Distinguishing minimal pairs

In languages that have tone systems with light functional loads, there are, nevertheless, sometimes a number of words that are distinguished from each other solely by means of tone. Minimal pairs like this can often create problems for reading comprehension if tone is not represented orthographically. Accordingly, one strategy to deal with this problem is not to mark lexical tone per se, but instead to distinguish one or the other member of a minimal pair with a diacritic mark. Bird 1999 cites Ewe [ewe], a Kwa language spoken in Togo and Ghana, and Kasem [xsm], a Gur language spoken in Ghana, as examples of orthographies that have adopted this approach, and he provides an enlightening discussion of the pros and cons associated with it. Similarly, Mary Pearce (personal communication) reports that orthographically distinguishing minimal pairs has worked well for a number of languages that belong to the Chadic language family.

On the other hand, a number of people with experience in teaching literacy to speakers of tone languages have criticized this strategy, including Wiesemann (1989), Mfonyam (1990), and the present author. Snider (2001) points out at least three problems with it:

(8) Three problems with distinguishing only minimal pairs
   a) Writers can't remember which words have a "partner" and which don't. So they never know which words to mark and which not to mark.
   b) Readers sometimes have difficulty remembering which member of the minimal pair a particular mark represents.
   c) Inevitably, more minimal pairs show up later which never get taught.

These conclusions are supported by Mfonyam's (1990:23) observation that, "people do not always think contrastively. When we write, we are not always conscious of potential ambiguities." In general, the strategy of only marking minimal pairs works better if the words in question are not nouns and verbs. Nouns and verbs, of course, constitute a vast number of words, and the relatively few that would have diacritical marks could very easily be forgotten.

To sum up, the strategy of marking only minimal pairs should only be employed if tone has a low functional load and testing indicates that people can read well using it.

4.3.3 Diacritic marking of grammatical constructions

Consider those languages that have both lexical tone and grammatical tone as defined above, and for which testing has determined that there is no need to represent lexical tone but that grammatical tone does need to be represented. If tonal differences are the sole means of distinguishing certain grammatical constructions, then diacritically distinguishing the constructions can work well if the associations between the diacritics and the grammatical meanings they represent are taught well and are completely memorized by the students. This strategy has been successfully employed in the following language development projects in Africa:

(9) Orthographic use of grammatical tone marking

Language	ISO	Classification	Location(s)	Reference
Budu	[buu]	Bantu	Dem. Rep. Congo	Kutsch Lojenga 2014
Shimakonde	[kde]	Bantu	Mozambique	Leach 2010
Kako	[kkj]	Bantu	Cameroon	Ernst 1996
Chumburung	[ncu]	Kwa	Ghana	Personal notes
Engenni	[enn]	Benue-Congo	Nigeria	Kutsch Lojenga 1993
Endo	[enb]	Nilotic	Kenya	Kisang' & Larsen n.d.
Sabaot	[spy]	Nilotic	Kenya	Sabaot Bible Translation and Literacy Staff 1990
Western Maninkakan	[mlq]	Mande	Mali, Senegal	Kutsch Lojenga 2014

In addition, it is used successfully in Mexico "by a number of Mixtec [mix] languages to mark grammatical meanings, such as negative, perfective, and imperfective" (Inga McKendry, personal communication). Finally, although diacritic marking of grammatical tone has not been adopted in the official orthography of Kabiye [kbp], a Gur language spoken in northern Togo, formal testing of a grammatical orthography vs. a tone orthography demonstrated that "writers performed quicker and with greater accuracy in the grammar group than in the tone group" (Roberts and Walter 2012).

One reason why diacritically distinguishing minimal pairs has proven more successful for grammatical tone than for lexical tone is that the number of grammatical contrasts in a language is a fixed and relatively low number compared to the lexical contrasts of, say, noun and verb roots. There is thus no concern about later discovering "new" minimal pairs which will need to be taught, and the relatively low number of grammatical contrasts means that the diacritic marking of such minimal pairs is more easily taught and remembered than is the case for lexical minimal pairs. In addition, the frequency with which any given grammatical form is used is much greater than it is for any given lexical form, and greater results in better remembering.

We first look at an example from the Chumburung orthography in which two grammatical constructions are distinguished diacritically. The fact that lexical tone is not represented has not proved to be a problem. However, there is a minimal pair between *mú* and *mù*, the 1S and 3S independent pronouns, respectively, of the noun class that denotes human beings. Since this distinction is clearly too important not to distinguish orthographically, a grave accent mark

4.3 Critiques of some strategies for marking tone

is placed above the 3S pronoun to distinguish the two. Although the phonological difference between the pronouns is tonal, the grave accent is not taught as a tone mark but rather as part of the spelling of the 3S pronoun. In other words, the accent indicates a difference in meaning, not a difference in pronunciation, and in this respect, it is not a lot different from the use of the question mark in the English orthography. This aspect of the Chumburung orthography has been in use now for more than 30 years and works well, from my point of view.

The Sabaot orthography uses an extensive array of punctuation marks to distinguish various grammatical differences that are differentiated only by tone. In a booklet designed to benefit those who can already read and write English (Sabaot Bible Translation and Literacy Staff 1990), the authors identify and illustrate the use of these marks in the following list.

(10) Diacritic marking of grammatical tone in Sabaot

:	Kumwoochi :choorweenyii	'His friend told him'
	Kumwoochi choorweenyii	'He told his friend'
/	/Kēēchāmē siruutēchu	'These writings are liked'
	Kēēchāmē siruutēchu	'We like these writings'
'	'Kēēsuus āmiik	'You fried the food'
	Kēēsuus āmiik	'He/she fried the food'
!	!Kaakas	'I really did see it/him'
	Kaakas	'I saw it/him'
+	+Māāmwoowook	'I shall tell you'
–	–Māāmwoowook	'I shall not tell you'

Finally, let us see in (11) how diacritical marking of grammatical constructions could be hypothetically applied to verbs in Kenyang if lexical tone is not marked.

(11) Hypothetical orthographic representation of Kenyang grammatical morphemes

Prefix	Dieresis on 2P prefix vowel
2P	bä-
3P	ba-

Tense/aspect	Diacritic on 1st vowel of verb stem
Imperfective	grave accent
Perfect	acute accent
Perfective	no accent

One might distinguish the 2P and 3P subject prefixes with a dieresis on the 2P prefix (least frequently occurring prefix of the two) and no accent on the 3P prefix. Similarly, one might place grave and acute accents, respectively, on the first vowel of verb stems to represent the imperfective and perfect tense/aspects, together with no accents on the stems of perfective verbs (most frequently occurring tense/aspect). Here is how the representations in (11) would appear when applied to the examples in (12).

(12) Hypothetical orthographic representation of Kenyang examples
a. 2P verbs

	Surface	Orthographic	Gloss
Imperfective	bǎ-tè	bä-tè	'you were standing'
	bǎ-ꜜpá	bä-pà	'you were spitting'
Perfect	bǎ-ꜜté	bä-té	'you have stood'
	bǎ-pà	bä-pá	'you have spat'
Perfective	bǎ-tê	bä-te	'you stood'
	bǎ-pá	bä-pa	'you spat'

b. 3P verbs

	Surface	Orthographic	Gloss
Imperfective	bá-tè	ba-tè	'they were standing'
	bá-ꜜpá	ba-pà	'they were spitting'
Perfect	bá-ꜜté	ba-té	'they have stood'
	bá-pà	ba-pá	'they have spat'
Perfective	bá-tê	ba-te	'they stood'
	bá-pá	ba-pa	'they spat'

In this case, the diacritic marks do not represent tones, per se, but rather grammatical distinctions. The 2P prefix on the verb is consistently represented with a dieresis, and the 3P prefix on the verb is consistently represented with no diacritic marking. Regardless of what the underlying tone patterns of the verbs are, and regardless of any tonal alternations that take place, verbs in the imperfective aspect are consistently represented with a grave accent, verbs in the perfect tense with an acute accent, and verbs in the perfective aspect with no accent. See also Snider 1992 for further discussion of this strategy.

While it is sometimes the case that one can successfully employ strategies such as those discussed above that do not distinguish all contrastive tone patterns, it is also sometimes the case that one cannot. Sometimes, all tonal contrasts need to be distinguished. Once this has been established, one needs to carefully consider the implications of the linguistic analysis. This next section proposes a phonologically ideal strategy for representing tone orthographically when the strategies discussed above are not feasible.

4.4 Phonologically ideal orthography

There are two primary considerations to keep in mind when establishing a linguistically ideal tone orthography. The first concerns the tonal entity that needs to be represented (i.e., tones or tone patterns), and the second concerns the level of phonological depth at which the native speaker is most aware of that entity (i.e., deep, as opposed to shallow, etc.).

Perusing the literature on orthography, it is striking that few of the recent proposals for orthography design take advantage of developments in linguistic theory more recent than that of generative phonology (Chomsky and Halle 1968). Since then, however, two theories (discussed below) have emerged that have significant implications for orthography development in tone languages. The first one, Autosegmental Phonology (Goldsmith 1976, Leben 1973) has implications for the first consideration mentioned above (viz. the tonal entity that needs to be represented), and the second one, Lexical Phonology (Kiparsky 1982 and Mohanan 1982, 1986), together with its more recent evolution into Stratal Optimality Theory (Kiparsky 2000,

4.4 Phonologically ideal orthography

2015 and Bermúdez-Otero 2011) has implications for the second consideration (viz. the level of phonological depth upon which one should base an orthography).

4.4.1 Tonal entity of representation

Although most linguists recognize the value of employing autosegmental theory for tone analysis, its implications for orthography development are often overlooked. This is perhaps due in part to the fact that many people do not recognize the value of representing a word's complete tone pattern in the orthography. Recall the discussion of the Mende data in chapter 1, repeated here in (13). In Mende nouns, there are five underlying tone patterns that are phonetically realized in different ways, depending on how many syllables there are in the noun root.

(13) Contrastive tone patterns in Mende monomorphemic nouns

	One Syllable		Two Syllables		Three Syllables	
/H/	[⁻] kɔ	'war'	[⁻ ⁻] pɛlɛ	'house'	[⁻ ⁻ ⁻] hawama	'waistline'
/L/	[_] k͡pa	'debt'	[_ _] bɛlɛ	'trousers'	[_ _ _] k͡pakali	'tripod chair'
/HL/	[\] m͡bu	'owl'	[⁻ _] ŋgila	'dog'	[⁻ _ _] felama	'junction'
/LH/	[/] m͡ba	'rice'	[_ ⁻] fande	'cotton'	[_ ⁻ ⁻] ndavula	'sling'
/LHL/	[/\] m͡ba	'companion'	[_ \ ] nyaha	'woman'	[_ ⁻ _] nikili	'groundnut'

From these data, one can see that regardless of how many syllables there are in each noun root, there are only five possible tone patterns for it. As explained in chapter 1, it is more helpful to think of the phoneme of tone as being the complete underlying tone pattern (e.g., H, LH, LHL) associated with a morpheme, rather than the individual tone associated with a TBU. How that underlying pattern is realized phonetically is determined in each language by the number and types of syllables in each morpheme, as well as by any phonological processes that might apply.

When representing tone orthographically, it is therefore important to recognize the unitary nature of the pattern, and to represent tone patterns associated with words, as opposed to individual tones associated with TBUs. How to represent those patterns is, of course, a separate issue. Representing the correct entity (pattern vs. tone) is particularly important when one considers the level of phonological depth at which the native speaker is most aware of that pattern. We look at that now.

4.4.2 Historical overview of orthography and phonological depth issues

For purposes that relate to orthography development, recent linguistic history can be divided into two broadly defined periods: the earlier structuralist era and the later generative era. The generative era, in turn, can also be divided into two periods: the earlier SPE (*The Sound Pattern of English,* Chomsky and Halle 1968) era and the later stratal phonology era of Lexical Phonology and Stratal Optimality Theory. Regrettably, the implications of the lexical/stratal phonology era for orthography development have largely gone unexplored until relatively recently.

With regard to the level of phonological representation upon which to base an orthography, although orthography developers during the structuralist era had two options available in principle, the phonetic (i.e., surface) level and the phonemic level, in practice they really had only one. As discussed above, representing the phonetic level was not realistic because native speakers are simply not aware of many phonetic distinctions (e.g., aspirated vs. non-aspirated stops in English).[4] So, as the title to Pike's 1947 *Phonemics: A Technique for Reducing Languages to Writing* implies, many structuralists strongly advocated basing orthographies on the phonemic level (e.g., Sapir 1933, 1949; Pike 1947; Nida 1954; and Gudschinsky 1958, 1970, 1973).

It was only with the advent of the generative era that a serious challenge to the phoneme emerged, viz. the underlying form, which was a morphophonemic representation. Early generativists also had two levels of phonological representation to choose from, in principle, the underlying level and the surface level. However, for the same reasons that the structuralists rejected the phonetic level, the generativists rejected the surface level, choosing instead to base orthographies on the underlying level (Chomsky and Halle 1968,[5] Newman 1968, and Venezky 1970). Choosing the underlying level resulted in single representations for each morpheme, which made it significantly different in this regard from the structuralists' phonemic level. So while everyone more or less agreed that the phonetic/surface level was not the ideal basis for an orthography, there was sharp disagreement as to which was better: the structuralists' phonemic level or the generativists' underlying (morphophonemic) one. The orthography developer of the early generative era was therefore left with two serious options: writing phonemically or writing morphophonemically.

More recently, the orthography discussions concerning phonological depth have continued, albeit with somewhat different nomenclature (e.g., Liberman et al. 1980; Katz and Feldman 1983; Frost, Katz, and Bentin 1987; Katz and Frost 1992). Today, orthographies are usually described as being either "shallow" or "deep." Shallow orthographies are basically phonemic, and deep orthographies are basically morphophonemic, with each type being "tweaked" in one way or another to best fit the situation. Katz and Frost 1992 further describe the difference between them in this way:

> In summary, all alphabetic orthographies can be classified according to the transparency of their letter-to-phoneme correspondence, a factor that has been referred to as orthographic depth (Liberman, Liberman, Mattingly, and Shankweiler 1980). An orthography in which the letters are isomorphic to phonemes in the spoken word (completely and consistently), is orthographically shallow. An orthography in which the letter-phoneme relation is substantially equivocal is said to be deep (e.g., some letters have more than one sound and some phonemes can be written in more than one way or are not represented in the orthography). (Katz and Frost 1992:71)

---

[4] Although it is not always clear what native speakers are or are not aware of, my experience suggests that over time, much of what native speakers are aware of eventually reveals itself to observant field workers. That being said, formal testing (and publishing of the results) to either discover or to confirm elements of native awareness is always informative.

[5] Although *The Sound Pattern of English* was not a treatise on orthography per se, the authors nevertheless appeal repeatedly to the closeness of the English orthography to their underlying representations as justification for those representations. That they considered the underlying form to be optimal for orthography development may be seen in the following: "In this case, as in many other cases, English orthography turns out to be rather close to an optimal system for spelling English. In other words, it turns out to be rather close to the true phonological representation, given the nonlinguistic constraints that must be met by a spelling system" (Chomsky and Halle 1968:184, fn. 19).

Shallow orthographies are often seen as better for beginning readers because their level of representation has a closer relationship to the spoken form. However, if a language has a lot of phrasal phenomena that result in phonemic alternations, advanced readers can sometimes have trouble with shallow orthographies because the visual images of many words can change, depending on the phonological contexts. Even beginning readers can have trouble in such cases, because native speakers tend not to be very aware of postlexical outputs, even when the output corresponds to a phoneme in the language. For example, although native speakers are aware of phonemic distinctions in most environments (e.g., /s/ vs. /z/ in English *sip* vs. *zip*), they are generally not aware of the distinction when the phoneme is the result of a postlexical process (e.g., *cat-s* vs. *dog-z*).[6] One could imagine that trying to teach children when to write <s> and when to write <z> for the English plural suffix would prove difficult. Moreover, history has demonstrated that having more than a single, consistent morphophonemic representation for this morpheme is unnecessary. So a strictly phonemic orthography is not always optimal.

By the same token, deep orthographies are sometimes thought of as being better for advanced readers because they maintain consistent visual images (constant morpheme-images and, therefore, logically, constant word-images). Consistent visual images allow advanced readers to read quickly by sight, since they can call up from memory visual images that correspond to particular meanings. On the other hand, such orthographies are not always helpful for beginning readers because the representations can sometimes be very different from the way native speakers actually pronounce words, or think they pronounce them. For example, a morphophonemic representation of the English negative prefix *in-* would result in its having a consistent single representation (i.e., <in>) for words like *in-tolerable, im-possible, il-logical,* and *ir-reverent,* etc. Native speakers, however, are very aware that they pronounce these allomorphs differently, and many are not even aware that they represent the same prefix. So consistently having a deep/morphophonemic orthography is also not always optimal.

4.4.3 Lexical Orthography Hypothesis

Since both shallow and deep orthographies have problems when applied to all languages and all situations, what is needed is an orthography that includes all distinctions of which native speakers are aware and which excludes all distinctions of which they are unaware. The Lexical Orthography Hypothesis, henceforth LOH (Snider 2014b), claims to do just that and offers a promising compromise between strictly phonemic and strictly morphophonemic orthographies.[7] The LOH proposes that the ideal level of phonological depth upon which to base an orthography is the output of the lexical phonology, as set forth in the theory of Lexical Phonology[8] (Kiparsky 1982; Mohanan 1982, 1986) and its more recent developement into Stratal Optimality Theory (Kiparsky 2000, 2015; Bermúdez-Otero 2011).

The theory of Lexical Phonology recognizes two main types of processes, lexical and postlexical, with lexical rules sensitive to lexical contexts, and postlexical rules sensitive to phrasal contexts. Theoretical issues aside, from a practical standpoint, native speakers appear to be much more aware of sounds that result from the application of lexical processes than they are of those that result from postlexical ones. Snider 2014b explains why as follows:

---

[6] For discussions on devoicing processes that result in phonemic sounds of which native speakers are not fully aware (including in English), see Lombardi 1991, 1996, 1999; Torres 2001; and Van Oostendorp 2007.

[7] Snider 2014b is not the first study to advocate the LOH. Snider 2001 and Roberts 2008a also explore the implications of Lexical Phonology for orthography development, and I have also advocated it for many years in linguistics workshops, seminars, and courses.

[8] For the interested reader, Kenstowicz 1994 provides a good introduction to the theory of Lexical Phonology.

Postlexical processes, such as the English one that aspirates voiceless stops in different environments, often begin their "lives" as unconscious attempts on the part of native speakers to make the sounds or combinations of sounds in their languages easier to pronounce in different phonological environments. In other words, the processes have phonological conditioning, and native speakers are usually not even aware that they pronounce certain sounds differently. Thus, most English speakers are unaware of the difference between the aspirated and unaspirated *p*'s in English [pʰɪt] 'pit' and [spɪt] 'spit'.

Later, conditioning environments for some of these processes may become lost, or they become obscure due to their interactions with other processes…In some cases, grammatical conditioning partially replaces phonological conditioning…In other cases, exceptions to certain postlexical processes begin to creep in for various reasons. As a result, some phonological processes begin to lack complete phonetic motivation, other processes apply only when certain grammatical conditions are met, and still others apply idiosyncratically for undetermined reasons. As a result, [phonological] contrasts emerge between those lexical forms that undergo the processes and those forms that do not. As native speakers become aware of these contrasts, the forms that undergo the processes become lexicalized in their minds and the processes themselves become lexical processes (see Hyman 1976; Zec 1993; Kiparsky 1995).

Whereas native speakers are relatively unaware of the output of postlexical processes, they are much more aware of the output of lexical ones, and this explains why native speakers often prefer to write words as they are realized after they have undergone lexical processes and before they have undergone postlexical ones (Mohanan 1982, 1986). The output of the lexical phonology, whether that of the rule-based Lexical Phonology or that of the constraint-based Stratal OT, therefore promises to be an excellent level of representation upon which to base an orthography. (Snider 2014b:30–31)

(Subsequently, of course, there may need to be modifications motivated by various factors, e.g., political, social.)

Despite the fact that not a lot of testing has yet been carried out to confirm or debunk the LOH (but see Roberts et al. 2015),[9] anecdotal evidence to support it can be found in the literature at least as early as Gudschinsky 1958. In this article, Gudschinsky documents how a Soyaltepec Mazatec [vmp] speaker demonstrated awareness of "internal sandhi (mechanical tone changes within the word)," but was unaware of "external sandhi (mechanical tone changes between words)" (Gudschinsky 1958:342–343). From a lexical theory perspective, internal and external tone sandhi occur lexically and postlexically, respectively.

Being able to distinguish between lexical and postlexical processes is therefore crucial. Fortunately, it is not necessary to have a complete grasp of the theories of Lexical Phonology and Stratal Optimality Theory in order to do so. Since the two types of processes have different characteristics, a simplified summary of a number of distinguishing criteria, distilled from Mohanan 1982, Kiparsky 1982, and Pulleyblank 1986, appears in (14).

---

[9] Roberts et al. 2015 presents the results of orthography testing carried out with 97 secondary students in Kara, Togo who are native speakers of Kabiye. Three tentative tone orthographies were compared, each of which represented a different phonological depth: (1) underlying forms (i.e., inputs to the lexical level), (2) the outputs of the lexical phonology, and (3) phonemic forms. The results of the testing showed that the orthography representing the output of the lexical phonology outperformed the other orthographies "in three of the error types associated with adding diacritics, although [it] performed less well on one of the error types associated with writing segmental vowel length." It is hoped that the present work will encourage further testing along these lines.

4.4 Phonologically ideal orthography

(14) Criteria for distinguishing lexical and postlexical processes
   A. Lexical processes
      1. If there are genuine exceptions to a phonological process, it must be lexical. Exceptions may be single words or morphemes that are simply exceptions to the process, or they may be classes of morphemes or classes of words that fail to undergo the process.
      2. If a process lacks phonetic motivation, it must be lexical.
      3. If it is necessary to refer to a morpheme boundary when describing a process, it must be lexical.
      4. If linguistically naïve native speakers are fully aware of the output or effect of a process, it must be lexical.

   B. Postlexical processes
      1. If the output of a process results in a noncontrastive sound (i.e., a sound that is not phonemic), it must be postlexical.
      2. If a process occurs across a word boundary, it must be postlexical.
      3. If a process occurs only at the beginning or end of a phrase (this includes the beginning or end of words spoken in isolation), it must be postlexical.
      4. f the output of a process is gradient (e.g., partially voiced, partially aspirated), it must be postlexical.
      5. If linguistically naïve native speakers are totally ignorant of the output or effect of a process, it must be postlexical.

Despite the criteria provided in (14), determining whether a given process is lexical or postlexical can still be challenging. Imagine a scenario in which one is unable to determine whether linguistically naïve native speakers are aware of the output or effect of a process. Furthermore, let us assume that none of the other criteria are diagnostic either. How does one decide in cases like this? In such situations, the default choice is to consider the process postlexical because of how these processes come into being. Historically, postlexical processes become lexical processes for a reason. If no reasons manifest themselves (e.g., exceptions to processes, lack of phonological conditioning of processes), then there is no particular reason to assume that a process is lexical. For a more detailed discussion of these issues, see Snider 2014b.

To conclude this section, let us review which types of processes are responsible for the different levels of phonological depth (i.e., surface, phonemic, lexical, and underlying).

(15) Phonological processes responsible for different types of orthographies

Orthography type	Phonological processes responsible
Surface forms	have undergone all lexical processes, but also all postlexical processes.
Phonemic forms	have undergone all lexical processes, but also those postlexical processes that result in phonemic sounds.
Lexical forms	have undergone only lexical processes.
Underlying forms	have undergone no phonological processes.

Surface representations result from the application of all phonological processes that apply to underlying forms, including all allophonic ones, of which native speakers are unaware. Allophonic processes (e.g., aspiration of English stops) by their very nature are always postlexical. The opposite, however, is not true: not all postlexical processes are allophonic.

Even though phonemic representations are often similar to phonetic ones, they are much better for orthography purposes because they exclude the output of all allophonic processes, which, of course, are postlexical. Unfortunately, phonemic representations can also include the output of certain other (non-allophonic) postlexical processes of which native speakers are typically unaware (e.g., the difference between the phonemes /s/ and /z/ in English *cat-s* and *dog-z*).

Lexical representations, on the other hand, include the outputs of all lexical processes, of which native speakers are aware, and exclude the outputs of all postlexical processes, of which they are not aware. For this reason, native speakers are most aware of this level of representation. Another factor that makes this level ideal is that while the output does not result in a consistent morpheme-image, it does result in a consistent word-image, which is an important characteristic of good orthographies (Nida 1954, Voorhoeve 1962).

With regard to underlying representations, they are just that, underlying forms that have yet to undergo any and all processes. One advantage of underlying representations is that in providing consistent morpheme-images, they logically also provide consistent word-images. They are not ideal for orthography purposes, however, because they exclude the outputs of lexical processes, and thus do not necessarily correspond well to native speaker intuitions.

Since excluding postlexical processes is helpful for beginners and mature readers alike, the output of the lexical phonology is proposed as the ideal level of phonological representation upon which to base an orthography.[10] From there, the orthography can and should be adjusted as needed after testing has taken place.

4.5 Issues in representing tonal contrasts

I have often been asked questions such as, "In a two-tone language, is it necessary to mark both high and low tones, or can one just mark one of the tones? And if so, which tone should we mark, high or low?" Questions like these usually arise in reference to orthographies that are based on phonemic representations, with little or no regard for perhaps more important questions. In certain respects, this is like asking whether green cars are better than red cars. The colour of a car, of course, has little enough to do with its quality. Likewise, how one chooses to represent a particular entity isn't nearly as important as: a) determining whether tone needs to be represented at all, b) determining whether or not to mark grammatical distinctions diacritically, c) representing the correct entity (i.e., the pattern, as opposed to the individual tone), and d) representing the level of orthographic depth (viz. underlying, phonemic, lexical, or surface) of which the native speaker is most aware. Only once one has answered questions like these can one profitably move on to discuss how to implement the answers. Or, to continue the car analogy, only once one has determined what make and model of car is most suitable for one's particular needs does it make sense to discuss what colour it should be.

This, of course, is not to minimize the value of employing a good strategy for marking whatever contrasts are deemed appropriate to represent. In order to do this well, orthography developers should take into account findings from studies on the psychology of reading. Dave Roberts (personal communication) suggests three such types of studies that are relevant to tone orthographies: research on eye movement (e.g., Rayner 1998, Van Gompel et al. 2007), research on visual crowding (e.g., Pelli et al. 2007, Roberts 2009), and research on the relative salience of letter positions (e.g., Jordan et al. 2003).

With regard to relevant research on eye movement, Roberts notes that when salient information is placed beyond the range of parafoveal vision,[11] it can cause disruptive backtracking

---

[10] The reader should keep in mind that what is being advocated here (i.e., basing orthographies on the output of the lexical level of phonology) concerns only the extent to which phonology should inform orthography development. Other factors (e.g., political, social) also need to be taken into consideration.

[11] While foveal vision (what is seen at the point where the eye is fixated) communicates to readers the identities of orthographic symbols, parafoveal vision (what is seen beyond foveal vision) communicates "lower-level visual features, such as the length and the visual shape of words" (Hyönä 2012).

4.5 Issues in representing tonal contrasts

when reading. Positioning the Spanish question mark at the beginning of the sentence is an example of one strategy used to provide salient information in time to influence correct question intonation, as opposed to placing it at the end of the sentence where it might appear beyond the range of parafoveal vision. With regard to relevant research on visual crowding, Roberts (personal communication) notes that "the perception of any object decreases if multiple similar objects are located nearby." This, of course, has implications for the number and placement of tone marks that are similar to one another. Finally, with regard to relevant research on the relative salience of letter positions, Roberts (personal communication) notes that symbols exterior to the word, such as word initial plus signs, play a preferential role in reading. Orthographies that employ symbols exterior to the word to diacritically mark grammatical categories (cf. section 4.3.3) are therefore on solid psychological ground.

Kutsch Lojenga 2014:54–59 puts forward the following strategies that she has seen employed to represent tone: accents, punctuation marks, numbers, and unused consonant letters. We discuss each of these, in turn.

First, one can simply represent the patterns more or less as I have been doing throughout this chapter, using accent marks above each TBU to represent the different tones in the patterns. To the extent that one is representing the output of the lexical level of phonology, this has the advantage of helping beginning readers sound out, as they are reading, the different tone patterns in a manner that resonates with how they think the words sound. Equally helpful could be a variation of this that omits writing one or more of the tones in the patterns in such a manner that contrast is not lost between the patterns. This has the advantage of significantly reducing the density of marks in a text, thereby making it easier to write and less formidable to begin learning. From a psycholinguistic point of view, undoubtedly certain representations could be more advantageous than others; unfortunately, psycholinguistic considerations are beyond the scope of the present work. However, from a purely linguistic point of view, as long as each pattern is clearly distinguished, there would be no problem.

A further option, at least theoretically, would be to assign a single diacritic to each word pattern that is output from the lexical strata.[12] What is important is that the word pattern, rather than the morpheme pattern, be represented since readers seem to be more attuned to memorizing word shapes than morpheme shapes. Such a strategy would result in a number of different representations (e.g., number of word-syllable profiles multiplied by number of patterns that contrast at this stage). The number would nevertheless be limited, and for most tone languages, it would not necessarily be all that great.

One advantage of having a single diacritic for each syllable profile/tone pattern is that once the associations between the diacritics and the patterns are memorized, in principle it would speed up word recognition for advanced readers. An orthography designed along such lines, employing single diacritics to represent complete lexical patterns (i.e., complete word patterns as they are realized at the output of the lexical phonology) would be shallower than one that represented the underlying pattern of each morpheme, but deeper than one that represented all the tones of each lexical pattern. Such an orthography would, in principle, be slightly better suited for advanced readers than beginning readers, but it would undoubtedly be much more difficult to teach.

Second, one can employ punctuation marks before or after words or syllables to indicate tonal contrasts, and this has been employed in Côte d'Ivoire for a number of languages, including Attié [ati]. According to Kutsch Lojenga, this strategy works best for languages with predominantly monosyllabic words. Punctuation marks have also been used successfully in Sabaot (see above) as diacritics to encode grammatical distinctions.

Third, some languages in Mexico have used superscripted numbers after each syllable to represent tone heights (1=high, 4=low), although this system is apparently giving way to the use of accents (Kutsch Lojenga 2014:58–59).

---

[12] To my knowledge, this strategy has never been employed or even tested, but I put it out for consideration.

Fourth and finally, Kutsch Lojenga reports that some languages in Africa have employed "unused consonant letters" for marking tone, although this has not worked well, in part because many people in Africa have learned to read different European languages and have attached "a certain sound value to these consonants and find it, therefore impossible to start relating such symbols to pitch" (Kutsch Lojenga 2014:59).

Ultimately, whatever strategy one adopts, it is important to conduct extensive testing in order to see what type of orthography is best suited to the needs of the language community, and then to publish the results of that testing.[13]

4.6 Issues with teaching tone

One implication of representing complete tone patterns as they are realized at the output of the lexical phonology concerns how tone is taught. Most primers that I am aware of focus on contrasting individual phonemic tones associated to individual TBUs, with other phonemic tones (e.g., high tone vs. mid tone, vs. low tone, vs. falling tone). Teaching in this manner poses at least two problems.

First, native speakers of tone languages are not very aware of the individual tones in words with simple stems, let alone in words with compound and complex stems, so it is difficult to teach them how to read complicated patterns. When asked to identify the tone of a particular syllable or TBU in a word or short phrase, most trained native speakers will first say the utterance or whistle the tone pattern and then count out the number of beats until they arrive at the part of the pattern associated with the syllable in question. On the other hand, when asked to identify the complete pattern of a word, these same native speakers can usually do this readily without thinking.

The second problem with teaching materials that focus on individual tones as opposed to word patterns is that not enough time is spent teaching how to read tone. Many primers that I have reviewed provide no more than a lesson or two on each tone, in keeping with how consonants and vowels are taught. For an orthography designed along the lines advocated in the present work, a better approach would be to focus on teaching the contrasts between word patterns. Again, this is word patterns as they are realized at the output of the lexical phonology. Recall the Mende data from chapter 1, repeated above in this chapter as (13). In Mende, the traditional approach to teaching tone would devote possibly five or so lessons to teaching the five contrastive tones (viz., high, low, falling, rising, and rising-falling) found on monosyllabic words (see the first column in (13)). The approach advocated here would have at least fifteen lessons devoted to tone, one for each word pattern (five lexical patterns multiplied by three word syllable profiles). Not only would this approach correspond more closely to native speaker perception, but it would greatly increase the number of lessons devoted to tone, and this in itself would provide better reinforcement of the material taught.

4.7 Conclusion

Many people who are faced with the task of developing an orthography for a tone language are unfortunately intimidated by tone, and in many cases they lack an understanding of how to analyze a tone system. At this point, the reader will hopefully feel less threatened. In order to further reinforce the concepts taught in this book, here is a summary in point form of the essential steps for analyzing a tone language and developing an orthography for it. These are divided into two groups: linguistic analysis and orthography development.

---

[13] For an excellent summary and discussion of "thirty years of tone orthography testing in West African languages," see Roberts 2008b.

4.7 Conclusion

4.7.1 Linguistic analysis

Recall the discussions in chapter 2 concerning how best to carry out tone analysis.

(16) Steps for carrying out a proper tone analysis
   a) Elicit a substantial wordlist (at least 1,000 words) in the language.
   b) Preferably using a database, separate the words into groups, as outlined in chapter 2, so that the potentially influencing factors are the same for all the words in each group. This will ensure that any tonal differences between the words in each group are due to differences in their underlying tone patterns, as opposed to differences induced by outside factors.
   c) For each of these groups, identify the tone patterns that contrast within each group and determine their underlying forms (e.g., /H/, /LH/) to the best of your ability. If you are unable to assign a linguistically accurate label to every contrastive pattern, at least assign abstract labels to them (e.g., Pattern A, Pattern B).
   d) Elicit the different morphemes in your data in as many different morphological and syntactic environments as possible (see the discussions in chapter 2) and observe the tonal alternations that occur. This will include those environments that result in distinctions that are typically referred to as grammatical tone. At this point, it is more important to identify the different processes responsible for the different tonal alternations than to explain them in a fully worked out analysis.
   e) Finally, following the criteria presented above in (14), identify which processes are lexical and which are postlexical.

In a nutshell, determine the contrastive patterns for each category of morphemes in the language, taking into account their different environments; observe any alternations those patterns undergo in the different contexts in which they are found; and identify whether the processes/constraints responsible for those alternations are lexical or postlexical in nature.

4.7.2 Orthography development

Recall the discussions above in this chapter concerning how to develop an orthography.

(17) Steps for developing an orthography
   a) With tone totally unmarked in any way, conduct extensive testing with texts of different genres and differing degrees of complexity in order to determine whether there are any difficulties in oral reading and in comprehension. If there are no substantial problems, consider not representing tone orthographically.
   b) Testing may show that lexical tone does not need to be represented orthographically, but native speakers nevertheless have significant problems recognizing certain grammatical distinctions (e.g., person, tense/aspect) indicated solely by tone. In this case, consider representing only the different grammatical distinctions with diacritics or by other means. Such marking should be confined to distinguishing grammatical morphemes, not lexical items in large word categories.
   c) If testing with tonally unmarked texts reveals an unacceptable degree of difficulty in distinguishing lexical items with different tone patterns, try to determine the nature of the problem(s).
   d) Having identified the different phonological processes in the language, and having distinguished those processes that are lexical from those that are postlexical, work out practical spellings for the language, in a manner that excludes the effects of postlexical processes.

e) For languages that have grammatical tone, it is also important to work out spellings for words as they are realized in different conjugations (e.g., with different subject/object markers and in different tense/aspects). Again, be sure to exclude any effects of postlexical processes.

f) Finally, it is important to test the proposed orthography against texts that are unmarked for tone in order to confirm that the problems identified earlier are actually resolved. This testing should be carried out with sample sizes large enough to reveal the statistical significance of any differences. And of course, one should always publish the results of orthography testing in order to help the discipline aggregate its experience in refining test designs.

5
Phonological Analysis of Chumburung Tone

Recall from the earlier chapters that the object of tone analysis is: a) to discover the different underlying tone patterns that are potentially possible for any given morpheme, and b) to discover and explain the different ways in which those patterns link to TBUs and are realized phonetically in the various contexts in which they are found. This chapter sets out to discover the underlying tone patterns of noun roots in Chumburung, and to identify and explain the behaviour of those patterns in a number of different contexts, following the methodology introduced in chapter 2. Due to the pedagogical nature of the work there is detailed reference to the analysis procedures applied at each stage. However, this is not intended to serve as a reference work on Chumburung.[1] A standard reference work would include many more details, especially relating to verbs, most of which would not contribute further to understanding the essence of the tone system. Chumburung also has a noun class system in which all noun prefixes behave the same tonally. Once we learn how the noun prefixes behave in two or three classes, there is little to be gained pedagogically by repeating the analysis procedures for the remaining classes. Also, since the phonological processes that apply to noun tones are essentially the same as those that apply to verb tones, this study deals mainly with nouns, in order to avoid unnecessary repetition. Attention is therefore given to the verbal system only to the extent that it enhances our understanding of the nominal system.

As with all natural languages, there is a certain amount of "mess," and I have chosen not to include certain idiosyncrasies when accounting for them would detract from the overall goal of exemplifying the methodology. For other idiosyncratic data, I have chosen to include them, but only to the extent that they further the goals of the present work.

Chumburung is a Guang language spoken in Ghana. The Guang group, in turn, belongs to the Kwa family, part of the greater Niger-Congo family of languages. In order to better understand the discussion of nominal tone in Chumburung, the reader will find helpful the following pertinent information on the phonology and morphology of the language.

The surface vowel inventory of Chumburung is set out as follows:

---

[1] For a general, broad description of Chumburung phonology, morphology, and syntax, see Hansford 1988.

(1) Surface vowel inventory of Chumburung

	−ATR		+ATR	
+High	ɪ	ʊ	i	u
−High	ɛ	ɔ	e	o
	a		ə	

Although there are ten surface vowels, underlyingly there are only nine, with [ə] and [a] occurring in complementary distribution: [ə] only occurs to the left of +ATR (Advanced Tongue Root) vowels, and [a] never occurs to the left of +ATR vowels within phonological words. The vowels of words are normally either all +ATR or all −ATR. The only exceptions are compound forms in which two roots are from different harmony sets (e.g., kìsáríi-d͡ʒì 'finger', wúrú-bʷárì 'God'), or when [a] occurs to the right of a +ATR vowel (e.g., kùrùmá 'donkey'). In the case of kìsáríi-d͡ʒì, the +ATR vowel in the second root of the compound spreads its +ATR value to the preceding vowel in the first root, rendering it [i] instead of [ɪ] (cf. kɪ̀sárɪ́ 'arm').

ATR vowel harmony also exists between the vowels of stems and prefixes, the latter always harmonizing with the former with respect to ATR. In addition, the kI- noun class prefix harmonizes with the Round specification of the first vowel of the stem, unless the first consonant of the stem is Labial. When the first consonant of the stem is Labial, the harmony is optionally blocked. The following examples are illustrative.

(2) Vowel harmony between stems and kI- prefix in Chumburung

	−ATR		+ATR	
−Rd	kɪ̀-sɪ̀bɔ́	'ear'	kí-jí?	'tree'
	kí-kɛ́?	'headpad'	kì-té?	'story'
	kɪ̀-pá	'hat'	kì-jé?	'meat (chunk)'
+Rd	kʊ̀-kʊ̀tɔ̀	'claw'	kù-ŋú	'head'
	kʊ̀-kɔ́	'debt'	kú-d͡ʒó	'yam'

(3) Round harmony optionally blocked due to intervening labial consonant

−ATR		+ATR	
kɪ́-pʊ́ ~ kʊ́-pʊ́	'forest'	kì-bú ~ kù-bú	'stone'
kɪ́-fʊ́rɪ̂ ~ kʊ́-fʊ́rɪ̂	'rock'	kì-bòŋìrə́ŋ ~ kù-bòŋìrə́ŋ	'bell'

Vowel assimilation processes also occur across word boundaries within phonological phrases, and careful readers will notice that some of the outputs of these processes (only those that affect +High vowels, which are the easiest to hear) are represented in the phonetic transcriptions of the examples and the online Chumburung exercises. Here are the processes relevant to the representations in this chapter.[2] Whenever a +High, -ATR vowel occurs in a syllable across a word boundary from a syllable with a +ATR vowel, the -ATR vowel will be realized as +ATR, regardless of the order of the syllables. For example, /dápú kɪ́ké/ → [dápú kíké] 'hawk's basket' (1st syllable -ATR, 2nd syllable +ATR), and /bùnì kɪ̀pá/ → [bùnì kìpá] 'butterfly's hat' (1st syllable +ATR, 2nd syllable -ATR). Similarly, whenever a +High, -Rd vowel occurs in a syllable that is on the left side of a word boundary from a syllable with a +Rd vowel, it is realized as +Rd (e.g., /bùnì kùkùt͡ʃé/ → [bùnù kùkùt͡ʃé] 'butterfly's oyster'). If, however, the two vowels are separated by a labial consonant, the spreading only occurs optionally

---

[2] Since it is beyond the scope of this brief introduction to discuss these processes in depth, the interested reader will find a fuller discussion of this subject in Snider 1985, 1989.

(e.g., /kídʒí bùnì/ → [kídʒú búnì] ~ [kídʒí búnì] 'seed's butterfly'). Unlike the situation with +ATR assimilation, +Rd spreading only occurs leftward. So if a +High, -Rd vowel occurs in a syllable that is on the right side of a word boundary from a syllable with a +Rd vowel, +Rd spreading does not occur (e.g., /dápú kídʒá/ → [dápú kídʒá] 'hawk's market', *[dápú kúdʒá]).

Whenever two vowels are brought into adjacency in Chumburung, hiatus resolution occurs (Snider 1989). In essence, the nucleus of the resultant syllable consists of the second of the two vowels, which potentially undergoes two assimilatory processes prior to deletion of the first vowel: a) If the first vowel is +ATR and the second vowel is +High, the second vowel will be realized as +ATR, regardless of the second vowel's underlying specification for ATR; b) If the first vowel is -High, the second vowel will be realized as -High, regardless of the second vowel's underlying specification for height or ATR. Finally, if the vowel that is deleted is +Round, the preceding consonant is realized with a round off-glide. Examples of hiatus resolution, with the resultant vowels underlined, appear in (4).

(4) Vowel coalescence

First vowel +ATR, +High Second vowel -ATR, +High	First vowel +ATR, +High Second vowel -ATR, -High
ìwú ìsá → [ìwí‘sá] 'three thorns' thorns three	ə̀ŋú àsá → [ə̀ŋʷá‘sá] 'three heads' heads three
First vowel +ATR, -High Second vowel -ATR, +High	First vowel +ATR, -High Second vowel -ATR, -High
ídʒó ìsá → [ídʒʷèsá] 'three yams' yams three	ə́k͡pé àsá → [ə́k͡pàsá] 'three witches' witches three
First vowel -ATR, +High Second vowel -ATR, +High	First vowel -ATR, +High Second vowel -ATR, -High
ìbúrí ìsá → [ìbúrí‘sá] 'three voices' voices three	àɲárí àsá → [àɲárá‘sá] 'three names' names three
First vowel -ATR, -High Second vowel -ATR, +High	First vowel -ATR, -High Second vowel -ATR, -High
ìk͡páŋŋá ìsá → [ìk͡páŋŋé‘sá] 'three horses' horses three	átɔ́ àsá → [àtʷàsá] 'three things' things three

The final helpful piece of information concerns the behaviour of the glottal stop. The glottal stop only occurs pause initially (i.e., at the end of phrases), and this only in two environments: at the end of all negative phrases (see example (5a) immediately below), and at the end of certain words when they are the end of a phrase, including in isolation environments (see example (5b)). When these certain words are pronounced phrase medially, the mora that is assigned to the glottal stop when the word is pronounced phrase finally is instead assigned to the preceding vowel. In other words, the syllable that is phonetically realized as CVʔ when spoken phrase finally, is phonetically realized as CVV when spoken phrase medially.

(5) Behaviour of glottal stop in Chumburung

    a.   nàná má nú dápúʔ   'grandchild won't hear a hawk'   cf. dápú 'hawk'
        nàná má ŋú búnìʔ   'grandchild won't see a butterfly'   cf. bùnì 'butterfly'

    b.   kìsáríʔ   'arm/hand'   cf. kìsárìi-dʒì 'finger (lit. hand-child)'
        kìdʒàbúʔ   'cripple'   cf. kìdʒàbúu ‘dápú 'cripple's hawk'

With respect to morphology, most nouns are comprised of a segmental noun class prefix followed by a stem (cf. kí-pú 'forest' á-pú 'forests'). That prefixes are affixed to stems and not roots becomes evident when we consider non-simple stems. The word ɔ̀-tʃíʔ 'woman' belongs to the O- class, which designates human beings and important animals and birds. The root /tʃíɪ/ may be combined with the verb /k͡pá/ 'love, want', to form the compound stem [tʃíɪ-k͡pá]. The complete word, kà-tʃíɪ-k͡pá literally means, 'woman-love', or 'adultery (with a woman)'. Pertinent to the matter at hand, and perhaps contrary to expectation, the prefix for this word is not O-, but rather kA-. While the O- prefix is appropriate for ɔ̀-tʃíʔ because the referent is a human being, it is not appropriate for the concept of 'adultery', which belongs to the kA- class. The choice of kA- over O- for this class prefix clearly demonstrates that the choice of prefix is sensitive to the stem, as opposed to the immediately following root.

The methodology put forward in this work will make tonal phenomena more transparent, but in and of itself, it will not explain those phenomena. That is where linguistic theory makes its contribution. Theory is important, and everyone undertaking linguistic analysis views the results of their analysis through one theoretical lens or another. That being said, the present work intentionally refrains from providing explanations for many of the phenomena observed. This would certainly be a worthy goal of a reference work on Chumburung tone; however, the goal of the present work is simply to teach a methodology of tone analysis that will reveal phenomena and make them amenable to theoretical explanations.

In this chapter, section 5.1 introduces the Chumburung word list that forms the basis for the analysis and discusses their entries in the different relevant database fields. Section 5.2 provides a full analysis of the first set of words chosen for analysis. This first set is a subset of the nouns, and the analysis takes into account their isolation forms, their plural forms, and their surface realizations when spoken in different phrasal contexts. Section 5.3 analyzes all remaining words in the database in their isolation forms, section 5.4 analyzes all remaining words as they are spoken in other morphological environments (i.e., the plural forms of nouns and the nominalized forms of verbs), and section 5.5 analyzes all remaining words as they are spoken in other phrasal (i.e., non-isolation) environments. Finally, section 5.6 pulls things together with a summary of the analysis and a discussion of certain data that I found perplexing for far too long.

5.1 Setting up the database and entering data

This section demonstrates in table format how to enter into a database data that are relevant to tone analysis.

Since consonant-tone interaction is not known to play a role in Guang languages, our "database" does not include a field for stem consonants. And although our database does include a field for the underlying tone patterns of the roots, this field is not shown in table 1 because at this stage of the analysis, this information is not known. Also, since Chumburung does not have a verb class system, the class field is not filled in for verbs. Abbreviations that appear in this table are as follows:

N   Noun
V   Verb
S   Simple stem
Cp Compound stem
Cx Complex stem

The data for this database are a set of Chumburung words, carefully selected with a view to demonstrating the methodology discussed in chapter 2.

5.1 Setting up the database and entering data

Table 1. Chumburung database

Ref.	Gloss	Segments	Pitch	Sing. Class	Pl. Seg.	Pl. Pitch	Gram. Cat.	Pl. Class	Stem Syll. Profile	Stem Type
001	breast	kɪ[ɲapʊ]		kɪ-	a[ɲapʊ]		N	A-	CVCV	S
002	nose	[mʊrɔbɔ]		NULL	ɪ[mʊrɔbɔ]		N	I-	CVCVCV	Cp
003	shoulder	kɪ[baʔ]		kɪ-	a[baʔ]		N	A-	CVC	S
004	hip	kɪ[laŋ]		kɪ-	a[laŋ]		N	A-	CVN	S
005	calf (of leg)	[tʃipi]		NULL	i[tʃipi]		N	I-	CVCV	S
006	heart	[duŋ]		NULL	i[duŋ]		N	I-	CVN	S
007	kidney	ki[tʃeʔ]		kɪ-	ə[tʃeʔ]		N	A-	CVC	S
008	vein	ki[tʃini]		kɪ-	ə[tʃini]		N	A-	CVCV	S
009	saliva (globule)	kʊ[tʃɔnɪ]		kɪ-	a[tʃɔnɪ]		N	A-	CVCV	S
010	phlegm (globule)	[wɛʔ]		NULL	ɪ[wɛʔ]		N	I-	CVC	S
011	cough (n.)	kʊ[wɔ]rɪ		kɪ-	a[wɔ]rɪ		N	A-	CV]CV	Cx
012	sore	[lɔ]		NULL	ɪ[lɔ]		N	I-	CV	S

106 — *Phonological Analysis of Chumburung Tone*

013	madness	ɪ[buŋ]	[-]	I-	ə[buŋ]	[-]	N		CVN	S
014	plan (n.)	kɪ[k͡pini]	[- -]	kɪ-	ə[k͡pini]	[- -]	N	A-	CVCV	S
015	name (n.)	kɪ[ɲa]rɪ	[- -]	kɪ-	a[ɲa]rɪ	[- -]	N	A-	CVJCV	Cx
016	fellow wife	[t͡ʃamʊna]	[- - -]	NULL	a[t͡ʃamʊna]	[- - -]	N	A-	CVCVCV	Cp
017	butcher (n.)	[naakɔsɪ]	[- - -]	NULL	a[naakɔsɪ]	[- - -]	N	A-	CVVCVCV	Cp
018	proverb	kɪ[k͡pa]rɪ	[/ -]	kɪ-	a[k͡pa]rɪ	[/ -]	N	A-	CVJCV	Cx
019	market	kɪ[d͡ʒa]	[/]	kɪ-	a[d͡ʒa]	[/]	N	A-	CV	S
020	farm (n.)	kʊ[dɔʔ]	[/]	kɪ-	a[dɔʔ]	[/]	N	A-	CVC	S
021	hat	kɪ[pa]	[/]	kɪ-	a[pa]	[/]	N	A-	CV	S
022	cloth	[wad͡ʒa]	[- ']	NULL	a[wad͡ʒa]	[- ']	N	A-	CVCV	S
023	piece	kɪ[tiŋ]	[/]	kɪ-	ə[tiŋ]	[/]	N	A-	CVN	S
024	meat (chunk)	kɪ[jeʔ]	[/]	kɪ-	ə[jeʔ]	[/]	N	A-	CVC	S
025	mortar	kɪ[pɪnɪ]	[- -]	kɪ-	a[pɪnɪ]	[- -]	N	A-	CVCV	S
026	clay bowl	[d͡ʒa]rɪ	[-]	NULL	ɪ[d͡ʒa]rɪ	[-]	N	I-	CVJCV	Cx

5.1 Setting up the database and entering data

ID	gloss	form1	tone1	prefix	stem	tone2	N	pref	syll	class
027	sack	[bɔtɪ]	[¬ ¬]	NULL	ɪ[bɔtɪ]	[¬ ¬ ¬]	N	I-	CVCV	S
028	basket	ki[ke]	[¬ /]	kɪ-	ə[ke]	[¬ ¬]	N	A-	CV	S
029	jug	kɪ[laŋ]	[¬ ¬]	kɪ-	a[laŋ]	[¬ /]	N	A-	CVN	S
030	compound	[lɔŋ]	[/]	NULL	ɪ[lɔŋ]	[¬ /]	N	I-	CVN	S
031	shelter (n.)	kɪ[dʒaŋ]	[¬ /]	kɪ-	a[dʒaŋ]	[¬ ′]	N	A-	CVN	S
032	room	kɪ[tʃaŋ]	[¬ /]	kɪ-	a[tʃaŋ]	[¬ /]	N	A-	CVN	S
033	doorway	[punɪ]	[¬ ¬]	NULL	ɪ[punɪ]	[¬ ¬ ¬]	N	I-	CVCV	S
034	doorway covering	ku[suŋ]	[¬ /]	kɪ-	ə[suŋ]	[¬ /]	N	A-	CVN	S
035	work (n.)	ku[suŋ]	[¬ /]	kɪ-	ə[suŋ]	[¬ /]	N	A-	CVN	S
036	needle	[basa]	[¬ ′]	NULL	ɪ[basa]	[¬ ¬ ′]	N	I-	CVCV	S
037	cutlass	kɪ[paŋ]	[¬ ′]	kɪ-	a[paŋ]	[¬ ′]	N	A-	CVN	S
038	bow (n.)	kɪ[ta]	[¬ ¬]	kɪ-	a[ta]	[¬ ¬]	N	A-	CV	S
039	throwing stick	[k͡puraka]	[¬]	NULL	ɪ[k͡puraka]	[¬ / ¬]	N	I-	CVCVCV	Cp
040	fish dam	[wuɹri]	[¬ ¬]	NULL	i[wuɹri]	[¬ ¬ ¬]	N	I-	CVJCV	Cx

041	debt	kʊ[kɔ]	[—]		a[kɔ]	[—]	N	A-	CV	S
042	paddle (n.)	kɪ[baŋ]	[╱]	kɪ-	a[baŋ]	[╲]	N	A-	CVN	S
043	headpad	kɪ[kɛʔ]	[—]	kɪ-	a[kɛʔ]	[—]	N	A-	CVC	S
044	war	kɪ[naʔ]	[—]	kɪ-	a[naʔ]	[—]	N	A-	CVC	S
045	cemetery	[purek͡pa]	[— ╱]	NULL	i[purek͡pa]	[— ╱]	N	I-	CVCVCV	Cp
046	monkey	[kɔtɪ]	[—]	NULL	a[kɔtɪ]	[— —]	N	A-	CVCV	S
047	antelope	[foʝrɪ]	[╱]	NULL	a[foʝrɪ]	[— ╱]	N	A-	CVJCV	Cx
048	guinea fowl	[t͡ʃaŋ]	[—]	NULL	a[t͡ʃaŋ]	[— —]	N	A-	CVN	S
049	hawk	[dapʊ]	[—]	NULL	a[dapʊ]	[— —]	N	A-	CVCV	S
050	snake	kʊ[wɔ]	[—]	kɪ-	a[wɔ]	[— —]	N	A-	CV	S
051	python	kɪ[t͡ʃaʔ]	[—]	kɪ-	a[t͡ʃaʔ]	[— —]	N	A-	CVC	S
052	lizard	[keʝri]	[— ╱]	NULL	i[keʝri]	[— —]	N	I-	CVJCV	Cx
053	oyster	ku[kut͡ʃe]	[— —]	kɪ-	ə[kut͡ʃe]	[— —]	N	A-	CVCV	S
054	louse	[k͡pabʊ]	[—]	NULL	ɪ[k͡pabʊ]	[— —]	N	I-	CVCV	S

5.1 Setting up the database and entering data

055	butterfly	[buni]	[-́]	NULL	i[buni]	[-́]	N	I-	CVCV	S
056	horn	kʊ[tʃɔ]rɪ	[-̀ -́]	kɪ-	a[tʃɔ]rɪ	[-̀ -́]	N	A-	CV]CV	Cx
057	hump (of cow)	kʊ[kɔŋ]	[-̀ -̀]	kɪ-	a[kɔŋ]	[-̀ -̀]	N	A-	CVN	S
058	animal track	kɪ[bʊ]rɪ	[-̀ -́]	kɪ-	a[bʊ]rɪ	[-̀ -́]	N	A-	CV]CV	Cx
059	feather	ki[teʔ]	[-̀ -̀]	kɪ-	ə[teʔ]	[-̀ -̀]	N	A-	CVC	S
060	shell	kɪ[dʒafʊ]	[-̀ -̀]	kɪ-	a[dʒafʊ]	[-̀ -̀]	N	A-	CVCV	S
061	nest	kɪ[saʔ]	[-̀ -̀]	kɪ-	a[saʔ]	[-̀ -̀]	N	A-	CVC	S
062	coconut palm	[kube]	[-̀ -̀]	NULL	ə[kube]	[-̀ -̀]	N	A-	CVCV	S
063	thorn tree	kʊ[wiʔ]	[-̀ -̀]	kɪ-	ə[wiʔ]	[-̀ -̀]	N	A-	CVC	S
064	thorn	[wu]	[-̀]	NULL	i[wu]	[-̀]	N	I-	CV	S
065	grass	ɪ[fa]	[-̀]	I-			N		CV	S
066	cavity (in tree)	kʊ[lɔŋ]	[-̀ -́]	kɪ-	a[lɔŋ]	[-̀ -́]	N	A-	CVN	S
067	seed	ki[dʒi]	[-̀ -̀]	kɪ-	ə[dʒi]	[-̀ -̀]	N	A-	CV	S
068	bud	ki[fu]ri	[-̀ -́]	kɪ-	ə[fu]ri	[-̀ -́]	N	A-	CV]CV	Cx

110   *Phonological Analysis of Chumburung Tone*

069	yam shoot	[baʔ]	[ˉ]	NULL	ɪ[baʔ]	[ˉ]	N	I-	CVC	S
070	orange (n.)	kʊ[kuti]	[ˉ ˉ]	kɪ-	ə[kuti]	[ˉ ˉ]	N	A-	CVCV	S
071	rubber (globule)	kɪ[maʔ]	[ˉ ˉ]	kɪ-	a[maʔ]	[ˉ ˉ]	N	A-	CVC	S
072	path	[k͡pa]	[ˉ]	NULL	ɪ[k͡pa]	[ˉ]	N	I-	CV	S
073	edge (n.)	[kɛʔ]	[ˉ]	NULL			N	A-	CVC	S
074	forest	kɪ[pʊ]	[ˉ ˉ]	kɪ-	a[pʊ]	[ˉ ˉ]	N	A-	CV	S
075	mountain	kɪ[brʔ]	[ˉ ˉ]	kɪ-	a[brʔ]	[ˉ ˉ]	N	A-	CVC	S
076	rock	kɪ[fʊ]rɪ	[ˉ ╱]	kɪ-	a[fʊ]rɪ	[ˉ ╱]	N	A-	CV]CV	Cx
077	stone	kɪ[bu]	[ˉ ˉ]	kɪ-	ə[bu]	[ˉ ˉ]	N	A-	CV	S
078	pool	kɪ[pa]rɪ	[ˉ ╱]	kɪ-	a[pa]rɪ	[ˉ ╱]	N	A-	CV]CV	Cx
079	river	[bʊŋ]	[ˉ]	NULL	ɪ[bʊŋ]	[ˉ]	N	I-	CVN	S
080	cloud	kʊ[wʊ]rɪ	[ˉ ╱]	kɪ-	a[wʊ]rɪ	[ˉ ╱]	N	A-	CV]CV	Cx
081	see	[ɲu]	[╱]				V		CV	S
082	hit	[da]	[╱]				V		CV	S

5.1 Setting up the database and entering data

083	twist	[kiʔ]	–	V	CVC	S
084	eat	[d͡ʒi]	／	V	CV	S
085	bite	[duŋ]	／	V	CVN	S
086	cut	[tɪŋ]	／	V	CVN	S
087	roast	[tɔ]	／	V	CV	S
088	fry	[kɪʔ]	–	V	CVC	S
089	want	[k͡pa]	／	V	CV	S
090	get	[ɲa]	／	V	CV	S
091	lose	[paŋ]	／	V	CVN	S
092	send	[suŋ]	／	V	CVN	S
093	prevent	[kuŋ]	／	V	CVN	S
094	hatch	[bo]	／	V	CV	S
095	chase	[d͡ʒa]	／	V	CV	S
096	give	[sa]	／	V	CV	S

097	take	[ta?]	[−]			V		CVC	S
098	buy	[sɔ?]	[−]			V		CVC	S
099	bewitch	[t͡ʃɔ]	[´]			V		CV	S
100	capsize	[buŋ]	[´]			V		CVN	S

5.1 Setting up the database and entering data

Although most of the information in table 1 is self-explanatory, the reader will nevertheless find the following discussion helpful.

Noun stems in Chumburung are identified by comparing singular nouns with their plural counterparts. For example, in the case of 001 *kí[ɲápû]* 'breast', since the plural form is *á[ɲápû]* (cf. section 5.4), the morpheme division is relatively straightforward. Similarly, in the case of 002 *múrɔ́bɔ́* 'nose', since the plural form is *ì[múrɔ́bɔ́]*, the division is again straightforward. There are two non-count nouns, 013 *ì[búŋ]* 'madness' and 065 *í[fá]* 'grass', listed with the singular forms, and both begin with vowels. All noun stems in Chumburung begin with consonants, so we can safely say that these nouns belong to the *I*- class (cf. the plural class of words such as *múrɔ́bɔ́/ ì[múrɔ́bɔ́]*). The process of deciding what constitutes a root, as opposed to a stem, is more involved and is discussed immediately below. In addition, there is another word, 073 *kɛ́ʔ* 'edge', that does not take a plural. The reason for this is so far unknown.

In the Stem type field, the following five nouns are marked as having compound stems.

(6) Compound stems

002	'nose'	[mʊrɔbɔ]	⎡ - - - ⎤
016	'fellow wife'	[t͡ʃamʊna]	⎡ - - ⎤
017	'butcher (n.)'	[naakɔsɪ]	⎡ - - ⎤
039	'throwing stick '	[k͡pʊraka]	⎡ - ⎺ \ ⎤
045	'cemetery'	[purek͡pa]	⎡ - - \ ⎤

As discussed in chapter 2, for most Niger-Congo languages, any stem with three or more syllables is most certainly compound or complex, even if it is not possible to recognize the different components of the stem. Of the stems in (6), four have a CVCVCV syllable profile and one, *nààkɔ̀sí* 'butcher', has CVVCVCV. The stem syllable profile of *nààkɔ̀sí* is completely different from that of all other stems in the database, and this idiosyncrasy is a strong indication that this stem is a compound composed of two or more roots. It is also the case that the remaining four nouns all have different pitch patterns. Again, the idiosyncratic nature of these syllable and pitch patterns is strongly indicative that the stems are compounds. Of these, although there is no definitive proof, the syllable *bɔ́* of *múrɔ́bɔ́* 'nose' is probably the noun *bɔ́* 'hole' (not included in the present database). The word *púrékpâ* 'cemetery' is most certainly composed of the verb *pùré* 'bury' (not part of the present database and perhaps a compound itself) and the noun root /k͡pà/ 'place' (cf. *dìŋk͡pà* 'fire place', *d͡ʒéekpâ* 'bathing place', words again not included in the present database). Although the constituent parts of the remaining two nouns, *t͡ʃàmʊ̀ná* 'fellow wife' and *k͡pʊ̀ráka̋* 'throwing stick', are unknown, due to the trisyllabic nature of their stems, the low frequency of the CVCVCV stem syllable profile, and the idiosyncratic nature of their tone patterns, we will categorically assume that these stems are not simple. Since more information is required to analyze these nouns further, and since that information is not readily available, we will not discuss these words further.

The following words are listed as having complex stems. In the Segments field, brackets are placed around roots in order to make recognizing them easier for both machine and man.

(7) Complex stems

011	'cough (n.)'	kʊ[wɔ]rɪ	⁻[⁻]⁻
015	'name'	kɪ[ɲa]rɪ	⁻[⁻]⁻
018	'proverb'	kɪ[k͡pa]rɪ	⁻[⁻]\
026	'clay bowl'	[d͡ʒa]rɪ	[⁻]⁻
040	'fish dam'	[wu]ri	⁻[⁻]⁻
047	'antelope'	[fʊ]rɪ	⁻[⁻]⁻
052	'lizard'	[ke]ri	[⁻]\
056	'horn'	kʊ[t͡ʃɔ]rɪ	⁻[⁻]⁻
058	'animal track'	kɪ[bʊ]rɪ	⁻[⁻]\
068	'bud'	ki[fu]ri	⁻[⁻]⁻
078	'pool'	kɪ[pa]rɪ	⁻[⁻]⁻
080	'cloud'	kʊ[wʊ]rɪ	⁻[⁻]\
091	'rock'	kɪ[fʊ]rɪ	⁻[⁻]\

These words are considered to be complex because they all end in what looks to be a suffix *-rI*, realized as either *-rɪ* or *-ri*, depending on whether the root is respectively –ATR or +ATR. Admittedly, if it is a suffix, it is difficult to ascribe a meaning to it. But given that of the 30 nouns whose stems are CVCV there are 13 (43%) whose second syllable is either *rɪ* or *ri*, this strongly suggests that we are dealing with at least an old suffix (or suffixes, since we can't rule out the possibility that there is more than one), even if we can't assign any meaning to it/them.[3] Similar to the treatment of compounds in the present work, since more information is required to analyze these nouns further, and since that information is again not readily available, we will not discuss these words further.

5.2 Full analysis of preliminary words

The principles discussed in chapter 2 can be applied to the data in table 1 in order to identify the first group of words that should be analyzed. With respect to which grammatical category to begin with, Chumburung nouns typically have the structure [Noun class prefix [Stem]],

---

[3] This figure is similar to that of my personal Chumburung database as of the time of this writing. In that database, of the 203 nouns whose stems are CVCV, there are 79 (39%) whose second syllable is either rɪ or ri.

5.2 Full analysis of preliminary words

while verbs typically have at least the following, more complex structure [Subject prefix [Aspect marker [Stem]]]. Given that there are fewer unknown elements in unanalyzed nouns than in unanalyzed verbs, we will begin with nouns.

With respect to which noun class to begin with, the largest class is the *kI-* class, with its four segmental allomorphs: *ki-, kɪ-, ku-,* and *kʊ-,* assuming that the *kI-* prefix doesn't split into two underlyingly, one prefix with underlying high tone, and the other with underlying low. On the other hand, the class with the simplest inflectional morphology would appear to be the NULL class, which takes no segmental class prefix, although as discussed elsewhere, there is always the possibility of a floating tone affix. Although we cannot be sure at this stage if the NULL (Ø-) class is indeed morphologically simple, we choose to begin with it because at this point, there is no evidence that it is not morphologically simple, and it is the second largest class. With respect to which "stem type" is the simplest, we obviously want to begin with simple (single root) stems, as best they are known.

With respect to which "syllable profile" is the longest in Chumburung, there are three choices, each of which consists of two moras. First, there are simple disyllabic stems with the profile CVCV. Then, there are simple monosyllabic stems with the profile CVN, and finally, there are simple monosyllabic stems with profile CVʔ. We favour the first two over the last one because while the coda of the CVʔ profile is moraic, it is not sonorant and is therefore less likely to reveal underlying tone patterns. In deciding which of the first two to begin with, all things being equal, we would prefer CVN (monosyllabic) over CVCV (disyllabic) in order to minimize the risk of the stem being morphologically complex. However, since in our chosen noun class there are three patterns represented by ten nouns in the CVCV group, but only two patterns represented by four nouns in the CVN group, we will go with the CVCV syllable profile despite the greater risk of morphological complexity because there are more nouns associated with it and hence a better chance that we will be working with all available underlying tone patterns.

Since there is no reason to suspect that stem consonants play any role in the tone analysis beyond that just discussed, our database does not include this field. To sum up, the first group of words that we will examine in Chumburung will be nouns with simple stems from the NULL class, beginning with those that have the CVCV syllable profile.

5.2.1 Analysis of isolation forms of preliminary words

We begin the actual analysis of Chumburung tone by looking at the surface pitch patterns of the words in (8), our preliminary group.

(8) Nouns, simple stems, NULL class, CVCV root profile

Isolation pattern 1		Isolation pattern 2		Isolation pattern 3	
$\begin{bmatrix} ‾\ ‾ \end{bmatrix}$		$\begin{bmatrix} \_\ ‾ \end{bmatrix}$		$\begin{bmatrix} ‾\ \searrow \end{bmatrix}$	
pʊnɪ	'doorway'	tʃipi	'calf (of leg)'	wadʒa	'cloth'
dapʊ	'hawk'	bɔtɪ	'sack'	basa	'needle'
k͡pabʊ	'louse'	kɔtɪ	'monkey'	buni	'butterfly'
		kube	'coconut palm'		

In (8) we find three contrastive patterns. Since we have carefully controlled for all the factors that can affect tone, any surface tone differences between these words can only be due to differences in the underlying patterns of their roots. It is possible that some of these words might, in fact, have floating tones and therefore be different from others that sound like them in their isolation forms, but since there is nothing to indicate that at this point, we will assume this is not the case, as we await further evidence. Certainly, it is clear that there are at least three underlying patterns. As discussed in chapter 2, we expect to find at least the patterns /H/ and /L/ in contrast.

Isolation pattern 1 [¯ ¯] looks like a good candidate for the underlying pattern /H/, and Isolation pattern 3 [- ˬ] for the underlying pattern /L/, although the final falling pitch might suggest to some a potential composite pattern rather than a single level tone. At this point we need to take into account what is known about African languages in general: in many, if not all African languages, low tones fall from low to an even lower level in pre-pausal environments. So the fact that potentially low-toned words in Chumburung show a final fall in their isolation forms would not be at all unusual. Furthermore, we do have more data at our disposal to check this hypothesis. A cursory look at all the words in our database reveals that there are, in fact, no level low tones at the end of words except for those ending in glottal stops. Since glottal stops are not sonorant, we have a natural explanation for why a low tone should not fall in those pre-pausal environments: the lack of voicing in the final TBU of the low tone cuts off the fall. Given these facts, we have no good reason not to propose the underlying pattern /L/ for Isolation pattern 3.

Isolation pattern 2 [- ¯] is a good candidate for either /LH/ or /LM/ (but not /HL/). Although the second half of the pattern is phonetic mid, rather than high, this fact is irrelevant since mid and high do not contrast in this environment: a cursory scan of the words in table 1 reveals that only low and mid pitches follow low pitch; high pitches never follow low. So, since there is no phonological contrast between the mid and high pitch levels (cf. the discussion on phonological contrast in chapter 1), we will call high anything that contrasts with low in this environment. We therefore tentatively assign the underlying pattern /LH/ to this surface pattern.

Next, we examine the surface patterns of the remaining groups of NULL class nouns. In the data at our disposal, we find only four words from the NULL class that have the syllable profile CVN.

(9) NULL class, CVN stem

Isolation pattern 1		Isolation pattern 2	
[ˋ]		[¯ \ ]	
duŋ	'heart'	t͡ʃaŋ	'guinea fowl'
lɔŋ	'compound'	buŋ	'river'

For the reasons discussed above, we will tentatively assign Isolation pattern 1 the underlying pattern /L/. Although we have not yet discussed an underlying pattern /HL/, for obvious reasons, Isolation pattern 2 presents itself as an excellent candidate for this pattern.

The remaining two syllable profiles from the NULL class that occur in our data set are CVʔ and CV. These appear in (10) and (11).

5.2 Full analysis of preliminary words

(10) NULL class, CV? stems

Isolation pattern 1

$\begin{bmatrix} - \end{bmatrix}$

wɛʔ	'phlegm (globule)'
baʔ	'yam shoot'
kɛʔ	'edge (n.)'

(11) NULL class, CV stems

Isolation pattern 1

$\begin{bmatrix} - \end{bmatrix}$

lɔ	'sore'
k͡pa	'path'
wu	'thorn'

With no evidence to the contrary, for the CV? stems in (10) we will tentatively assign the underlying pattern /H/ to all three words with CV? stems. Similarly, we assign the pattern /H/ to all three words with CV stems in (11). Here is a summary of our analysis so far of the isolation forms of NULL class nouns.

(12) Tentative underlying tone patterns discovered in NULL class nouns

CVCV	/L/	/H/	/LH/	
CVN	/L/			/HL/
CV?		/H/		
CV		/H/		

Although there are a number of unexplained "holes" in these patterns, we will not be overly concerned right now since the NULL class is not the largest class and would not be expected to necessarily have all tone patterns represented for all syllable profiles.

5.2.2 Analysis of plural forms of preliminary words

Compare the singular and plural forms for NULL class nouns that have the syllable profile CVCV in (13).

(13) Plurals from NULL class with simple CVCV stems

Tentative underlying pattern of stem	Singular		Plural	
/H/	$\begin{bmatrix} - - \end{bmatrix}$		$\begin{bmatrix} \_ - - \end{bmatrix}$	
	pʊnɪ	'doorway'	ɪ-pʊnɪ	'doorways'
	dapʊ	'hawk'	a-dapʊ	'hawks'
	k͡pabʊ	'louse'	ɪ-k͡pabʊ	'lice'
/LH/	$\begin{bmatrix} \_ - \end{bmatrix}$		$\begin{bmatrix} - - \_ \end{bmatrix}$	
	tʃipi	'calf (of leg)'	i-tʃipi	'calves (of legs)'
	kɔtɪ	'monkey'	a-kɔtɪ	'monkeys'
	kube	'coconut palm'	ə-kube	'coconut palms'
	bɔtɪ	'sack'	ɪ-bɔtɪ	'sacks'
/L/	$\begin{bmatrix} - \ \backslash \end{bmatrix}$		$\begin{bmatrix} - - \ \backslash \end{bmatrix}$	
	wad͡ʒa	'cloth'	a-wad͡ʒa	'cloths'
	basa	'needle'	ɪ-basa	'needles'
	buni	'butterfly'	i-buni	'butterflies'

In section 5.2.1, we tentatively assigned the underlying patterns /H/, /LH/, and /L/ to singular patterns 1, 2, and 3, respectively, of CVCV noun stems in the NULL class. In (13) it is shown that two of the plural surface patterns (viz. [_ - -] and [¯ ¯ \]) are actually different from their singular counterparts. At this point it is worth noting that the tone of *A-* class plurals never differs from that of *I-* class plurals when they are affixed to stems with the same singular patterns. This strongly suggests that the *A-* and *I-* prefixes have the same underlying tone patterns. This will therefore be assumed throughout the remainder of this study until/unless evidence to the contrary should emerge. If we assume the tentative underlying patterns of (13), comparison of the singular and plural forms of the words in (13) reveals the following phonological alternations.

(14) Alternating tone patterns

/Prefix pattern/ →   [L] before /H/ and /LH/
                               [H] before /L/

Stem pattern /H/ →   [M] after prefixes with surface low patterns
                                 [H] elsewhere

Stem pattern /LH/ →   [LM] in all environments

Stem pattern /L/ →   [HH-L] after prefixes with surface high patterns
                                 [L] elsewhere

This returns us to the question of whether there might actually be two segmentally identical prefixes: one with underlying high tone, and one with underlying low. From the observations

5.2 Full analysis of preliminary words

in (14), it is clear that for these data at least, the high and low variants do not contrast, but are rather in complementary distribution: the prefix tone is [H] when the underlying stem pattern is /L/ (e.g., í-básâ 'needles', cf. bàsà 'needle'), and low elsewhere, i.e., when there is a high tone anywhere in the underlying stem pattern (e.g., à-kɔ̀tí 'monkeys' cf. kɔ̀tí 'monkey' and à-dápú 'hawks' cf. dápú 'hawk'). It remains to be seen whether the remaining data support this conclusion.

If we review the observations in (14), it is clear that the presence or absence of a prefix causes the stem patterns themselves to alternate: /H/ is realized as [M] when the prefix is phonetically low (e.g., ɪ-pʊnɪ [‾ ‾ ‾] 'doorways' cf. pʊnɪ [‾ ‾] 'doorway') and /L/ is realized as [H] when the prefix is phonetically high (e.g., a-wad͡ʒa [‾ ‾ \] 'cloths', cf. wad͡ʒa [- ˷] 'cloth').

The fact that the tentative stem pattern /H/ is realized as mid when it follows a low tone and as high elsewhere is strong confirmation that the underlying form is /H/, and that the lowering to a mid level (it is actually downstepped high) is an assimilation to the preceding low tone: the alternative, i.e. that the underlying tone is /M/ raised to high elsewhere, caused by some unknown factor, is much less likely.

Let us sum up the analysis so far for NULL class nouns with simple CVCV stems. When the stem pattern is underlyingly /H/ or /LH/, the prefix is realized with low level pitch. Any high tones that follow a low tone are realized with a mid pitch. When the stem pattern is /L/, the prefix is realized with a high pitch, and the stem pattern itself is realized with a high, high falling pitch.

Let us next compare the isolation patterns of the remaining NULL class nouns (i.e., those with the syllable profiles CVN, CV?, and CV) with their plural counterparts. We begin in (15) with CVN profiles.

(15) Plural forms of NULL class nouns with simple CVN stems

Tentative underlying pattern of stem	Singular		Plural	
/L/	[˷]		[‾ ‾ \]	
	lɔŋ	'compound'	ɪ-lɔŋ	'compounds'
	duŋ	'heart'	i-duŋ	'hearts'
/HL/	[‾ \]		[- ‾ \]	
	t͡ʃaŋ	'guinea fowl'	a-t͡ʃaŋ	'guinea fowls'
	bʊŋ	'river'	ɪ-bʊŋ	'rivers'

In section 5.2.1, we tentatively assigned the underlying patterns /L/ and /HL/ to the stems of these words. When we compare the singular and plural forms of the underlyingly low-toned stems with their CVCV counterparts in (13), it confirms our previous analysis that the underlying pattern is /L/. It also reinforces what we previously discovered, that when the underlying pattern of the stem is /L/, the prefix is realized with high tone; this high tone then spreads rightward to the underlying low tone of the stem, causing it to be realized with a high falling pitch. With regard to the words with underlying /HL/ stems, their tonal behaviour is in keeping with what we have learned so far: if there is a high tone anywhere in the stem, the prefix will be low, and if the prefix is low, the high tone in the stem will be lowered to a mid level. This reinforces our analysis of this pattern as underlyingly /HL/.

The next words for examination are the plural forms of nouns from the NULL class that have simple stems and the syllable profile CV?. These appear in (16).

(16) Plural forms of NULL class nouns with simple CV? stems

Tentative underlying pattern of stem	Singular		Plural	
/H/	$\begin{bmatrix} - \end{bmatrix}$		$\begin{bmatrix} - & - \end{bmatrix}$	
	baʔ	'yam shoot'	ɪ-baʔ	'yam shoots'
	kɛʔ	'edge (n.)'		
	wɛʔ	'phlegm (globule)'	ɪ-laʔ	'phlegm (globules)'

The singular and plural surface patterns of these words behave similarly to what we would expect, given the tonal behaviour in the other groupings. Although kɛ́ʔ doesn't have a plural form, there is no reason at this point to assume that its root is anything other than /H/.

Finally, in (17), we examine singular and plural nouns from the NULL class with simple CV stems.

(17) Plural forms of NULL class nouns with simple CV stems

Tentative underlying pattern of stem	Singular		Plural	
/H/	$\begin{bmatrix} - \end{bmatrix}$		$\begin{bmatrix} - & - \end{bmatrix}$	
	lɔ	'sore'	ɪ-lɔ	'sores'
	k͡pa	'path'	ɪ-k͡pa	'paths'
	wu	'thorn'	i-wu	'thorns'

When we compare the singular and plural surface patterns of the words in (17), we again find what we would expect, given the tonal behaviour in the other groupings. Moreover, there is no evidence, so far, of any of the NULL class nouns having a floating tone singular prefix. It remains, nevertheless, to be seen whether such evidence emerges later when these words are placed in different phrasal contexts.

The initial conclusions reached regarding the plural patterns of NULL class nouns with CVCV simple stems are confirmed by examining the other syllable profiles for this noun class. So, from the NULL class noun data we conclude that the underlying tone of the *A*- class prefix is identical to that of the *I*- class prefix because they are always the same when affixed to stems with identical singular patterns. We further conclude that the high and low pitch variants of the prefixes do not contrast, but are rather in complementary distribution.

5.2.3 Analysis of phrasal environments of preliminary words

We now expand the phrasal environments of nouns beyond their isolation forms. The most productive grammatical construction in Chumburung for varying the tonal environment of nouns in phrasal contexts is the possessive construction. Possession is shown in two ways depending on whether the item possessed is a kinship term or not. If the item possessed is *not* a kinship term, possession is expressed through simple adjacency, with the word order Noun1 Noun2. In this case, Noun1 is the possessor noun and Noun2 the possessed noun, and the phrase may be translated as 'Noun1's Noun2'. This is unlike Bantu languages, for example, which have a reversed word order with an associative marker (AM) between the two nouns, yielding a translation 'Noun2 of Noun1'. So, while in Bantu languages a literal translation of

5.2 Full analysis of preliminary words

Kofi's house would be 'house of Kofi', in Chumburung it would simply be 'Kofi house'. On the other hand, if the item possessed is a kinship term, then possession is expressed as follows: Noun1 POSS Noun2, in which POSS is a possessive pronoun (e.g., mì 'his/her'). Thus 'Kofi's wife/grandchild, etc.' is expressed as 'Kofi his wife/grandchild, etc.'

Given the latitude that the non-kinship possessive construction provides for placing almost any noun adjacent to any other noun, this is an ideal grammatical construction for observing tonal behaviour in noun phrases; any one nominal tone pattern can be placed adjacent to any other nominal tone pattern. Following the suggested four environments of chapter 2 for expanding phrasal environments, and employing the possessive construction, (18) provides four frames in which to compare words.

(18) Four Chumburung frames that employ the possessive construction

    a. ____ dápú   '__'s hawk'
    b. ____ bùnì   '__'s butterfly'
    c. dápú ____   'hawk's __'
    d. bùnì ____   'butterfly's __'

Although we cannot be sure that *dápú* and *bùnì* do, in fact, have the underlying patterns /H/ and /L/, respectively, these patterns are the best options among our data, and there is no good reason at this stage to suspect that they are not /H/ and /L/. Notice that as best we can determine, each of these words has a single tone for its pattern and each is monomorphemic, that is, it has a simple stem with no known prefix or suffix. Both 'hawk' and 'butterfly' also promise to be reasonable fits semantically, as possessors and things to be possessed. Assuming then that the pattern of each frame environment is as stated, the unknown patterns in each phrase are thereby reduced to whatever appears in the "slots" that precede or follow the frame words.

The examples in table 2 illustrate the use of the four frames from (18) for constructing a complete paradigm for the NULL class. The isolation patterns are repeated in the first column, and the slot words are underlined. In addition to tonal processes, the reader will notice that a number of segmental processes are also triggered across word boundaries (see discussion in the introduction). For additional discussion of these processes, the interested reader is referred to Snider 1989.

Table 2. NULL class, CVCV, tentative /H/

Tentative stem pattern /H/	___ dápú '__'s hawk'	___ bùnì '__'s butterfly'	dápú ___ 'hawk's __'	bùnì ___ 'butterfly's __'
[− −] pʊnɪ 'doorway'	[− − − −] pʊnɪ dapʊ	[− − − ↘] pʊnɪ buni	[− − − −] dapʊ pʊnɪ	[− − − −] buni pʊnɪ
[− −] dapʊ 'hawk'	[− − − −] dapʊ dapʊ	[− − − ↘] dapʊ buni	[− − − −] dapʊ dapʊ	[− − − −] buni dapʊ
[− −] kpabʊ 'louse'	[− − − −] kpabʊ dapʊ	[− − − ↘] kpabʊ buni	[− − − −] dapʊ kpabʊ	[− − − −] buni kpabʊ

The most immediate observation is that all three slot words behave the same in the four different frames, or phrasal contexts, and this suggests that these words all share the same underlying pattern. Indeed, this is also the case for table 3 and table 4. Based on their behaviour in lexical environments, the words in table 2 have tentatively been assigned the underlying pattern /H/. Working from left to right in the paradigm, when these words appear to the left of *dápú* in the first frame, they are realized at the same phonetic pitch as *dápú*. In light of this, there is nothing that refutes our hypothesis that these stems are underlyingly high-toned.

In the second frame, we see that when the low-toned *bùnì* follows these high-toned nouns, the high tone of the first word spreads across the word boundary onto the first TBU of the second word, *bùnì*. Here too, the 'high' hypothesis holds. Moreover, we have learned something new: when low tones follow high tones across word boundaries, high tone spreading takes place across the word boundary onto the first TBU only of the second word.

There is nothing new to be learned from the third frame, since all of the words being investigated have the same tone as the frame word. The fourth frame, however, does add something new: whenever a high tone follows a low tone across a word boundary, the pitch of the high tone is lowered. This is in keeping with the fact that in none of the data so far do we find any instances of a surface pattern LH; in each case, whenever an underlying high tone follows a low tone, the high is lowered, as suggested by our initial hypothesis in section 5.2.2.

Next, we examine NULL class nouns with CVCV stems and tentative underlying pattern /L/.

Table 3. NULL class, CVCV, tentative /L/

Tentative stem pattern /L/	___ dápú '__'s hawk'	___ bùnì '__'s butterfly'	dápú ___ 'hawk's __'	bùnì ___ 'butterfly's __'
[− ↘] wadʒa 'cloth'	[− − − −] wadʒa dapʊ	[− − − ↘] wadʒa buni	[− − − ↘] dapʊ wadʒa	[− − − ↘] buni wadʒa
[− ↘] basa 'needle'	[− − − −] basa dapʊ	[− − − ↘] basa buni	[− − − ↘] dapʊ basa	[− − − ↘] buni basa
[− ↘] buni 'butterfly'	[− − − −] buni dapʊ	[− − − ↘] buni buni	[− − − ↘] dapʊ buni	[− − − ↘] buni buni

5.2 Full analysis of preliminary words

Similar to table 2, we notice in table 3 that all three slot words behave identically in the four environments, which confirms that they have the same underlying patterns. Moving across the frames from left to right, we notice that the tonal behaviour is very much in keeping with our expectations. In the first frame, high-toned *dápú* is lowered after the low-toned slot words. In the second and fourth frames, we learn that the falling low pitch at the end of words is, in fact, a phrase-final phenomenon: we note that low-toned words that occur in other than pre-pausal positions do not end in low falling pitches. The third frame again confirms that high tones spread rightward across word boundaries to the first syllable only of the second word.

At this point, we move to study the tentative stem pattern /LH/ in table 4.

Table 4. NULL class, CVCV, tentative /LH/

Tentative stem pattern /LH/	___ dápú '__'s hawk'	___ bùnì '__'s butterfly'	dápú ___ 'hawk's __'	bùnì ___ 'butterfly's __'
[- ⁻] tʃipi 'calf (leg)'	[⁻ - - ⁻] tʃipi dapʊ	[⁻ - - ⸜] tʃipi buni	[- - ⁻ ⁻] dapʊ tʃipi	[- - - ⁻] buni tʃipi
[- ⁻] bɔtɪ 'sack'	[⁻ - - ⁻] bɔtɪ dapʊ	[⁻ - - ⸜] bɔti buni	[- - ⁻ ⁻] dapʊ bɔtɪ	[- - - ⁻] buni bɔtɪ
[- ⁻] kɔtɪ 'monkey'	[⁻ - - ⁻] kɔtɪ dapʊ	[⁻ - - ⸜] kɔti buni	[- - ⁻ ⁻] dapʊ kɔtɪ	[- - - ⁻] bunu kɔtɪ
[- ⁻] kube 'palm'	[⁻ - - ⁻] kube dapʊ	[⁻ - - ⸜] kube buni	[- - ⁻ ⁻] dapʊ kube	[- - - ⁻] bunu kube

In the first frame, when high-toned *dápú* is placed after *kɔ̀tí*, the pitch of *dápú* is at the same pitch (i.e., mid) as the second syllable of *kɔ̀tí*. Given the hypothesis that the underlying pattern for each of these three TBUs is /H/, this is not surprising. We do learn one additional fact, though, and that is that the lowering observed above when a high tone follows a low tone is likely due to "automatic downstep," a common tonal phenomenon in African languages (cf. Stewart 1965, 1983, 1993). This term describes the process whereby the phonetic pitch of a high tone that follows a low tone is lowered (usually to a mid level), and this lowering also affects any high tones that immediately follow the first lowered high tone. It seems as if we are indeed dealing with automatic downstep in Chumburung: a cursory look at all the data assembled so far shows no instances of a lowered high tone followed by a nonlowered high tone.

With regard to the data in the second frame, the (downstepped) high tone at the end of the first word spreads rightward onto the first syllable of *bùnì*, in keeping with the phrasal high tone spreading process observed in data previously studied. This confirms that the second syllable of *kɔ̀tí* is underlyingly high-toned. It also confirms that the lowering that occurs following low tones is indeed automatic downstep: not only has the pitch of the high tone been lowered following the low tone, but the pitch of the low tone of the final syllable of *bùnì* has also been lowered, as indicated by the fact that it is lower than the pitch of the preceding low tone of *kɔ̀tí*. From this it can be seen that the lowering that follows this initial low tone is not confined to the high tone that immediately follows it, but rather affects the tonal register of all following tones. Automatic downstep has just this effect, lowering not only the highs that follow a low, but affecting all subsequent tones in the utterance, including lows. In other words, the low tone lowers the tonal register of all following tones.

The third frame demonstrates the phenomenon known as "non-automatic downstep," i.e., downstep that is triggered by a floating low tone (cf. Stewart 1965, 1983). In this case, the high tone from *dápú* spreads rightward across the word boundary onto the first syllable of the slot word, which is underlyingly low, causing this low tone to "float." Its presence is indicated solely by its lowering, or downstepping, effect on the following high tone of *kɔ́tí*.

In the fourth frame, we see that the underlying low tone of the first syllable of the slot word is realized at the same low phonetic height as the preceding low-toned word, *bùnì*. This further confirms that the first syllable of these slot words is low-toned, and that their underlying pattern is, in fact, /LH/.

While the corpus appears to have a reasonable number of words in the NULL class with CVCV syllable profiles, there are holes in the patterns of other syllable profiles. Table 5 presents how the two low-toned nouns in the corpus with the syllable profile CVN behave in the different phrasal environments.

Table 5. NULL class, CVN, tentative /L/

Tentative stem pattern /L/	____ dápú '__'s hawk'	____ bùnì '__'s butterfly'	dápú ____ 'hawk's __'	bùnì ____ 'butterfly's __'
[ˋ] duŋ 'heart'	[- - -] dun dapʊ	[- - ˋ] dum buni	[- - \ ] dapu duŋ	[- - ˋ] bunu duŋ
[ˋ] lɔŋ 'compound'	[- - -] lɔn dapʊ	[- - ˋ] lɔm buni	[- - \ ] dapʊ lɔŋ	[- - ˋ] bunu lɔŋ

We note that the tonal behaviour of these two words in the four different phrasal environments of the study is very much in keeping with that of the low-toned words in table 3, and so we conclude that their underlying pattern is indeed /L/.

Moving on to NULL class CVN nouns with the tentative underlying pattern /HL/, we see that the two words in table 6 behave identically, so we conclude that they have the same underlying pattern.

Table 6. NULL class, CVN, tentative /HL/

Tentative stem pattern /HL/	____ dápú '__'s hawk'	____ bùnì '__'s butterfly'	dápú ____ 'hawk's __'	bùnì ____ 'butterfly's __'
[\ ] t͡ʃaŋ 'guinea fowl'	[- - -] t͡ʃan dapʊ	[- - ˋ] t͡ʃam buni	[- - \ ] dapu t͡ʃaŋ	[- - \ ] buni t͡ʃaŋ
[\ ] bʊŋ 'river'	[- - -] bʊn dapʊ	[- - ˋ] bʊm buni	[- - \ ] dapʊ bʊŋ	[- - \ ] bunu bʊŋ

The tentative assignment of /HL/ to the stems of *t͡ʃâŋ* and *bʊ̂ŋ* was based on the fact that the pitch descends from high to low through the length of a completely sonorant syllable. In the first frame of table 6, these words occur in phrase-initial position. Since they are realized with a phonetic high pitch in this environment, this helps to confirm that the first tone of their pattern is indeed high. And the fact that *dápú* is downstepped when it follows these words helps to confirm that their last tone is indeed low.

5.2 Full analysis of preliminary words

In the second frame, the fact that *bùnì* does not undergo high tone spreading, as it would if the tone immediately to its left were high (cf. *dápú búnì* 'hawk's butterfly' in table 2), strongly suggests that the tone to its left is indeed low, again adding strength to the hypothesis that the underlying patterns of *tʃâŋ* and *bôŋ* are /HL/.

Finally, in the third and fourth frames, the phonetic realization of a high falling pitch following a high tone, and of a downstepped high falling pitch following a low tone, is further confirmation that the underlying pattern of these words is /HL/.

Next, we investigate NULL class nouns with the stem syllable profile CVʔ that have the tentative underlying pattern /H/ (cf. discussion of the examples in (10)).

Table 7. NULL class, CVʔ, tentative /H/

Tentative stem pattern /H/	____ dápú '__'s hawk'	____ bùnì '__'s butterfly'	dápú ____ 'hawk's __'	bùnì ____ 'butterfly's __'
[⁻] wɛʔ 'phlegm (globule)'	[⁻ ⁻ ⁻] wɛɛ dapʊ	[⁻ ⁻ ↘] wɛɛ buni	[⁻ ⁻ ⁻] dapʊ wɛʔ	[⁻ ⁻ ⁻] buni wɛʔ
[⁻] baʔ 'yam shoot'	[⁻ ⁻ ⁻] baa dapʊ	[⁻ ⁻ ↘] baa buni	[⁻ ⁻ ⁻] dapʊ baʔ	[⁻ ⁻ ⁻] buni baʔ
[⁻] kɛʔ 'edge'	[⁻ ⁻ ⁻] kɛɛ dapʊ	[⁻ ⁻ ↘] kɛɛ buni	[⁻ ⁻ ⁻] dapʊ kɛʔ	[⁻ ⁻ ⁻] buni kɛʔ

Regarding the alternation of the glottal stop with vowel length in these examples, the reader will recall the discussion above where it is noted that the glottal stop only occurs phrase finally. Elsewhere it is realized as length on the preceding vowel. One of the first things to notice in table 7 is that these nouns do not behave identically in all environments. The behaviour of *kɛ́ʔ* 'edge' is different from that of *wɛ́ʔ* and *báʔ* in the first and second frames. We note that the behaviour of *kɛ́ʔ* is very much in keeping with that of the nouns in table 2 that are analyzed as underlyingly /H/ (e.g., *dápú* and *kpábú*). Like those words, *kɛ́ʔ* triggers high tone spreading across a word boundary to a following low-toned word (second frame), it undergoes downstepping when it follows a low tone (fourth frame), and it is realized elsewhere with high pitch. In short, these facts allow us to conclude that for *kɛ́ʔ*, the previously tentative underlying pattern of /H/ is indeed correct.

With regard to *wɛ́ʔ* and *báʔ*, like *kɛ́ʔ*, they are both realized with high surface pitches in their isolation forms. Unlike *kɛ́ʔ*, however, they cause downstep in the first frame, when followed by high-toned *dápú*. It is also the case that the high tones of these words do not spread rightward across the word boundary in the second frame, when followed by the low-toned *bùnì*. In this respect they act much like *tʃâŋ* and *bôŋ* in table 6, which are analyzed as underlyingly /HL/. Accordingly, we will reanalyze these stems as underlyingly /HL/.

It is at this juncture that the difference between sonorant and non-sonorant codas reveals itself. While *tʃâŋ* 'guinea fowl' and *báʔ* 'yam shoot' both belong to the same (NULL) noun class, both have CVC roots, and both are analyzed as underlyingly /HL/, their phonetic realizations are different when pronounced in isolation (i.e., high falling vs. level high) because *tʃâŋ* has a sonorant coda and *báʔ* does not. One way to explain these pitch differences is to think of the two moras in each root as each bearing one of the two tones in the /HL/ pattern: the H is associated to the nucleus, and the L to the coda. In the case of *tʃâŋ*, since both moras are sonorant, both tones are heard. In the case of *báʔ*, the H is associated to the nucleus and is therefore heard, but since the L of the pattern is associated to the non-sonorant coda, it is not heard. The fact that it is there, however, is clear by its effect on following tones, as demonstrated above in table 7.

Table 8 presents NULL class nouns with the syllable profile CV and tentative underlying pattern /H/ in the different phrasal environments.

Table 8. NULL class, CV noun stems, tentative /H/

Tentative stem pattern /H/	____ dápʊ́ '__'s hawk'	____ bùnì '__'s butterfly'	dápʊ́ ____ 'hawk's __'	bùnì ____ 'butterfly's __'
[−] lɔ 'sore'	[− − −] lɔ dapʊ	[− − ˋ] lɔ buni	[− − −] dapʊ lɔ	[− − −] bunu lɔ
[−] k͡pa 'path'	[− − −] k͡pa dapʊ	[− − ˋ] k͡pa buni	[− − −] dapʊ k͡pa	[− − −] buni k͡pa
[−] wu 'thorn'	[− − −] wu dapʊ	[− − ˋ] wu buni	[− − −] dapu wu	[− − −] bunu wu

The nouns in table 8 are tentatively analyzed in section 5.2.1 above as having the underlying pattern /H/, and there is nothing here to challenge that conclusion: the high tones spread rightward across word boundaries when the following words begin with low tones, and they undergo downstep when preceded by low tones. There is no evidence of any floating tones. So we conclude that they are underlyingly /H/.

The paradigm in (19) provides one example from each underlying tone pattern/syllable profile associated with the nouns in the data corpus that belong to the NULL class. Notice that baʔ [⁻] 'yam shoot', previously analyzed as underlyingly /H/, has been re-analyzed as underlyingly /HL/.

5.3 Analysis of isolation forms of remaining words

(19) Examples of tonal contrasts in NULL class nouns

Underlying pattern	CV	CVʔ	CVN	CVCV
/L/			$[\ \grave{}\ ]$ lɔŋ 'compound'	$[\ ^{-}\ \grave{}\ ]$ wad͡ʒa 'cloth'
/H/	$[\ ^{-}\ ]$ lɔ 'sore'	$[\ ^{-}\ ]$ kɛʔ 'edge'		$[\ ^{-}\ ^{-}\ ]$ dapʊ 'hawk'
/HL/		$[\ ^{-}\ ]$ baʔ 'yam shoot'	$[\ \grave{}\ ]$ t͡ʃaŋ 'guinea fowl'	
/LH/				$[\ _{-}\ ^{-}\ ]$ kɔtɪ 'monkey'

A glance at the patterns in this summary quickly reveals a number of holes. While some of these are undoubtedly accidental, due perhaps to the fact that the NULL class of nouns is not the largest class, other holes may be systematic, due to factors unknown to us at this point.

5.3 Analysis of isolation forms of remaining words

5.3.1 Analysis of isolation forms of *kI-* class nouns

Having investigated the tonal patterns of Chumburung nouns that do not take a singular prefix, we continue the analysis by looking at the isolations forms of those nouns that do take a prefix in both their singular and plural forms. Again, we begin by looking at those with the syllable profile CVCV. These appear in (20).

(20) *kI-* class, CVCV stems

Isolation pattern 1		Isolation pattern 2		Isolation pattern 3	
$[\ ^{-}\ ^{-}\ ^{-}\ ]$		$[\ ^{-}\ _{-}\ ^{-}\ ]$		$[\ ^{-}\ ^{-}\ \grave{}\ ]$	
ki-k͡pini	'plan (n.)'	kɪ-d͡ʒafʊ	'shell'	kɪ-ɲapʊ	'breast'
kʊ-t͡ʃɔnɪ	'saliva globule'	kʊ-kut͡ʃe	'oyster'	kɪ-pɪnɪ	'mortar'
		kʊ-kuti	'orange (n.)'	ki-t͡ʃini	'vein'

Interestingly enough, with this syllable profile we again find only three contrastive surface patterns, similar to its NULL class counterpart. As with the NULL class, because we have controlled for all the factors that affect tone in Chumburung, we conclude that the differences observed in the surface patterns must be due to differences in the underlying patterns of the different roots, although again, it is possible that underlyingly, the *kI-* prefix has two variants, a high-toned one and a low-toned one. Given at least three underlying root patterns, we will make the hypothesis that one of them is /L/, one of them /H/, and the remaining one either /LH/ or /HL/ (cf. the discussion in chapter 2). Which underlying pattern corresponds to which surface pattern is not clear with these words because they consist not only of a simple stem, but of a prefix as well. This means there are two unknown patterns in each word, unlike the situation with their NULL class counterparts.

In the case of the prefix, we see that, like the A- and I- plural prefixes, it is sometimes realized with low pitch (e.g., kì-k͡pínî 'plan (n.)') and at other times with high pitch (kí-ŋápû 'breast'). As mentioned, we must entertain the possibility that there are two *kI-* prefixes that are identical segmentally but different tonally. We need to wait until we have more information before speculating further.

In (21), we look at *kI-* class nouns with simple CVN stems.

(21) *kI-* class, CVN stems

Isolation pattern 1		Isolation pattern 2	
$\begin{bmatrix} - & - \end{bmatrix}$		$\begin{bmatrix} - & \bar{}\backslash \end{bmatrix}$	
kʊ-kɔŋ	'hump'	kɪ-baŋ	'paddle'
ku-suŋ	'work (n.)'	ku-suŋ	'doorway covering'
kɪ-laŋ	'jug'	ki-tiŋ	'piece'

Isolation pattern 3		Isolation pattern 4	
$\begin{bmatrix} - & \bar{}\backslash \end{bmatrix}$		$\begin{bmatrix} - & \diagdown \end{bmatrix}$	
kɪ-laŋ	'hip'	kɪ-d͡ʒaŋ	'shelter (n.)'
kɪ-t͡ʃaŋ	'room'	kɪ-paŋ	'cutlass'
kʊ-lɔŋ	'cavity (in tree)'		

Unlike their NULL class counterparts, these *kI-* class nouns have four contrastive patterns. Following the logic presented in chapter 2, the hypothesis is that these four patterns will have underlying representations of L, H, LH, and HL, assuming that there are not two prefixes. Again, it remains to be seen which underlying pattern corresponds to which surface form. The remaining groups of nouns with simple stems in the *kI-* class appear in (22) and (23).

5.3 Analysis of isolation forms of remaining words

(22) kI- class, CVʔ stems

Isolation pattern 1		Isolation pattern 2		Isolation pattern 3	
$\begin{bmatrix} - & ^- \end{bmatrix}$		$\begin{bmatrix} ^- & - \end{bmatrix}$		$\begin{bmatrix} ^- & ^- \end{bmatrix}$	
kɪ-baʔ	'shoulder'	kɪ-saʔ	'nest'	ki-t͡ʃeʔ	'kidney'
ki-jeʔ	'meat (chunk)'	kɪ-maʔ	'rubber (globule)'	kɪ-kɛʔ	'headpad'
ki-teʔ	'feather'			kɪ-naʔ	'war'
kɪ-t͡ʃaʔ	'python'			kʊ-dɔʔ	'farm (n.)'
kɪ-bɪʔ	'mountain'				
ku-wiʔ	'thorn tree'				

(23) kI- class, CV stems

Isolation pattern 1		Isolation pattern 2	
$\begin{bmatrix} - & ^- \end{bmatrix}$		$\begin{bmatrix} ^- & ^- \end{bmatrix}$	
kɪ-pa	'hat'	kɪ-d͡ʒa	'market'
kɪ-ta	'bow'	ki-ke	'basket'
kʊ-kɔ	'debt'	kɪ-pɔ	'forest'
kʊ-wɔ	'snake'	ki-d͡ʒi	'seed'
ki-bu	'stone'		

With respect to the underlying patterns of (22) and (23), we will assume that there are at least three underlying patterns assigned to CVC stems and two to CV ones. And we have yet to rule out there being two segmentally identical kI- prefixes. We hypothesize that for each of the syllable profiles, one of the underlying patterns will be /L/ and another one will be /H/, although again without specifying which is which.

5.3.2 Analysis of isolation forms of *I-* class nouns

The remaining noun class in our non-plural data is the small *I-* class. Our database includes only two examples, and these words belong to two different syllable profiles, CVN and CV.

(24) *I-* class

Isolation pattern 1	Isolation pattern 2
$\begin{bmatrix} - & ^- \end{bmatrix}$	$\begin{bmatrix} ^- & ^- \end{bmatrix}$
ɪ-bʊŋ	ɪ-fa
'madness'	'grass'

There is little we can say at this point about their underlying patterns beyond the observation that ì-búŋ 'madness' is similar to words like kì-láŋ 'jug', assigned to Pattern 1 in (21), and í-fá 'grass' is similar to words like kí-d͡ʒí 'seed', assigned to Pattern 2 in (23).

At this stage of the analysis we have looked at the isolation form patterns of all non-plural nouns that have simple stems. We will not worry too much at this point about analyzing the remaining five nouns (i.e., those with compound stems) until we know more about the tonal behaviour of simple stems.

5.3.3 Analysis of isolation forms of verbs

The remaining groups of isolation forms are verbs, and since there are no verb classes in Chumburung, all verbs belong to the same "class." In the data at our disposal, however, verbs with simple stems have three different syllable profiles, CVN, CVʔ, and CV. These appear in (25) in their isolation forms (imperative construction).

(25) Imperative verbs (isolation patterns)

CVN stem $\begin{bmatrix} \ \grave{\ } \ \end{bmatrix}$		CVʔ stem $\begin{bmatrix} \ ^- \ \end{bmatrix}$		CV stem $\begin{bmatrix} \ \grave{\ } \ \end{bmatrix}$	
kuŋ	'prevent'	taʔ	'take'	ŋu	'see'
suŋ	'send'	kɪʔ	'fry'	d͡ʒi	'eat'
tɪŋ	'cut'	sɔʔ	'buy'	tɔ	'roast'
buŋ	'capsize'	kiʔ	'twist'	ɲa	'get'
duŋ	'bite'			da	'hit, kick'
paŋ	'lose'			k͡pa	'want, love'
				bo	'hatch'
				d͡ʒa	'chase'
				sa	'give'
				t͡ʃɔ	'bewitch'

Looking at the data in (25), it is clear that there is no tonal contrast between the verbs of any given syllable profile. We therefore conclude that verbs do not contrast with each other tonally (i.e., they are underlyingly toneless) or that the isolation (in this case the imperative) environment is neutralizing whatever underlying contrasts there are. In the latter case, we would expect those contrasts to appear when we place those verbs into other environments, but for the moment, without further data, we cannot know which analysis is correct.

This concludes the study of the surface patterns of Chumburung words as they are pronounced in their isolation forms. Although we have not yet confirmed the underlying patterns of these words, we have nevertheless learned from investigating simple noun stems from the *kI-* class (the largest class) that there are at least four different underlying patterns for CVN nouns, at least three for CVCV and CVʔ nouns, and at least two for CV nouns. This is all assuming, of course, that there is only one underlying prefix. With regard to the verbs, no tonal contrasts emerged during the analysis of their isolation forms.

5.4 Analysis of remaining words in other morphological environments

5.4.1 Analysis of plural forms of *kI-* class nouns

All *kI-* class nouns in our database take their plural forms from the *A-* class, as do some of the NULL class nouns. In (26), the singular forms of those *kI-* class nouns with simple CVCV stems appear together with their plural forms.

5.4 *Analysis of remaining words in other morphological environments* 131

(26) Plurals from *kI*- class with simple CVCV stems

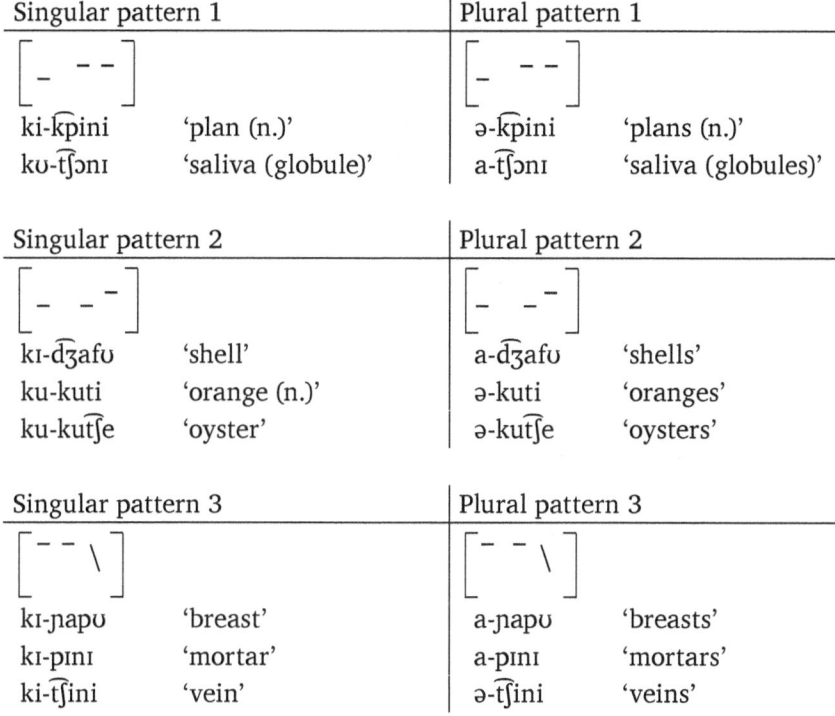

Singular pattern 1		Plural pattern 1	
ki-k͡pini	'plan (n.)'	ə-k͡pini	'plans (n.)'
kʊ-t͡ʃɔnɪ	'saliva (globule)'	a-t͡ʃɔnɪ	'saliva (globules)'

Singular pattern 2		Plural pattern 2	
kɪ-d͡ʒafʊ	'shell'	a-d͡ʒafʊ	'shells'
ku-kuti	'orange (n.)'	ə-kuti	'oranges'
ku-kut͡ʃe	'oyster'	ə-kut͡ʃe	'oysters'

Singular pattern 3		Plural pattern 3	
kɪ-ɲapʊ	'breast'	a-ɲapʊ	'breasts'
kɪ-pɪnɪ	'mortar'	a-pɪnɪ	'mortars'
ki-t͡ʃini	'vein'	ə-t͡ʃini	'veins'

It is immediately apparent that the surface patterns of the plural forms are identical to those of their singular counterparts. Moreover, this holds true for all of the nominal prefixes in the language, regardless of their class, provided there are prefixes involved with both singular and plural forms. Further evidence of this may be seen in the remaining *kI*- class data of (27) through (29).

(27) Plurals from *kI-* class with simple CVN stems

Singular pattern 1		Plural pattern 1	
$\begin{bmatrix} - & - \end{bmatrix}$		$\begin{bmatrix} - & - \end{bmatrix}$	
kʊ-kɔŋ	'hump'	a-kɔŋ	'humps'
ku-suŋ	'work (n.)'	ə-suŋ	'works (n.)'
kɪ-laŋ	'jug'	a-laŋ	'jugs'

Singular pattern 2		Plural pattern 2	
$\begin{bmatrix} - & \bar{\backslash} \end{bmatrix}$		$\begin{bmatrix} - & \bar{\backslash} \end{bmatrix}$	
kɪ-baŋ	'paddle'	a-baŋ	'paddles'
ku-suŋ	'door covering'	ə-suŋ	'door coverings'
ki-tiŋ	'piece'	ə-tiŋ	'pieces'

Singular pattern 3		Plural pattern 3	
$\begin{bmatrix} - - \bar{\backslash} \end{bmatrix}$		$\begin{bmatrix} - - \bar{\backslash} \end{bmatrix}$	
kɪ-laŋ	'hip'	a-laŋ	'hips'
kɪ-t͡ʃaŋ	'room'	a-t͡ʃaŋ	'rooms'
kʊ-lɔŋ	'cavity (in tree)'	a-lɔŋ	'cavities (in trees)'

Singular pattern 4		Plural pattern 4	
$\begin{bmatrix} - & \backslash \end{bmatrix}$		$\begin{bmatrix} - & \backslash \end{bmatrix}$	
kɪ-d͡ʒaŋ	'shelter (n.)'	a-d͡ʒaŋ	'shelters (n.)'
kɪ-paŋ	'cutlass'	a-paŋ	'cutlasses'

5.4 Analysis of remaining words in other morphological environments

(28) Plurals from *kI*- class with simple CV? stems

Singular pattern 1 $\begin{bmatrix} - \\ - \end{bmatrix}$		Plural pattern 1 $\begin{bmatrix} - \\ - \end{bmatrix}$	
kɪ-baʔ	'shoulder'	a-baʔ	'shoulders'
ki-jeʔ	'meat (chunk)'	ə-jeʔ	'meat (chunks)'
ki-teʔ	'feather'	ə-teʔ	'feathers'
kɪ-t͡ʃaʔ	'python'	a-t͡ʃaʔ	'pythons'
kɪ-bɪʔ	'mountain'	a-bɪʔ	'mountains'
ku-wiʔ	'thorn tree'	ə-wiʔ	'thorn trees'

Singular pattern 2 $\begin{bmatrix} - & - \end{bmatrix}$		Plural pattern 2 $\begin{bmatrix} - & - \end{bmatrix}$	
kɪ-saʔ	'nest'	a-saʔ	'nests'
kɪ-maʔ	'rubber (globule)'	a-maʔ	'rubber (globules)'

Singular pattern 3 $\begin{bmatrix} - & - \end{bmatrix}$		Plural pattern 3 $\begin{bmatrix} - & - \end{bmatrix}$	
ki-t͡ʃeʔ	'kidney'	ə-t͡ʃeʔ	'kidneys'
kɪ-kɛʔ	'headpad'	a-kɛʔ	'headpads'
kɪ-naʔ	'war'	a-naʔ	'wars'
kʊ-dɔʔ	'farm (n.)'	a-dɔʔ	'farms (n.)'

(29) Plurals from *kI-* class with simple CV stems

Singular pattern 1		Plural pattern 1	
$\begin{bmatrix} - & - \end{bmatrix}$		$\begin{bmatrix} - & - \end{bmatrix}$	
kɪ-pa	'hat'	a-pa	'hats'
kɪ-ta	'bow'	a-ta	'bows'
kʊ-kɔ	'debt'	a-kɔ	'debts'
kʊ-wɔ	'snake'	a-wɔ	'snakes'
ki-bu	'stone'	ə-bu	'stones'

Singular pattern 2		Plural pattern 2	
$\begin{bmatrix} - & - \end{bmatrix}$		$\begin{bmatrix} - & - \end{bmatrix}$	
kɪ-d͡ʒa	'market'	a-d͡ʒa	'markets'
ki-ke	'basket'	ə-ke	'baskets'
kɪ-pɔ	'forest'	a-pɔ	'forests'
ki-d͡ʒi	'seed'	ə-d͡ʒi	'seeds'

The main problem in trying to analyze nouns with prefixes is that until at least one of the patterns is figured out (prefix or stem), there are always two unknown patterns to analyze. Moreover, since there is no alternation between singular and plural patterns, there is no way of knowing to what extent the prefix patterns might be influencing the stem patterns and/or vice versa. Also, the fact that the surface prefix patterns alternate between low and high pitches makes the analysis even more difficult because it is not clear if there is one prefix or two.

What is really needed in this situation is to see what the surface patterns of the stems would be like if one of the forms had a prefix and the other didn't. This would help to determine what influence, if any, the prefix patterns have on the stems, thus making the analyses of both patterns easier. Fortunately in Chumburung, the NULL class (see analysis in section 5.2) provides us with just this scenario. The question, of course, that remains at this point is whether the *kI-* prefix is truly a single prefix, tonally equatable with the *I-* and *A-* plural prefixes of the NULL class nouns.

In (30) the three contrastive patterns of NULL class nouns with CVCV syllable profiles are compared with the three contrastive patterns of *kI-* class nouns that also have CVCV syllable profiles.

5.4 *Analysis of remaining words in other morphological environments*

(30) NULL class CVCV patterns compared with *kI-* class CVCV patterns

	NULL class		**kI- class**	
	Singular	Plural	Singular	Plural
/H/	[¯ ¯] dapʊ 'hawk'	[¯ ¯ ¯] a-dapʊ 'hawks'	[¯ ¯ ¯] ki-k͡pini 'plan (n.)'	[¯ ¯ ¯] ə-k͡pini 'plans (n.)'
/LH/	[_ ¯] kɔtɪ 'monkey'	[_ _ ¯] a-kɔtɪ 'monkeys'	[_ _ ¯] ku-kuti 'orange (n.)'	[_ _ ¯] ə-kuti 'oranges'
/L/	[_ ↘] buni 'butterfly'	[¯ ¯ ↘] ə-buni 'butterflies'	[¯ ¯ ↘] kɪ-ɲapʊ 'breast'	[¯ ¯ ↘] a-ɲapʊ 'breasts'

In (30), we see that these NULL and *kI-* class nouns form their plurals with the same *A-* class prefix: in addition, we find the same three contrastive surface patterns wherever there is a prefix. Everything therefore points to the underlying patterns as being /H/, /LH/ and /L/.

Underlying tone patterns in Chumburung appear to be comprised of only two tones, H and L. We would therefore expect to find at least four underlying patterns associated with disyllabic stems: /H/, /LH/, /HL/, and /L/ (cf. the discussion in chapter 2). But this is not the case: we have so far found no evidence of /HL/. Given the combined large size of the *kI-* and NULL classes, holes like these are surely not accidental. We return to this matter below.

Next, we compare the two contrastive patterns of *kI-* class nouns that correspond to those of the NULL class nouns that have CVN syllable profiles.

(31) NULL class CVN patterns compared with *kI-* class CVN patterns

	NULL class		**kI- class**	
	Singular	Plural	Singular	Plural
/L/	[↘] lɔŋ 'compound'	[¯ ↘] ɪ-lɔŋ 'compounds'	[¯ ↘] kɪ-laŋ 'hip'	[¯ ↘] a-laŋ 'hips'
/HL/	[↘] t͡ʃaŋ 'guinea fowl'	[¯ ↘] a-t͡ʃaŋ 'guinea fowls'	[¯ ↘] kɪ-baŋ 'paddle'	[¯ ↘] a-baŋ 'paddles'

Applying the reasoning in the discussion of (15) above to the data in (31), it becomes clear that *kI-* class nouns like *kɪ-laŋ* [¯ ↘] 'hip' and *kɪ-baŋ* [_ ↘] 'paddle' must have underlyingly /L/ and /HL/ stems, respectively. Furthermore, since all high falling contours to this point have been analyzable as high tones and low tones conjoined on single TBUs, as in (15), the proposal of /HL/ to account for the high falling pattern on the final TBU of *kì-bâŋ* is very reasonable.

In (32) and (33), the contrastive patterns of NULL class nouns with CVʔ and CV syllable profiles are compared with their *kI-* class counterparts.

(32) NULL class CV? patterns compared with kI- class CV? patterns

	NULL class		kI- class	
	Singular	Plural	Singular	Plural
/H/	$\begin{bmatrix} - \end{bmatrix}$	$\begin{bmatrix} - \ - \end{bmatrix}$	$\begin{bmatrix} - \ - \end{bmatrix}$	$\begin{bmatrix} - \ - \end{bmatrix}$
	ba?	ɪ-ba?	ki-je?	ə-je?
	'yam shoot'	'yam shoots'	'meat (chunk)'	'meat (chunks)'

(33) NULL class CV patterns compared with kI- class CV patterns

	NULL class		kI- class	
	Singular	Plural	Singular	Plural
/H/	$\begin{bmatrix} - \end{bmatrix}$	$\begin{bmatrix} - \ - \end{bmatrix}$	$\begin{bmatrix} - \ - \end{bmatrix}$	$\begin{bmatrix} - \ - \end{bmatrix}$
	lɔ	ɪ-lɔ	kʊ-wɔ	a-wɔ
	'sore'	'sores'	'snake'	'snakes'

Again, comparing the singular and plural surface patterns of the words in (32) and (33), it is clear that they behave similarly to what we would otherwise expect, given the tonal behaviour in the other groupings.

With regard to the tonal variants of the *kI-* prefix, a perusal of the data in (30) through (33) reveals a number of things. First, the word pitch patterns of both singular and plural forms are always identical (e.g., *kɪ-ɲapʊ* [¯ ¯ \] 'breast', *a-ɲapʊ* [¯ ¯ \] 'breasts'). Since in these cases, both the singular and plural forms take the same stems, the fact that their surface word patterns are always identical means that their prefixes (viz. *kI-* and *A-*) must also be identical.

Secondly, given that the patterns of the *kI-* and *A-* prefixes are underlyingly identical, if the stem of *buni* [– ↙] 'butterfly' (pl. *ə-buni* [¯ ¯ \] 'butterflies') is indeed underlyingly /L/, then the stem of *kɪ-ɲapʊ* [¯ ¯ \] 'breast' (pl. *a-ɲapʊ* [¯ ¯ \] 'breasts') in (30) is also underlyingly /L/, based on the fact that their plural patterns are identical.

Since we previously concluded that the high and low tonal variants of the *I-* and *A-* prefixes were in complementary distribution (i.e., they did not contrast), we can equally conclude for the same reason that the high and low variants of the *kI-* class do not contrast either. Further support for there being only one *kI-* prefix comes from the fact that when comparing the different data sets in the *kI-* class, for any given syllable profile there is never more than one tone pattern that has a high-toned prefix. If there were indeed two prefixes with different underlying tones, we would expect to find more than one stem pattern associated with each prefix (i.e., we would expect to find contrast). Instead, there is complete complementary distribution between the stem patterns. There is therefore no reason to further suspect the presence of two *kI-* prefixes, and additional data such as nominalized verbs (see below) will only further corroborate this conclusion. Given that the study of NULL class plurals reveals that the tones of the *I-* and *A-* prefixes are identical, we can now conclude that all noun class prefixes investigated so far have the same underlying tone pattern, even if we don't yet know what it is.

To summarize how the underlying tone patterns of simple CVCV stems are phonetically realized when their singular forms belong to the *kI-* class, the paradigm in (34) provides one example from each tentative pattern/syllable profile.

5.4 Analysis of remaining words in other morphological environments   137

(34) Tentative tonal contrasts of *kI*- class nouns with simple stems

Underlying pattern	CV	CVʔ	CVN	CVCV
/L/	[¯ ¯] kɪ-d͡ʒa 'market'	[¯ ¯] ki-t͡ʃeʔ 'kidney'	[¯ ¯\] kɪ-laŋ 'hip'	[¯ ¯ \] kɪ-pɪnɪ 'mortar'
/H/	[_ ¯] kɪ-pa 'hat'	[_ ¯] kɪ-baʔ 'shoulder'	[_ ¯] kʊ-kɔŋ 'hump'	[_ ¯ ¯] ki-k͡pini 'plan (n.)'
/HL/			[_ ¯\] kɪ-baŋ 'paddle'	
/LH/				[_ _¯] ku-kuti 'orange (n.)'
/?/		[_ _] kɪ-saʔ 'nest'	[_ \] kɪ-paŋ 'cutlass'	

For some of the forms, we are fairly confident of the underlying pattern. For others, we are not sure. And of course, there are many pattern holes to be explained.

5.4.2 Analysis of nominalized verbs

Finally, let us expand the lexical environments of the verb roots in our data. There are two productive nominalization processes in Chumburung that permit this: gerundization and agentization. Gerundization involves affixation of the *kI*- noun class prefix to the verb stem. Grammatically, the resultant nominalized verb functions very much like a gerund in English, and translates readily as '__-ing' (e.g., sùŋ 'send' / kù-súŋ 'sending'). Agentization involves two separate actions, the first of which affixes the suffix -*pʊ* to the verb root. Unlike other affixes in Chumburung, the -*pʊ* suffix does not harmonize with the ATR value of the root, but always retains its own –ATR value. The second action affixes the *O*- class prefix to the now derived stem. The *O*- prefix is normally affixed to nouns that denote human beings, deities, and important animals and birds (e.g., ɔ̀-ɲárí 'man', ɔ̀-ɟáasɛ́ 'leopard', and ò-lùŋ 'eagle'). This second type of nominalized verb translates as an agent, '__-er' or, 'one who does __' (e.g., sùŋ 'send' / ò-súm-pʊ́ 'sender'). The nominalized forms of the twenty verbs in our database are shown in (35) through (37).

(35) Nominalized CVN verbs

	Imperative		Gerundized		Agentized	
/H/	[ˋ]		[− −]		[− − −]	
	suŋ	'send'	ku-suŋ	'sending'	o-sum-pʊ	'sender'
	paŋ	'lose'	kɪ-paŋ	'losing'	ɔ-pam-pʊ	'loser'
/L/	[ˋ]		[− ˋ]		[− − ˋ]	
	kuŋ	'prevent'	ku-kuŋ	'preventing'	o-kum-pʊ	'preventer'
	tɪŋ	'cut'	kɪ-tɪŋ	'cutting'	ɔ-tɪm-pʊ	'cutter'
	buŋ	'capsize'	ku-buŋ	'capsizing'	o-bum-pʊ	'capsizer'
	duŋ	'bite'	ku-duŋ	'biting'	o-dum-pʊ	'biter'

(36) Nominalized CVʔ verbs

	Imperative		Gerundized		Agentized	
/L/	[−]		[− −]		[− − ˋ]	
	kɪʔ	'fry'	kɪ-kɪʔ	'frying'	ɔ-kɪɪ-pʊ	'fryer'
	sɔʔ	'buy'	kʊ-sɔʔ	'buying'	ɔ-sɔɔ-pʊ	'buyer'
	kiʔ	'twist'	ki-kiʔ	'twisting'	o-kii-pʊ	'twister'
	taʔ	'take'	kɪ-taʔ	'taking'	ɔ-taa-pʊ	'taker'

(37) Nominalized CV verbs

	Imperative		Gerundized		Agentized	
/H/	[ˋ]		[− −]		[− − −]	
	da	'hit'	kɪ-da	'hitting'	o-da-pʊ	'hitter'
	k͡pa	'want'	kɪ-k͡pa	'wanting'	ɔ-k͡pa-pʊ	'wanter'
	sa	'give'	kɪ-sa	'giving'	ɔ-sa-pʊ	'giver'
	tɔ	'roast'	kʊ-tɔ	'roasting'	ɔ-tɔ-pʊ	'roaster'
	ɲa	'get'	kɪ-ɲa	'getting'	ɔ-ɲa-pʊ	'getter'
/L/	[ˋ]		[− −]		[− − ˋ]	
	ŋu	'see'	ku-ŋu	'seeing'	o-ŋu-pʊ	'see-er'
	d͡ʒi	'eat'	ki-d͡ʒi	'eating'	o-d͡ʒi-pʊ	'eater'
	d͡ʒa	'chase'	kɪ-d͡ʒa	'chasing'	ɔ-d͡ʒa-pʊ	'chaser'
	t͡ʃɔ	'bewitch'	kʊ-t͡ʃɔ	'bewitching'	ɔ-t͡ʃɔ-pʊ	'bewitcher'
	bo	'hatch'	ku-bo	'hatching'	o-bo-pʊ	'hatcher'

Recall from the data in (25) above, which shows verbs in their isolation environments, that all imperative verbs that end in sonorant segments (i.e., vowels or nasal consonants) have low falling pitches, and those that end in non-sonorant segments (viz. glottal stops) have non-falling low pitches. A cursory look at the forms in (35) through (37), however, reveals that the CVN and CV groups each split into two when the surface patterns of their gerundized and agentized forms are taken into account. A closer look reveals that the surface patterns of these derived nouns are identical to many of those discovered in the nominal data previously analyzed. Given what we know regarding the interaction of nominal prefix tones and stem tones in Chumburung, it is clear that the data to this point reveal no more than a two-way distinction, /H/ and /L/, between the verbs of any single syllable profile. Of particular interest at this point is the similarity between the gerundized forms of (tentatively assigned) low-toned CV verbs (e.g., kú-ŋú 'seeing') and (tentatively assigned) low-toned kI- class CV nouns (e.g., kí-pú 'forest'). Although both end in sonorant segments and both are tentatively assigned underlying patterns of /L/, neither of these ends with a falling pitch, as might otherwise be expected of underlyingly low-toned stems that end in sonorant segments (e.g., kí-ɲápô 'breast', kí-tʃâŋ 'room'). We discuss this further below.

At this point, the underlying tone pattern assigned to each group of verbs is based entirely on the similarity between the nominalized forms of the verbs and the forms of the nouns to which they correspond tonally. Further insight into the tone systems of both nouns and verbs is needed, and this is best done by investigating phrasal environments.

5.5 Analysis of remaining words in phrasal environments

With the knowledge gained from examining morphologically simple nouns in different phrasal contexts, we are now in a better position to examine morphologically more complex nouns in those same environments.

5.5.1 *kI-* class nouns in phrasal environments

Table 9 presents *kI-* class CVCV nouns with tentative underlying pattern /H/ in the same environments to which their NULL class counterparts were exposed. Again, as in the tables above, the slot words are underlined.

Table 9. *kI-* class, CVCV noun stems, tentative /H/

Tentative stem pattern /H/	___ dápú '__'s hawk'	___ bùnì '__'s butterfly'	dápú ___ 'hawk's __'	bùnì ___ 'butterfly's __'
[- - -] ki-k͡pini 'plan (n.)'	[- - - - -] kik͡pini dapʊ	[- - - - ↘] kik͡pini buni	[- - - - -] dapʊ kik͡pini	[- - - - -] buni kik͡pini
[- - -] kʊ-t͡ʃɔnɪ 'saliva (globule)'	[- - - - -] kʊt͡ʃɔnɪ dapʊ	[- - - - ↘] kʊt͡ʃɔnɪ buni	[- - - - -] dapʊ kʊt͡ʃɔnɪ	[- - - - -] bunu kʊt͡ʃɔnɪ

It is readily apparent from table 9 that both nouns behave the same in the different frames, or phrasal contexts. Again, this further confirms that these words have the same underlying patterns. The tonal behaviour of these words is entirely consistent with their stems having an underlying /H/ pattern, given the behaviour of their NULL class counterparts.

Table 10 presents the phrasal behaviour of *kI-* class CVCV nouns with tentative underlying pattern /LH/.

Table 10. *kI*- class, CVCV noun stems, tentative /LH/

Tentative stem pattern /LH/	___ dápú '__'s hawk'	___ bùnì '__'s butterfly'	dápú ___ 'hawk's __'	bùnì ___ 'butterfly's __'
[- -ˉ] kɪ-d͡ʒafʊ 'shell'	[-ˉ- -ˉ] kɪd͡ʒafʊ dapʊ	[-ˉ- -ˉ\ ] kɪd͡ʒafu buni	[-ˉ-ˉ -ˉ] dapʊ kɪd͡ʒafʊ	[-ˉ- -ˉ-ˉ] buni kɪd͡ʒafʊ
[- -ˉ] ku-kut͡ʃe 'oyster'	[-ˉ- -ˉ] kukut͡ʃe dapʊ	[-ˉ- -ˉ\ ] kukut͡ʃe buni	[-ˉ-ˉ -ˉ] dapu kukut͡ʃe	[-ˉ- -ˉ-ˉ] bunu kukut͡ʃe
[- -ˉ] ku-kuti 'orange (n.)'	[-ˉ- -ˉ] kukuti dapʊ	[-ˉ- -ˉ\ ] kukuti buni	[-ˉ-ˉ -ˉ] dapu kukuti	[-ˉ- -ˉ-ˉ] bunu kukuti

Like their NULL class counterparts, these nouns behave exactly as expected for /LH/ CVCV stems. The first syllable of the stem is always low in the different environments, confirming that it is indeed underlyingly low-toned. When preceding the high-toned *dápú*, the final syllables are phonetically realized at the same pitch as *dápú*, and when preceding the low-toned *bùnì*, the first syllable of *bùnì* undergoes high tone spreading from the final high-toned syllables, confirming that these stems indeed end in high tones. Table 11 presents /L/, the final contrastive pattern for *kI*- class CVCV nouns with simple stems.

Table 11. *kI*- class, CVCV noun stems, tentative /L/

Tentative stem pattern /L/	___ dápú '__'s hawk'	___ bùnì '__'s butterfly'	dápú ___ 'hawk's __'	bùnì ___ 'butterfly's __'
[-ˉ-\ ] kɪ-ɲapʊ 'breast'	[-ˉ-ˉ-ˉ --] kɪɲapʊ dapʊ	[-ˉ-ˉ-ˉ -\ ] kɪɲapu buni	[-ˉ-ˉ-ˉ-ˉ\ ] dapʊ kɪɲapʊ	[--ˉ -ˉ-ˉ\ ] buni kɪɲapʊ
[-ˉ-\ ] kɪ-pɪnɪ 'mortar'	[-ˉ-ˉ-ˉ --] kɪpɪnɪ dapʊ	[-ˉ-ˉ-ˉ -\ ] kɪpɪnɪ buni	[-ˉ-ˉ-ˉ-ˉ\ ] dapʊ kɪpɪnɪ	[-- -ˉ-ˉ\ ] buni kɪpɪnɪ
[-ˉ-\ ] ki-t͡ʃini 'vein'	[-ˉ-ˉ-ˉ --] kit͡ʃini dapʊ	[-ˉ-ˉ-ˉ -\ ] kit͡ʃini buni	[-ˉ-ˉ-ˉ-ˉ\ ] dapu kit͡ʃini	[-- -ˉ-ˉ\ ] buni kit͡ʃini

The fact that these stems begin with high pitch when they are preceded by a prefix is dealt with above in section 5.2.2. In that discussion, the high falling pitch of the final syllable of the isolation forms was seen to be due to the high tone of the prefix spreading rightward over the course of the stem and joining together with the low tone on the final syllable. In the examples in table 11, this final low tone on the stem is confirmed by the downstepping of the following high-toned *dápú* (e.g., *kíɲápú ꜝdápú*) and by the blocking of the rightward spread of the high tone to the low-toned *bùnì* (e.g., *kíɲápú bùnì*).

The next nouns to be examined are those with *kI*- prefixes and CVN stems, which appear in the next four tables. We begin with the tentative stem pattern /H/.

5.5 Analysis of remaining words in phrasal environments 141

Table 12. *kI-* class, CVN noun stems, tentative /H/

Tentative stem pattern /H/	____ dápʋ́ '__'s hawk'	____ bùnì '__'s butterfly'	dápʋ́ ____ 'hawk's __'	bùnì ____ 'butterfly's __'
[¯ ¯] kʋ-kɔŋ 'hump'	[¯ ¯ ¯ ¯] kʋkɔn dapʋ	[¯ ¯ ¯ ˋ] kʋkɔm buni	[¯ ¯ ¯ ¯] dapʋ kʋkɔŋ	[¯ ¯ ¯ ¯] bunu kʋkɔŋ
[¯ ¯] kɪ-laŋ 'jug'	[¯ ¯ ¯ ¯] kɪlan dapʋ	[¯ ¯ ¯ ˋ] kɪlam buni	[¯ ¯ ¯ ¯] dapʋ kɪlaŋ	[¯ ¯ ¯ ¯] buni kilaŋ
[¯ ¯] kʋ-sʋŋ 'work (n.)'	[¯ ¯ ¯ ¯] kusun dapʋ	[¯ ¯ ¯ ˋ] kusum buni	[¯ ¯ ¯ ¯] dapu kusʋŋ	[¯ ¯ ¯ ¯] bunu kusʋŋ

From the tonal behaviour shown, there is nothing to suggest that the underlying pattern is anything but /H/. There is also really nothing new to be learned here, given what is already known from examining other phrasal paradigms.

We move on to CVN stems whose surface tones in isolation were initially puzzling to us, but to which we now tentatively assign the pattern /LH/.

Table 13. *kI-* class, CVN noun stems, tentative /LH/

Tentative stem pattern /LH/	____ dápʋ́ '__'s hawk'	____ bùnì '__'s butterfly'	dápʋ́ ____ 'hawk's __'	bùnì ____ 'butterfly's __'
[¯ ˋ] kɪ-d͡ʒaŋ 'shelter (n.)'	[¯ ¯ ¯ ¯] kɪd͡ʒan dapʋ	[¯ ¯ ¯ ˋ] kɪd͡ʒam buni	[¯ ¯ ¯ ˋ] dapʋ kɪd͡ʒaŋ	[¯ ¯ ¯ ˋ] buni kid͡ʒaŋ
[¯ ˋ] kɪ-paŋ 'cutlass'	[¯ ¯ ¯ ¯] kɪpan dapʋ	[¯ ¯ ¯ ˋ] kɪpam buni	[¯ ¯ ¯ ˋ] dapʋ kɪpaŋ	[¯ ¯ ¯ ˋ] buni kipaŋ

These stems give every appearance in their isolation forms of being simply low-toned, underlyingly. Indeed, in the different phrasal environments, there is still no reason to suspect a high tone anywhere, floating or otherwise. In every respect these words behave tonally as do words with CVCV syllable profiles from the NULL class that are underlyingly low-toned (cf. table 4). They have, nevertheless, been assigned the underlying pattern /LH/ for two reasons. First, it is difficult to find a better candidate pattern, particularly since /L/ has already been assigned to a different pattern for good reasons. Also, there is already excellent support for the other underlying patterns /H/, and /HL/. Moreover, the pattern /LH/ is already known to exist for the stem profile CVCV (e.g., *kù-kùt͡ʃé* 'oyster'), but otherwise is so far absent for the profile CVN. So assigning /LH/ to this pattern nicely fills an existing hole. The second reason for assigning /LH/ to this pattern is that elsewhere throughout the language, the prefix is only realized as low if there is a high tone somewhere in the stem pattern, even when the high tone belongs only to the second part of a compound stem (see section 5.6.2). When all morphemes in a stem are known to be low-toned, the prefix is always high.

We next examine CVN stems with the underlying pattern /HL/.

Table 14. *kI-* class, CVN noun stems, tentative /HL/

Tentative stem pattern /HL/	____ dápʊ́ '__'s hawk'	____ bùnì '__'s butterfly'	dápʊ́ ____ 'hawk's __'	bùnì ____ 'butterfly's __'
$\begin{bmatrix} - \ \bar{} \\ \ \backslash \end{bmatrix}$ kɪ-baŋ 'paddle'	$\begin{bmatrix} - \ \bar{} \ \ \ - \ - \end{bmatrix}$ kɪban dapʊ	$\begin{bmatrix} - \ \bar{} \\ \ \ \ - \ \backslash \end{bmatrix}$ kɪbam buni	$\begin{bmatrix} - \ - \ - \\ \ \ \ \bar{} \backslash \end{bmatrix}$ dapʊ kɪbaŋ	$\begin{bmatrix} - \ - \ - \ \bar{} \backslash \end{bmatrix}$ buni kɪbaŋ
$\begin{bmatrix} - \ \bar{} \\ \ \backslash \end{bmatrix}$ ku-suŋ 'door covering'	$\begin{bmatrix} - \ \bar{} \ \ \ - \ - \end{bmatrix}$ kusun dapu	$\begin{bmatrix} - \ \bar{} \\ \ \ \ - \ \backslash \end{bmatrix}$ kusum buni	$\begin{bmatrix} - \ - \ - \\ \ \ \ \bar{} \backslash \end{bmatrix}$ dapu kusuŋ	$\begin{bmatrix} - \ - \ - \ \bar{} \backslash \end{bmatrix}$ bunu kusuŋ
$\begin{bmatrix} - \bar{} \backslash \end{bmatrix}$ ki-tiŋ 'piece'	$\begin{bmatrix} - \ \bar{} \ \ \ - \ - \end{bmatrix}$ kitin dapʊ	$\begin{bmatrix} - \ \bar{} \\ \ \ \ - \ \backslash \end{bmatrix}$ kitim buni	$\begin{bmatrix} - \ - \ - \\ \ \ \ \bar{} \backslash \end{bmatrix}$ dapu kitiŋ	$\begin{bmatrix} - \ - \ - \ \bar{} \backslash \end{bmatrix}$ buni kitiŋ

In the case of the first frame, *kìbán ꜝdápú* 'paddle's hawk', the final low of *kì-báŋ* is shown to be present but floating in the non-automatic downstep of the following high-toned *dápú*. In *kìbám bùnì* 'paddle's butterfly', the floating low blocks the spread of the high tone of *kì-báŋ* onto the first TBU of *bùnì*. In both cases, the low tone is not present in the surface forms but is revealed, nevertheless, by its effect on the tones that follow it.

Finally, we consider those CVN stems that have the underlying pattern /L/.

Table 15. *kI-* class, CVN noun stems, tentative /L/

Tentative stem pattern /L/	____ dápʊ́ '__'s hawk'	____ bùnì '__'s butterfly'	dápʊ́ ____ 'hawk's __'	bùnì ____ 'butterfly's __'
$\begin{bmatrix} \bar{} \ - \\ \ \backslash \end{bmatrix}$ kɪ-laŋ 'hip'	$\begin{bmatrix} \bar{} \ - \ \ \ - \ - \end{bmatrix}$ kɪlan dapʊ	$\begin{bmatrix} \bar{} \ - \\ \ \ \ - \ \backslash \end{bmatrix}$ kɪlam buni	$\begin{bmatrix} - \ - \ \bar{} \ - \\ \ \ \ \ \ \backslash \end{bmatrix}$ dapʊ kɪlaŋ	$\begin{bmatrix} - \ - \ \bar{} \ \backslash \end{bmatrix}$ buni kɪlaŋ
$\begin{bmatrix} \bar{} \ \bar{} \\ \ \backslash \end{bmatrix}$ kɪ-t͡ʃaŋ 'room'	$\begin{bmatrix} \bar{} \ \bar{} \\ \ \ \ - \ - \end{bmatrix}$ kɪt͡ʃan dapʊ	$\begin{bmatrix} \bar{} \ \bar{} \\ \ \ \ - \ \backslash \end{bmatrix}$ kɪt͡ʃam buni	$\begin{bmatrix} - \ - \ \bar{} \ - \\ \ \ \ \ \ \backslash \end{bmatrix}$ dapʊ kɪt͡ʃaŋ	$\begin{bmatrix} - \ - \ \bar{} \ \backslash \end{bmatrix}$ buni kɪt͡ʃaŋ
$\begin{bmatrix} \bar{} \ \bar{} \\ \ \backslash \end{bmatrix}$ kʊ-lɔŋ 'cavity (in tree)'	$\begin{bmatrix} \bar{} \ \bar{} \ \ \ - \end{bmatrix}$ kʊlɔn dapu	$\begin{bmatrix} \bar{} \ \bar{} \\ \ \ \ - \ \backslash \end{bmatrix}$ kʊlɔm buni	$\begin{bmatrix} - \ - \ \bar{} \ - \\ \ \ \ \ \ \backslash \end{bmatrix}$ dapʊ kʊlɔŋ	$\begin{bmatrix} - \ - \ \bar{} \ \backslash \end{bmatrix}$ bunu kʊlɔŋ

In isolation forms, the high tone spreads lexically from the prefix onto the stem and creates a high falling contour. It is important to realize that isolation forms are also in pre-pausal (phrase-final) position. Alternatively, it could be said that the lexical spreading creates a floating low tone, which manifests itself in several ways: by triggering downstep of a following high tone, by blocking high-tone spread to a following low tone, and by appearing as a falling contour in pre-pausal position.

Next, we examine nouns with *kI-* prefixes that have stems with CVʔ syllable profiles. These appear in the next three tables.

We begin with those stems that are tentatively assigned the underlying pattern /H/.

5.5 Analysis of remaining words in phrasal environments

Table 16. *kI*- class, CV? noun stems, tentative /H/

Tentative stem pattern /H/	___ dápú '__'s hawk'	___ bùnì '__'s butterfly'	dápú ___ 'hawk's __'	bùnì ___ 'butterfly's __'
[- -] ki-jeʔ 'meat (chunk)'	[- - - -] kijee dapʊ	[- - - -↘] kijee buni	[- - - -] dapu kijeʔ	[- - - -] buni kijeʔ
[- -] ki-teʔ 'feather'	[- - - -] kitee dapʊ	[- - - -↘] kitee buni	[- - - -] dapu kiteʔ	[- - - -] buni kiteʔ
[- -] kɪ-tʃaʔ 'python'	[- - - -] kɪtʃaa dapʊ	[- - - -↘] kɪtʃaa buni	[- - - -] dapʊ kɪtʃaʔ	[- - - -] buni kɪtʃaʔ
[- -] ku-wiʔ 'thorn tree'	[- - - -] kuwii dapʊ	[- - - -↘] kuwii buni	[- - - -] dapʊ kuwiʔ	[- - - -] bunu kuwiʔ
[- -] kɪ-bɪʔ 'mountain'	[- - - -] kɪbɪɪ dapʊ	[- - - -↘] kɪbii buni	[- - - -] dapu kɪbɪʔ	[- - - -] buni kibɪʔ
[- -] kɪ-baʔ 'shoulder'	[- - - -] kɪbaa dapʊ	[- - - -↘] kɪbaa buni	[- - - -] dapʊ kɪbaʔ	[- - - -] buni kɪbaʔ

As we have seen in the phrasal paradigms so far, most words that share the same pitch patterns in isolation share the same pitch patterns in the different phrasal environments. The one set of exceptions was the NULL class counterparts (table 7) of these CV? nouns. Like the nouns of table 7, the nouns of table 16 also divide into two groups, based on their tonal behaviours. The last two nouns in table 16, *kì-bíʔ* 'mountain' and *kì-báʔ* 'shoulder', exhibit behaviours consistent with their tentative underlying /H/ patterns; i.e., they do not cause following high tones to be downstepped, and they spread their final high tone onto low-toned TBUs that follow them. The first three nouns of table 16, however, behave differently.

When we consider the behaviour of *kì-jéʔ* 'meat (chunk)', *kì-téʔ* 'feather', and *kì-t͡ʃáʔ* 'python', we see two things that suggest that their underlying stem tone patterns are not the tentatively assigned /H/. First, when the high-toned *dápú* 'hawk' is placed after these words, its surface pattern is downstepped relative to that of the immediately preceding pitches. If their underlying patterns were indeed /H/, we would expect the pitch of *dápú* to be at the same level as the preceding pitch, as it is in the case of *kì-bíʔ* 'mountain' and *kì-báʔ* 'shoulder'. The fact that it is lower suggests that the underlying patterns of *kì-jéʔ*, *kì-téʔ*, and *kì-t͡ʃáʔ* are actually /HL/ instead of /H/, and that the low tone of the pattern is causing the downstep, as happens elsewhere in the language.

Secondly, when *bùnì* 'butterfly' is placed after *kì-jéʔ*, *kì-téʔ*, and *kì-t͡ʃáʔ*, high tone spreading does not take place across the word boundary, as it does when *bùnì* is placed after *kì-bíʔ* and *kì-báʔ*. The failure of high tone spreading to take place here confirms that these words do not end in a high tone. Taken together, these data suggest that the underlying stem patterns of *kì-jéʔ*, *kì-téʔ*, and *kì-t͡ʃáʔ*, are better analyzed as /HL/ instead of /H/.

We next look at the words in table 17.

Table 17. *kI-* class, CV? noun stems, tentative /LH/

Tentative stem pattern /LH/	____ dápʊ́ '__'s hawk'	____ bùnì '__'s butterfly'	dápʊ́ ____ 'hawk's __'	bùnì ____ 'butterfly's __'
[− −] kɪ-saʔ 'nest'	[− − − −] kɪsaa dapʊ	[− − − ↘] kɪsaa buni	[− − ⁻ −] dapʊ kɪsaʔ	[− − − −] buni kisaʔ
[− −] kɪ-maʔ 'rubber (globule)'	[− − − −] kɪmaa dapʊ	[− − − ↘] kɪmaa buni	[− − ⁻ −] dapʊ kɪmaʔ	[− − − −] buni kimaʔ

Recall the discussion of the tonal behaviour of *kì-d͡ʒàŋ* 'shelter (n.)' and *kì-pàŋ* 'cutlass' (cf. table 13, above) in which the underlying patterns in those cases were determined to be /LH/. We observe the same kind of behaviour with the nouns listed here, and so we conclude that here too the underlying pattern is /LH/.

Table 18 presents *kI-* class simple stems with the syllable profiles CV? that have tentatively been assigned the underlying pattern /L/.

Table 18. *kI-* class, CV? noun stems, tentative /L/

Tentative stem pattern /L/	____ dápʊ́ '__'s hawk'	____ bùnì '__'s butterfly'	dápʊ́ ____ 'hawk's __'	bùnì ____ 'butterfly's __'
[− −] ki-t͡ʃeʔ 'kidney'	[− − − −] kit͡ʃee dapʊ	[− − − ↘] kit͡ʃee buni	[− − − −] dapu kit͡ʃeʔ	[− − − −] buni kit͡ʃeʔ
[− −] kɪ-kɛʔ 'headpad'	[− − − −] kɪkɛɛ dapʊ	[− − − ↘] kɪkɛɛ buni	[− − − −] dapʊ kɪkɛʔ	[− − − −] buni kikɛʔ
[− −] kɪ-naʔ 'war'	[− − − −] kɪnaa dapʊ	[− − − ↘] kɪnaa buni	[− − − −] dapʊ kɪnaʔ	[− − − −] buni kinaʔ
[− −] kʊ-dɔʔ 'farm (n.)'	[− − − −] kʊdɔɔ dapʊ	[− − − ↘] kʊdɔɔ buni	[− − − −] dapʊ kʊdɔʔ	[− − − −] bunu kʊdɔʔ

The stems in table 18 are tentatively assigned the underlying pattern /L/ because the prefix tone is high. The stem tone is also high due to the process of lexical high tone spreading whereby the high-toned prefix spreads rightward onto the stem. Although these words might look like they are underlyingly high-toned in their isolation forms, the underlying /L/ pattern is further confirmed by the downstepping that takes place on following high-toned words such as *dápʊ́*. This noticeable lowering is due to the presence of the intervening (albeit now floating) low tone. Additional evidence for this floating tone is provided by the failure of the final high tone to spread onto any following low-toned words (e.g., *kʊ́dɔ́ɔ bùnì* 'farm's butterfly', cf. *dápʊ́ búnì* 'hawk's butterfly'). Much of this behaviour has been seen previously with other tentatively /L/ assigned nouns, e.g. in table 15.

The final two groups from the *kI-* class contain nouns with CV syllable profiles. We begin with those that are tentatively /H/.

5.5 *Analysis of remaining words in phrasal environments* 145

Table 19. *kI-* class, CV noun stems, tentative /H/

Tentative stem pattern /H/	____ dápʊ́ '___'s hawk'	____ bùnì '___'s butterfly'	dápʊ́ ____ 'hawk's ___'	bùnì ____ 'butterfly's ___'
[- -] kɪ-pa 'hat'	[- - - -] kɪpa dapʊ	[- - - -] kɪpa buni	[- - - -] dapʊ kɪpa	[- - - -] buni kipa
[- -] kɪ-ta 'bow'	[- - - -] kɪta dapʊ	[- - - -] kɪta buni	[- - - -] dapʊ kɪta	[- - - -] buni kita
[- -] kʊ-kɔ 'debt'	[- - - -] kʊkɔ dapʊ	[- - - -] kʊkɔ buni	[- - - -] dapʊ kʊkɔ	[- - - -] bunu kukɔ
[- -] kʊ-wɔ 'snake'	[- - - -] kʊwɔ dapʊ	[- - - -] kʊwɔ buni	[- - - -] dapʊ kʊwɔ	[- - - -] bunu kuwɔ
[- -] ki-bu 'stone'	[- - - -] kibu dapʊ	[- - - -] kibu buni	[- - - -] dapu kibu	[- - - -] buni kibu

Looking at the tonal behaviour of nouns in this group, there is nothing to suggest they are not /H/. The high-toned stems themselves are realized at the same pitch as following high tones (e.g., *kʊ̀wɔ́ dápʊ́* 'snake's hawk'), the high tones spread to following low-toned syllables (e.g., *kʊ̀wɔ́ búnì* 'snake's butterfly'), and they also undergo downstep when there are intervening floating low tones between them and preceding high-toned syllables (e.g., *dápʊ́ kʊ́⁺wɔ́* 'hawk's snake').

We next look at nouns with CV syllable profiles that are tentatively /L/.

Table 20. *kI-* class, CV noun stems, tentative /L/

Tentative stem pattern /L/	____ dápʊ́ '___'s hawk'	____ bùnì '___'s butterfly'	dápʊ́ ____ 'hawk's ___'	bùnì ____ 'butterfly's ___'
[- -] kɪ-d͡ʒa 'market'	[- - - -] kɪd͡ʒa dapʊ	[- - - -] kɪd͡ʒa buni	[- - - -] dapʊ kɪd͡ʒa	[- - - -] buni kid͡ʒa
[- -] ki-ke 'basket'	[- - - -] kike dapʊ	[- - - -] kike buni	[- - - -] dapu kike	[- - - -] buni kike
[- -] kɪ-pɔ 'forest'	[- - - -] kɪpɔ dapʊ	[- - - -] kɪpɔ buni	[- - - -] dapu kɪpɔ	[- - - -] buni kipɔ
[- -] ki-d͡ʒi 'seed'	[- - - -] kid͡ʒi dapʊ	[- - - -] kid͡ʒi buni	[- - - -] dapu kid͡ʒi	[- - - -] buni kid͡ʒi

The high-toned prefix here suggests that the stem tone for these nouns is /L/ (cf. section 5.4). However, unlike the underlyingly low-toned CVN and CVʔ stems of table 15 and table

18, there is nothing further to suggest that these stems are, in fact, underlying low-toned (i.e., there is no evidence of a floating low tone here). The high tones of these stems are realized at the same pitch as following high tones (e.g., kíbɔ́ dápú 'neck's hawk'), the high tones spread rightward across word boundaries to underlyingly low-toned syllables (e.g., kíbɔ́ búnì 'neck's butterfly'), and the high tones are lowered following low tones (e.g., bùnì kíbɔ́ 'butterfly's neck'). Moreover, high tones that follow these words are not downstepped, as they are when they follow other underlyingly low-toned words (cf. table 15 and table 18). Whereas the underlying low tone is retained and triggers downstep of following high tones when the stem is CVʔ (i.e., when the stem consists of two moras), the underlying low tone appears to be completely replaced when the stem is CV (i.e., when the stem consists of a single mora).

In addition, however, to the surface forms of the prefixes being high, evidence that these stems actually are underlyingly /L/ comes from the nominalized forms of verbs. Recall the discussion of the tonal behaviour of nominalized verbs in (37) in which underlyingly low-toned verbs such as ŋù 'see' are realized as kú-ŋú 'seeing' in their gerundial forms. We observe the same kind of behaviour with the nouns listed here, and so we conclude that to the extent that verbs such as ŋù truly are underlyingly low, here too the underlying pattern is /L/. Evidence for such verbs being truly low emerges when they are placed in expanded verb phrase contexts (cf. section 5.5.3, below).

The chart in (38) provides a summary of the different underlying patterns that we have discovered for each syllable profile in the kI- class.

(38) Underlying simple stem tone patterns discovered in kI-class nouns

CVCV	/H/	/L/	/LH/	
CVN	/H/	/L/	/LH/	/HL/
CVʔ	/H/	/L/	/LH/	/HL/
CV	/H/	/L/		

The absence of the /LH/ and /HL/ patterns on CV stems is perhaps understandable, since they consist of only one mora. The language thus provides evidence of a lexical constraint against the underlying association of multiple tones with single moras, or TBUs. Notably absent from this summary, however, is an expected /HL/ pattern for CVCV stems. We return to this matter below.

5.5.2 *I-* class nouns in phrasal environments

The final nouns we need to examine in phrasal environments are the two non-count nouns that belong to the *I-* class. Although the stems of these two nouns have different syllable profiles and different tone patterns, they are placed in the same table since there are only two.

5.5 Analysis of remaining words in phrasal environments   147

Table 21. *I-* class nouns in phrasal environments

Tentative stem pattern /H/	____ dápú '__'s hawk'	____ bùnì '__'s butterfly'	dápú ____ 'hawk's __'	bùnì ____ 'butterfly's __'
[- -̄] ɪ-bʊŋ 'madness'	[- -̄ - -] ɪbʊn dapʊ	[- - - -̀] ɪbum buni	[- -̄ -] dapʷ ɪbʊŋ	[- - -] bun ɪbʊŋ

Tentative stem pattern /L/	____ dápú '__'s hawk'	____ bùnì '__'s butterfly'	dápú ____ 'hawk's __'	bùnì ____ 'butterfly's __'
[- -] ɪ-fa 'grass'	[-- - -] ɪfa dapʊ	[-- - -̀] ɪfa buni	[- - -] dapʷ ɪfa	[- - -] bun ɪfa

In the discussion of these nouns in their isolation environments, the stem of *ì-búŋ* 'madness' was assigned the tentative underlying pattern /H/ and *ì-fá* 'grass' the tentative pattern /L/, based on their respective similarity to *kI-* class counterparts *kì-láŋ* 'jug' and *kí-dʒí* 'seed' (cf. section 5.3.2). Given the similarity of the tonal behaviour of *ì-búŋ* in the phrasal environments of table 21 to that of *kì-láŋ* 'jug' in table 12 and of *ì-fá* to *kí-dʒí* in table 20, the respective assignments of /H/ and /L/ to these stems is further reinforced.

5.5.3 Verbs in phrasal environments

Let us now observe the tonal behaviour of the verbs in different phrasal contexts. While the possessive construction in Chumburung permits a great deal of flexibility with nouns, there is much less flexibility with respect to verbs. One of the simplest ways to expand the phrasal environments of verbs is to employ a frame with the structure of (39).

(39) Structure of verb phrase frame

[dápú]_Subject [[[má] _Neg/Imperf Aspect_ [Verb]]_Predicate_ [Noun]_Object_]_Verb Phrase_
'hawk will not predicate object'

While the frame in (39) allows manipulation of the environment on the right edge of the verb, the left edge of the verb is restricted to the high-toned negative imperfective aspect marker. Not being as flexible as the possessive construction, this frame nevertheless allows the placement of any noun after any verb within the verb phrase. This, in turn, permits comparison of the phonetic pitch height of the verb with the phonetic pitch height of any noun to its right within the same phrase.

We should be aware of potential contexts for high tone spreading. For example, does it occur between the verb and the object? It will be noticed that the high tone of the aspect marker does indeed spread onto low-toned verbs. Although the surface high pitch of the verb in this environment will mask the verb's underlying tone pattern in many cases, we nevertheless expect to see effects of the underlying patterns on the following objects. If the verb is underlyingly high-toned, we would expect high tone spreading to take place between the verb and a low-toned object. And if the verb is underlyingly low-toned, we would expect high tone spreading not to occur and the pitch of a following high-toned object to be downstepped.

The different verbs appear in table 22 through table 26 before a high-toned object, *dápú* 'hawk', and a low-toned object *bùnì* 'butterfly'.

Table 22. CVN verb stems, tentative /H/, in phrasal environments

Tentative stem pattern /H/	dápʋ́ má ___ dápʋ́ 'hawk will not ___ hawk'	dápʋ́ má ___ bùnì 'hawk will not ___ butterfly'
[ˋ] suŋ 'send'	[⁻ ⁻ ⁻ ⁻ ⁻ ⁻] dapʋ ma sun dapʋ?	[⁻ ⁻ ⁻ ⁻ ⁻ ⁻] dapʋ ma sum buni?
[ˋ] paŋ 'lose'	[⁻ ⁻ ⁻ ⁻ ⁻ ⁻] dapʋ ma pan dapʋ?	[⁻ ⁻ ⁻ ⁻ ⁻ ⁻] dapʋ ma pam buni?

Table 23. CVN verb stems, tentative /L/, in phrasal environments

Tentative stem pattern /L/	dápʋ́ má ___ dápʋ́ 'hawk will not ___ hawk'	dápʋ́ má ___ bùnì 'hawk will not ___ butterfly'

[ˋ]
kuŋ 'prevent'
	[⁻ ⁻ ⁻ ⁻
	         ⁻ ⁻]
	dapʋ ma kun dapʋ?
		[⁻ ⁻ ⁻ ⁻
		         ⁻ ⁻]
		dapʋ ma kum buni?

[ˋ]
tɪŋ 'cut'
	[⁻ ⁻ ⁻ ⁻
	         ⁻ ⁻]
	dapʋ ma tɪn dapʋ?
		[⁻ ⁻ ⁻ ⁻
		         ⁻ ⁻]
		dapʋ ma tum buni?

[ˋ]
buŋ 'capsize'
	[⁻ ⁻ ⁻ ⁻
	         ⁻ ⁻]
	dapʋ ma bun dapʋ?
		[⁻ ⁻ ⁻ ⁻
		         ⁻ ⁻]
		dapʋ ma bum buni?

[ˋ]
duŋ 'bite'
	[⁻ ⁻ ⁻ ⁻
	         ⁻ ⁻]
	dapʋ ma dun dapʋ?
		[⁻ ⁻ ⁻ ⁻
		         ⁻ ⁻]
		dapʋ ma dum buni?

Table 24. CVʔ verb stems, tentative /L/, in phrasal environments

Tentative stem pattern /L/	dápʋ́ má ___ dápʋ́ 'hawk will not ___ hawk'	dápʋ́ má ___ bùnì 'hawk will not ___ butterfly'

[⁻]
kɪʔ 'fry'
	[⁻ ⁻ ⁻ ⁻
	         ⁻ ⁻]
	dapʋ ma kɪɪ dapʋ?
		[⁻ ⁻ ⁻ ⁻
		         ⁻ ⁻]
		dapʋ ma kii buni?

[⁻]
sɔʔ 'buy'
	[⁻ ⁻ ⁻ ⁻
	         ⁻ ⁻]
	dapʋ ma sɔɔ dapʋ?
		[⁻ ⁻ ⁻ ⁻
		         ⁻ ⁻]
		dapʋ ma sɔɔ buni?

[⁻]
kiʔ 'twist'
	[⁻ ⁻ ⁻ ⁻
	         ⁻ ⁻]
	dapʋ ma kii dapʋ?
		[⁻ ⁻ ⁻ ⁻
		         ⁻ ⁻]
		dapʋ ma kii buni?

[⁻]
taʔ 'take'
	[⁻ ⁻ ⁻ ⁻
	         ⁻ ⁻]
	dapʋ ma taa dapʋ?
		[⁻ ⁻ ⁻ ⁻
		         ⁻ ⁻]
		dapʋ ma taa buni?

5.5 Analysis of remaining words in phrasal environments

Table 25. CV verb stems, tentative /H/, in phrasal environments

Tentative stem pattern /H/	dápú má ___ dápú 'hawk will not ___ hawk'	dápú má ___ bùnì 'hawk will not ___ butterfly'
da 'hit'	dapʊ ma da dapʊ?	dapʊ ma da buni?
kpa 'want'	dapʊ ma kpa dapʊ?	dapʊ ma kpa buni?
sa 'give'	dapʊ ma sa dapʊ?	dapʊ ma sa buni?

Table 26. CV verb stems, tentative /L/, in phrasal environment

Tentative stem pattern /L/	dápú má ___ dápú 'hawk will not ___ hawk'	dápú má ___ bùnì 'hawk will not ___ butterfly'
ŋu 'see'	dapʊ ma ŋu dapʊ?	dapʊ ma ŋu buni?
dʒi 'eat'	dapʊ ma dʒi dapʊ?	dapʊ ma dʒi buni?
dʒa 'chase'	dapʊ ma dʒa dapʊ?	dapʊ ma dʒa buni?
tʃɔ 'bewitch'	dapʊ ma tʃɔ dapʊ?	dapʊ ma tʃɔ buni?

Observation of the tonal behaviour of the verbs in table 22 through table 26 confirms the earlier tentative hypotheses regarding the underlying patterns of the verb stems. The tonal processes that operate in noun phrases also operate in verb phrases. In sections 5.4.2 and 5.5.1, the similarity of patterns between gerundized underlyingly low-toned CV verbs like kú-ŋú 'seeing' and low-toned kI- class CV nouns like kí-pɔ́ 'forest' is noted. The fact that these words end in non-falling high pitches and do not cause following high tones to be downstepped casts doubt on whether the stems of these words are indeed underlyingly low. However, the behaviour of the CV verbs like ŋù 'see' in table 26 confirms that indeed they are underlyingly low. It also further confirms the correctness of the original analysis that the stems of nouns like kí-pɔ́ 'forest' are also underlyingly low.

The chart in (40) provides a summary of the two underlying patterns that we have discovered for each of the three syllable profiles of verbs.

(40) Underlying tone patterns of verbs

CVN	/H/	/L/
CV?		/L/
CV	/H/	/L/

5.6 Conclusions

Chapter 2 describes a methodology for discovering the underlying tone patterns in a language, as well as the phonological processes that occur in various contexts. This chapter illustrates that methodology with data primarily from the Chumburung nominal system. Due to the pedagogical nature of this work, the information about the Chumburung tone system is somewhat scattered throughout it. This section therefore represents an attempt to pull that information together into a form that better clarifies the goals of tonal analysis and reinforces the reasons for the methodology employed.

5.6.1 Underlying noun root patterns

Noun roots in Chumburung employ four underlying tone patterns that, together with segmental elements, conspire to produce the contrasts needed for effective communication. These four underlying patterns, in turn, are composed of two contrastive level tones, high and low, which together result in the patterns /L/, /H/, /HL/ and /LH/. How these patterns are realized phonetically when they are associated with the different root syllable profiles of the language is presented in (41). All of the examples in (41) are drawn from the kI- noun class.

(41) Underlying tone patterns phonetically realized on different syllable profiles

Underlying pattern	CV	CV?	CVN	CVCV
/L/	[- -] kɪ-d͡ʒa 'market'	[- -] ki-t͡ʃe? 'kidney'	[- -\] kɪ-laŋ 'hip'	[- - \] kɪ-pɪnɪ 'mortar'
/H/	[- -] kɪ-pa 'hat'	[- -] kɪ-ba? 'shoulder'	[- -] ku-kɔŋ 'hump'	[- - -] ki-k͡pini 'plan (n.)'
/HL/		[- -] kɪ-t͡ʃa? 'python'	[- -\] kɪ-baŋ 'paddle'	
/LH/		[- -] kɪ-sa? 'nest'	[- ↘] kɪ-paŋ 'cutlass'	[- - -] ku-kuti 'orange (n.)'

Since the prefixes of the examples in (41) are all the same, any isolation patterns that contrast within any given syllable profile immediately demonstrate contrastive underlying tone patterns (e.g., the difference between /L/ and /H/ in CV nouns). The fact that CV nouns

5.6 Conclusions

have only two contrastive patterns is not totally surprising, given that this is the only syllable profile that consists of a single mora; the other syllable profiles, whether consisting of one or two syllables, are comprised of two moras each. Taken together, these facts suggest that Chumburung, like many other languages, has a constraint against moras having more than one tone assigned to them underlyingly.

Moving on to the CV? syllable profile, there is no contrast between /H/ and /HL/ in isolation forms; however, when other words follow, the contrast between them manifests itself in the following ways. When a high tone follows the /HL/ pattern across a word boundary, the high tone is downstepped, whereas when a high tone follows the /H/ pattern, it is realized at the same phonetic pitch as the preceding high. Also, when a low tone follows the pattern /H/, it is realized at the same (high) pitch of the preceding high, whereas when a low tone follows the /HL/ pattern, it is realized at low pitch. This is presented in (42).

(42) /H/ and /HL/ patterns contrasted in CV? syllable profile

Underlying pattern	Isolation form	Before high tone	Before low tone
/H/	kɪ-baʔ 'shoulder'	kɪbaa dapʊ 'shoulder's hawk'	kɪbaa buni 'shoulder's butterfly'
/HL/	kɪ-t͡ʃaʔ 'python'	kɪt͡ʃaa dapʊ 'python's hawk'	kɪt͡ʃaa buni 'python's butterfly'

For the syllable profile CVN, while one might quarrel with the actual labels used to distinguish the patterns, the fact remains that there is a four-way contrast in its isolation forms and they must be labelled somehow. Given the behaviour of the noun class prefix (see discussion below), and the discussion immediately above regarding the /HL/ pattern, there are likely to be few objections to the assignment of the /L/, /H/, and /HL/ patterns to these roots. On the other hand, defending the pattern /LH/ is more controversial, given its assignment to words like kì-pàŋ 'cutlass', where there is minimal evidence of a high tone. Nevertheless, as discussed above, there are three points to be made in favour of this choice. The first is that the pattern /LH/ clearly does exist in the language, at least for CVCV roots, as evidenced by words like kù-kùtí 'orange (n.)'. Secondly, for CVN stems, /LH/ is the only remaining pattern of the four canonical ones, so to exclude it and label these forms with some fifth pattern would pose even more problems. What, exactly, would that fifth pattern be? All other things being equal, calling it /L/ would be an obvious choice, but then there are good reasons for calling one of the other three patterns /L/. Finally, the fact that the surface pattern of the prefix is low argues strongly in favour of there being a high tone somewhere in the stem pattern (we discuss this further below). These three points taken together make a clear case for assigning the /LH/ pattern to the roots of words like kì-sàʔ 'nest' and kì-pàŋ 'cutlass'.

Finally, with regard to the CVCV syllable profile, the assignments of /L/, /H/, and /LH/ are not controversial. However, we would normally expect to find the fourth pattern, /HL/, with this syllable profile, particularly since this profile consists of two sonorant moras. But this is clearly not the case (cf. the discussion above). However, we can speculate that historically there was a four-way contrast for this syllable profile and that the /H/ and /HL/ patterns underwent absolute neutralization following the development of lexical high tone spreading. There is some support for this, based on the fact that when high tones spread rightward lexically, the first syllable that undergoes the spreading (i.e., the syllable immediately to the right of the syllable that triggers the spreading) never shows evidence of a low tone (floating or otherwise). This is demonstrated in (43) and (44).

(43) Lexical high tone spreading

Underlying pattern	Isolation form	No downstep	High spread
/L/	[- -] kɪ-d͡ʒa 'market'	[- - - -] kɪd͡ʒa dapʊ 'market's hawk'	[- - - ↘] kɪd͡ʒa buni 'market's butterfly'

If there were a floating low tone at the right edge of kíd͡ʒá 'market', we would expect the high tone of dápú to be downstepped when it follows kíd͡ʒá. But this is not the case (cf. kíd͡ʒá dápú 'market's hawk'). We would also expect that high tone spreading would not take place as it does in kíd͡ʒá búnì 'market's butterfly'.

In (44), below, repeated from (35), above, there is again a complete lack of evidence of a low tone on the first syllable that follows the initial high tone that triggers high spreading.

(44) High tone spreading to suffix -pù

Underlying Pattern	Imperative verb		Gerund		Agentized	
/H/	[↘] sa k͡pa	'give' 'want'	[- -] kɪ-sa kɪ-k͡pa	'giving' 'wanting'	[- - -] ɔ-sa-pʊ ɔ-k͡pa-pʊ	'giver' 'wanter'
/L/	[↘] ŋu d͡ʒi	'see' 'eat'	[- -] ku-ŋu ki-d͡ʒi	'seeing' 'eating'	[- - ↘] o-ŋu-pʊ o-d͡ʒi-pʊ	'see-er' 'eater'

In this case, the evidence that we might otherwise expect to see would be a final high falling pitch on words like kú-ŋú 'seeing' (H originates with prefix) and ɔ́-sá-pú 'giver' (high originates with verb root and spreads onto the underlyingly low-toned agentive suffix -pù). By way of contrast, when -pù is affixed to low-toned verb roots, it is realized with a high falling pitch because it is not immediately adjacent to the high tone that triggers the spreading (e.g., ó-ŋú-pû 'see-er').

From this we conclude that the syllable profile CVCV has only three contrastive patterns, /L/, /H/, and /LH/, and that the fourth pattern, /HL/, has historically undergone absolute neutralization with /H/ due to the peculiar behaviour of high tone spreading in not leaving any trace of the underlying low tone on the first syllable that undergoes the spreading.

This reinforces the value of analyzing tone from the point of view of establishing the contrastive tone patterns (and their behaviour) associated with morphemes, as opposed to just establishing the contrastive tones (and their behaviour) associated with TBUs. When one analyzes tone only from the perspective of individual tones and TBUs, any holes that would otherwise emerge in a pattern analysis (e.g., the missing /HL/ and /LH/ patterns of CV noun roots and the missing /HL/ pattern of CVCV noun roots in Chumburung) would remain

5.6 Conclusions

unrecognized. And with that lack of recognition, those insights that would otherwise emerge when one attempts to account for those holes would also be missed.

5.6.2 Less transparent matters

One problem that often plagues beginning analysts of tone languages is that even when they organize their data correctly and follow all best practices for analysis, sometimes the resulting surface patterns appear bizarre and unexplainable. For example, one of the contexts that often works well in different languages for expanding phrasal environments is to place the noun next to a quantifier. In Chumburung, however, this results in tonal patterns quite unlike those of other phrasal constructions. Given a situation like this (discussed below), it is much more advantageous to set aside the perplexing data until there is a better understanding of the "easier" data. Later, there are often explanations for the "harder" cases. This is especially true for data with compound stems. Let us look now at some Chumburung data that have not been previously discussed.

Consider the kI- class compound noun kì-t͡ʃàndírósê 'bedroom'. Like its English counterpart, one of its constituents is the noun kí-t͡ʃâŋ 'room' (discussed above). However, the tones of 'bedroom' are confusing because while the surface pitches of kí-t͡ʃâŋ are respectively high and high falling due to high spreading from the prefix, those of their counterparts in the compound are low and low. Let us look more closely at each constituent.

(45) Compound stem of 'bedroom'
/t͡ʃàŋ-dí-rò-sè/
room-sleep-LOC-ADJ

As analyzed above, /t͡ʃàŋ/ 'room' is an underlyingly /L/ noun root. /dí/ 'lie down', on the other hand, is an underlyingly high-toned verb root (cf. dì 'lie down', kì-dí 'lying down', ò-dí-pú 'one who lies down'). The locative suffix -rɔ̀/-rò 'in' has a tone that is "polar," or opposite, to that of the preceding syllable. In this case, since the preceding tone is /H/, the surface pitch of the locative suffix is low. However, since it is immediately to the right of the high-toned verb, it undergoes lexical high tone spreading and is realized with a level high pitch. In this respect, its behaviour is similar to that of the underlyingly low-toned verb root /ŋù/ in ó-ŋú-pô 'see-er' (see discussion above). The final suffix, -sè, is derivational in nature. In this case, it derives the verb 'lie down' into an adjective that modifies the noun 'room'. Since this low-toned suffix is not adjacent to the high tone that triggers lexical high spreading, when it undergoes high spreading it is not realized with a high level pitch, but rather with a high falling pitch, comparable to the suffix -pò in ó-ŋú-pô 'see-er'. Considering the morphological make-up of this compound-complex stem, it can be translated something like 'lying down place room', or more simply, 'bedroom'.

At this point, things become interesting because in Chumburung, noun class prefixes are affixed to stems, not roots (recall the discussion above). Knowing what we know now, it is not difficult to understand why both the prefix and the first syllable of the stem of kì-t͡ʃàndírósê are low-pitched: the first syllable of the stem is low-pitched because it is underlyingly low, and the prefix is low because there is a high tone somewhere in the stem (in this case, the verb /dí/ 'lie down'). So knowing first how tone patterns behave in simple stems helps us understand what happens in compound and complex stems.

Next, we look at nouns and their quantifiers. In this construction, the stem for the quantifier 'one' does not take a prefix (although it does take the definite suffix -kú). The other modifiers do take prefixes, as explained below. Here are some examples.

(46) Nouns from different noun classes with quantifiers[4]

Stem patterns /L/	___ kúŋ-kʊ́ʔ 'one'	___ X-sá 'three'	___ kú-dú 'ten'
[- -] [- -] kɪ-pɔ a-pɔ 'forest' / 'forests'	[- - ⁻ -] kɪ-pɔ kʊŋ-kʊʔ	[- ⁻ -] a-pʷ a-sa (a-pɔ a-sa)	[- ⁻ ⁻ ⁻] a-pɔ ku-du
[- -] [- -] ku-d͡ʒo i-d͡ʒo 'yam' / 'yams'	[- - ⁻ -] ku-d͡ʒo kʊŋ-kʊʔ	[- ⁻ -] i-d͡ʒʷ e-sa (i-d͡ʒo ɪ-sa)	[- ⁻ ⁻ ⁻] i-d͡ʒo ku-du
[- -] [- -] ka-nɔ n-nɔ 'mouth' / 'mouths'	[- - ⁻ -] ka-nɔ kʊŋ-kʊʔ	[- ⁻ -] n-nɔ n-sa	[- ⁻ ⁻ ⁻] n-nɔ ku-du

When a noun is modified by *kúŋ-kʊ́ʔ* 'one', *kúŋ-kʊ́ʔ* does not take a prefix, even though the first syllable of *kúŋ-kʊ́ʔ* resembles the *kI*- prefix. In actual fact, the stem of *kúŋ-kʊ́ʔ* consists of the root *kúŋ* 'one' and the definite suffix *-kʊ́ʔ* 'certain'. That this word has no prefix becomes clear when we compare *kúŋkʊ́ʔ*, an adjective, with its derivative *kʊ̀-kúŋkʊ́ʔ* 'the one', a substantive adjective that does take the *kI*- class prefix. On the other hand, when a noun is modified by the numbers two through nine, the number modifier does have a noun class prefix that is concordant with the noun class prefix of the noun it modifies. In the case of 'ten', however, although the stem of *kú-dú* does take a prefix, the prefix is not concordant with the noun class of the noun that 'ten' modifies, but rather it is concordant with the noun class to which the stem /dú/ 'ten' belongs, i.e., the *kI*- prefix. In this respect, 'ten' is different from the lower numbers.

Now consider the data in (47). The phrases below translate as 'one hat', 'two hats', 'ten hats', etc.

(47) Two nouns and quantifiers

CV stem Stem pattern /H/	___ kúŋ-kʊ́ʔ 'one __'	___ à-ɲɔ́ 'two __'	___ kú-dú 'ten __'
[- ⁻] [- ⁻] kɪ-pa / a-pa 'hat' / 'hats'	[- ⁻ ⁻ -] k<u>ɪpa</u> kʊŋkʊʔ	[- ⁻ -] <u>ap</u> aɲɔ	[- ⁻ ⁻ -] <u>apa</u> kudu

CV stem Stem pattern /L/	___ kúŋ-kʊ́ʔ 'one __'	___ à-ɲɔ́ 'two __'	___ kú-dú 'ten __'
[- -] [- -] kɪ-pɔ / a-pɔ 'forest / forests'	[- - ⁻ -] k<u>ɪpɔ</u> kʊŋkʊʔ	[- ⁻ -] <u>apʷ</u> aɲɔ	[- ⁻ ⁻ ⁻] <u>apɔ</u> kudu

---

[4] In order to keep this study manageable, the nouns so far are all drawn from a very restricted set of noun classes. In addition to having no prefix (null class), Chumburung singular nouns may be prefixed with *kI-*, *kA-*, and *O-*, and a floating high tone, while plural nouns may be prefixed with *A-*, *I-*, and *N-*.

5.6 Conclusions

An examination of *kì-pá* 'hat' (underlying pattern /H/) reveals that when high-toned quantifiers like *kúŋkúʔ* 'one' and *kúdú* 'ten' follow it, they are realized at the same phonetic (high) pitch as *pá*. This behaviour, of course, is totally in keeping with expectations, given what we have seen of normal noun phrase constructions (e.g., *kìpá dápʊ́* 'forest's hawk' cf. *dápʊ́* 'hawk'). Similarly, when *àɲɔ́* 'two' is placed after *àpá,* the high tone of *pá* can be seen to have spread onto the first syllable of *àɲɔ́*, causing it to be realized with high pitch. In this environment, the final vowel of *àpá* is also deleted, following normal vowel hiatus resolution in Chumburung (see discussion above and also Snider 1989). The low tone of the prefix, set floating in this construction, causes the following high tone of *ɲɔ́* to be downstepped relative to the preceding high tone. All of this behaviour is exactly what we would otherwise expect.

A problem, however, arises when we examine underlyingly low-toned CV roots such as that of *kí-pɔ́* 'forest'. Here we see that when a quantifier is placed after *kípɔ́*, the tonal behaviour is quite unlike what would otherwise be expected. When the high-toned *kúŋkúʔ* is placed after *kípɔ́*, instead of all four TBUs being pronounced with high pitch, as is the case in the possessive construction (cf. *kípɔ́ dápʊ́* 'forest's hawk'), the TBUs of *kípɔ́* are instead pronounced with low pitch (cf. *kìpɔ̀ kúŋkú* 'one forest'), and the TBUs of *kúŋkú* are pronounced at the level of high tones that have been lowered due to automatic downstep. The same happens when *àɲɔ́* is placed after *ápɔ́* 'forests' (cf. *àpʷ àɲɔ́* 'two forests'). As if this isn't puzzling enough, when *kúdú* 'ten' is placed after *ápɔ́*, all four TBUs are realized at the same high pitch level (cf. *ápɔ́ kúdú* 'ten forests'), as would otherwise be expected. So what is going on?

Given our understanding now of how tone patterns behave in different constructions, we can deduce that phrases like *kìpɔ̀-kúŋkúʔ* and *àpʷ-àɲɔ́* each consist of one phonological word, and phrases like *ápɔ́ kúdú* each consist of two phonological words, similar to the possessive construction. The constituent structures of these two constructions are contrasted in (48).

(48) Two different quantifier constructions
    a. [[kì[pɔ̀-kúŋkúʔ]]STEM] WORD] PHRASE   'one forest'
    b. [[á[pɔ́]] WORD [kú[dú]] WORD] PHRASE   'ten forests'

In (48a), the root [pɔ̀] is part of a stem, the other part consisting of the modifying suffix -*kúŋkúʔ*. This results in the compound stem [pɔ̀-kúŋkúʔ] with the underlying pattern /LH/. To this stem is affixed the singular *kI*- prefix, which is realized with low pitch, in keeping with its normal realization when it is prefixed to stems with the pattern /LH/. This results in the phonological word (albeit with a compound stem) *kì-pɔ̀-kúŋkúʔ* 'one forest'. Forms like *à-pʷ-àɲɔ́* 'two forests' have a similar analysis, the only difference being the presence of the noun class prefix *à-*, which agrees with the class of the plural noun it modifies.

In (48b), the root [pɔ̀] is a simple stem, to which is affixed the *A-* prefix. This results in the phonological word *ápɔ́* 'forest'. *ápɔ́*, in turn, is modified by the following word *kúdú* 'ten', which has the same constituent structure as *ápɔ́*, and this results in the phonological phrase *ápɔ́ kúdú* 'ten forests'. Some readers might be skeptical that constructions as semantically similar as 'one forest' and 'ten forests' actually have such different constituent structures. Evidence that this is indeed the case, however, comes from the noun class concord patterns, also discussed above. Setting aside the quantifier 'one', which doesn't take a prefix, the quantifiers two through nine take prefixes that are concordant with the nouns they modify. The quantifier 'ten', however, has its own prefix. This difference strongly supports the claim that whereas the quantifiers 'one' through 'nine' form single phonological words with the nouns they modify, the quantifier 'ten' is an independent phonological word. This indicates that the grammatical tie between the noun and its semantic modifier is closer between the noun and the numbers one through nine than it is between the noun and the number ten. In fact, that close tie is identical to that of the constituents in a compound stem.

From this analysis of the tonal behaviour of nouns in the context of quantifiers, the reader can see how important it is to first analyze simple data before moving on to more complex data. When faced with perplexing tonal behaviour, rather than dwelling on it, one should not be overly discouraged. There are always reasons for everything, and when those reasons are not transparent one needs to be patient and continue the analysis with data whose behaviour are more transparent. In this case, having previously determined how tone patterns behave across morpheme boundaries within words, as well as across word boundaries within phrases, it is easier to analyze the tonal behaviour of nouns with non-simple stems, as well as that of noun-quantifier constructions. Further, the analysis of quantifier data in Chumburung also highlights the importance of conducting tone analysis in order to properly understand the different constituent structures of the grammar. Simply put, anyone who attempts to analyze the morphology and syntax of a tone language without also analyzing tone does so at serious risk to their analysis.

As stated elsewhere, this book describes a methodology that involves analyzing tone from the point of view of morphemes having contrastive tone patterns, as opposed to TBUs having contrastive tones. If Chumburung were analyzed from the syllable-tone perspective, one would discover little more than: a) the existence of two underlying tones: high and low, b) the phenomena of automatic and non-automatic downstep, and c) the lexical and postlexical versions of high tone spreading. However, when Chumburung is analyzed from the broader perspective of tone patterns associated with morphemes, additional facts and advantages emerge.

For example, one advantage of employing this approach is that compound and complex stems are more easily identified because the tone patterns of non-simple stems are often more complicated than those of simple stems. The number of words with non-simple stems that have each complicated pattern is significantly lower than the number of words with simple stems that have each simple pattern, and this is a further tip-off that words with complicated tone patterns do not have simple stems. By analyzing complete tone patterns instead of individual tones, facts like these emerge more easily and quickly.

Another fact about Chumburung that emerges more readily with this approach is that the high and low variants of each noun class prefix occur in complementary distribution: for any given syllable profile, high prefixes occur with only one tone pattern, whereas low-toned prefixes occur with other (different) patterns. For example, while the only pattern that can possibly occur with simple CVN stems that have a high prefix is [¯ \], CVN stems with low prefixes can have one of either [- ¯], [- \], or [- ⌣] patterns. If the high-toned variants of these prefixes were truly separate prefixes, one would expect to find contrastive tone patterns associated with their stems also. Again, when tone is analyzed from the point of view of patterns associated with morphemes, facts like these emerge much quicker than they otherwise would.

Finally, application of this methodology to tone languages can also reveal phenomena that might otherwise remain undiscovered. While discovering the existence of four underlying patterns associated with simple noun stems in Chumburung might not initially seem all that important, discovering that the /HL/ pattern is missing from CVCV stems is not insignificant. This fact would most likely remain unnoticed, together with whatever theoretical insights one might gain by explaining its absence, if one did not analyze tone from the perspective of morpheme patterns.

6

The Lexical Orthography Hypothesis Applied to Chumburung Tone

Chapter 4 of this book, devoted to the subject of tone and orthography, discusses different factors that must be taken into consideration when deciding whether or not to represent tone orthographically in any given tone language. It also discusses the pros and cons of different ways to represent tone, if indeed tone needs to be represented. A stated prerequisite to this, of course, is the need to first analyze the tone system of the language in question so that one knows what to represent.

In chapter 5, the tone analysis methodology of chapter 2 is applied to Chumburung, although no attempt is made to apply the knowledge gained from that analysis to developing a tone orthography for the language. And in actual fact, the Chumburung language community uses an orthography that was developed over thirty years ago, and with one minor exception, tone is not represented at all. The exception is that a diacritic mark is used to distinguish the first and third person singular pronouns, which are distinguished solely by tone in the language. But other than that, tone is excluded from representations, and native speakers of the language read quite all right without it. There are probably several reasons for this, but one major factor that contributes to this outcome is that the inventory of contrasts in each of the other (viz. non-tonal) domains that provide contrast (e.g., vowels, consonants, syllable profiles), together with the morphological redundancy built into the relatively rich noun class system, is great enough that the native speaker relies less on tonal distinctions to establish contrast than is the case in some other languages. Readers can therefore read fluently and with adequate comprehension without tone being marked.

So what follows is not a suggestion for revising the Chumburung orthography. Rather, what follows is a demonstration of how to apply to a tone system with which the reader is already familiar (viz. Chumburung) the Lexical Orthography Hypothesis (LOH), presented in chapter 4 as a solution for when simpler methods of representing tone fail. The reader will recall from chapter 4 that the LOH proposes that the level of phonological depth of which native speakers are psychologically the most aware, and hence which should be represented in the orthography, is the output of the lexical phonology, as set forth in the theories of Lexical Phonology and Stratal Optimality Theory.

6.1 Lexical and postlexical processes in Chumburung

As an important step in applying the LOH to Chumburung tone, we need to determine which phonological processes in the language apply lexically, and which apply postlexically. However, let us first review the different criteria, established in (14) of chapter 4 and repeated here as (1), for distinguishing lexical from postlexical processes.

(1) Criteria for distinguishing lexical from postlexical processes

   A. Lexical processes
   1. If there are genuine exceptions to a phonological process, it must be lexical. Exceptions may be single words or morphemes that are simply exceptions to the process, or they may be classes of morphemes or classes of words that fail to undergo the process.
   2. If a process lacks phonetic motivation, it must be lexical.
   3. If it is necessary to refer to a morpheme boundary when describing a process, it must be lexical.
   4. If linguistically naïve native speakers are fully aware of the output or effect of a process, it must be lexical.

   B. Postlexical processes
   1. If the output of a process results in a noncontrastive sound (i.e., a sound that is not phonemic), it must be postlexical.
   2. If a process occurs across a word boundary, it must be postlexical.
   3. If a process occurs only at the beginning or end of a phrase (this includes the beginning or end of words spoken in isolation), it must be postlexical.
   4. If the output of a process is gradient (e.g., partially voiced, partially aspirated), it must be postlexical.
   5. If linguistically naïve native speakers are totally ignorant of the output or effect of a process, it must be postlexical.

Next, let's review the different phonological processes that apply to tone in Chumburung (see preceding chapter) with a view to determining which apply lexically, and which apply postlexically. Recall the following facts:

(2) Chumburung facts pertinent to classifying phonological processes

   a) The data presented in chapter 5 demonstrate two underlying tone heights, low (L) and high (H).
   b) These two heights combine to yield the four contrastive tone patterns, /L/, /H/, /LH/, and /HL/, on noun roots.
   c) All noun class prefixes behave the same tonally and can be analyzed as having the underlying pattern /H/.

In addition, there are seven phonological processes that we examine in 6.1.1–6.1.7 with a view to determining their lexical/postlexical statuses. We discuss each of these in turn.

6.1.1 High tone dissimilation (lexical)

High tone dissimilation is a process whereby the high tone of a noun class prefix is phonetically realized as low when there is another high tone in the pattern of the noun stem. Elsewhere, when the stem pattern is low (or toneless, depending on one's theory), the prefix is realized as high. The examples in (3) are illustrative.

(3) High tone dissimilation (lexical)

$$\begin{bmatrix} - - - \\ \end{bmatrix} \quad \begin{bmatrix} - - - \\ \end{bmatrix} \quad \begin{bmatrix} - - \\ \searrow \end{bmatrix}$$

kí-párá → kɪpara   kú-kùtí → kukuti   kí-ɲàpʊ̀ → kɪɲapʊ
'loan'   'orange'   'breast'

High tone dissimilation is quite clearly a lexical process, given that it only happens to prefixes (cf. point A.1 in (1) when there is another H tone across the morpheme boundary in the pattern of the stem (see also point A.3 in (1)). By way of contrast, H tone dissimilation does not take place across word boundaries, as may be seen in (4).

(4) High tone dissimilation blocked across word boundaries

$$\begin{bmatrix} - - \quad - - \\ \end{bmatrix}$$

dápʊ́ k͡pábʊ́ →   dapʊ k͡pabʊ
hawk louse   'hawk's louse'

Since high tone dissimilation is a lexical process, its output needs to be represented orthographically.

6.1.2 High tone spreading across word boundaries (postlexical, but phonemic)

High tones spread rightward across word boundaries to the first TBUs of following words and delink low tones from those TBUs if any are present.

(5) High tone spreading across word boundaries

$$\begin{bmatrix} - - - \\ \searrow \end{bmatrix}$$

dápʊ́ bùnì →   dapʊ buni
hawk butterfly   'hawk's butterfly'

(High tone spreading across word boundaries is very clearly a postlexical process since it occurs across word boundaries (cf. point B.2 in (1)). Note that this is different from high tone spreading within words, discussed below.

The output of this process is also very much below the level of native awareness (cf. point B.5 in (1)). During the several years that I conducted linguistic analysis and literacy work in Ghana amongst native speakers of Chumburung, I trained some of them to transcribe tone accurately. I found it almost impossible, however, to train them to correctly transcribe high tone spreading across word boundaries; they just were not aware of the process. Since high tone spreading across word boundaries is a postlexical process, it would not be represented orthographically, even though its output is phonemic (i.e., H is a toneme in the language).

6.1.3 High tone spreading within words (lexical)

High tones also spread rightward within words. This can take place from the prefix, as may be seen in (6), but it is not limited to that, as may be seen in (7).

(6) High tone spreading from prefix to stem

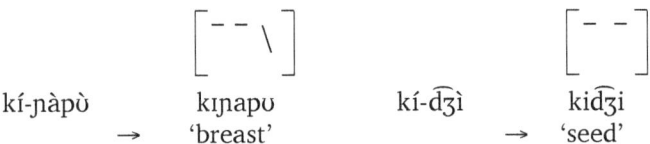

kí-ɲàpʊ̀   kɪɲapʊ   kí-d͡ʒì   kid͡ʒi
→ 'breast'   → 'seed'

(7) High tone spreading from root to suffix

ɔ́-sá-pʊ̀ → ɔsapʊ   'giver'

High tone spreading within words is a lexical process. Native speakers are very aware of this process and after transcription training have no problem transcribing the resultant pitches accurately (cf. point A.4 in (1)). In addition, the target of the lexical process is the final TBU of the stem, whereas the postlexical process, described in section 4.5.2, only targets the first TBU of the following word. In other words, while the lexical process applies iteratively to more than one TBU, the postlexical process applies noniteratively to only one TBU. Since H tone spreading within words is a lexical process, its output needs to be represented orthographically.

6.1.4 Automatic downstep (postlexical, allophonic)

Automatic downstep occurs in such a manner that the complete tonal register is lowered whenever a low tone follows a high tone. Accordingly the downstepped low is lower than any low that precedes it in the utterance and all high tones that follow the low are lower than any high tones that precede the low. Here is a good example of automatic downstep in Chumburung. Notice also that high tone spreading occurs across word boundaries, spreading the high tone of the final syllable of *nàná* onto the following underlyingly low-toned *mì*.

(8) Automatic downstep

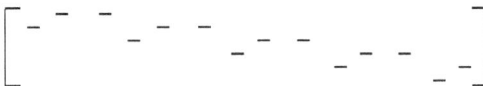

nàná mì nàná mì nàná mì nàná mì nàná →   nana mɪ nana mɪ nana mɪ nana mɪ nana
grandfather 3S.POSS grandfather 3S.POSS   'grandfather's grandfather's grandfather's
grandfather 3S.POSS grandfather 3S.POSS   grandfather's grandfather'
grandfather

In (8), the lowering of the tonal register at each juncture of HL is evident in the graphic display of the pitch. Recall that any given process is considered postlexical unless there is reason to assume otherwise. In this case, there is no evidence that automatic downstep is lexical. Furthermore, it occurs across word boundaries (cf. point B.2 in (1)). The output of the process is also very much below the level of native awareness (cf. point B.5 in (1)). Since automatic downstep is a postlexical process, its output would not be represented orthographically.

6.1.5 Non-automatic downstep (postlexical, but represents displaced contrast)

Non-automatic downstep (downstep attributable to a floating low tone) is essentially the same phenomenon as automatic downstep: both lower the tonal register to the same degree[1] and both occur after low tones. Also, both occur postlexically, although the phenomena that give rise to the floating tones in the case of non-automatic downstep are often the result of lexical processes.

Floating low tones can be created diachronically through the historical loss of a TBU, or synchronically by means of vowel elision or by high tone spreading accompanied by low tone delinking. While the outputs of diachronic processes are always lexical, their synchronic counterparts can be either lexical or postlexical, and in what follows we will examine examples of both.

In example (10), the floating low responsible for downstep is attributable to the postlexical spreading of a high tone across a word boundary and its consequent delinking of the low tone.

(9) Non-automatic downstep attributable to postlexical processes

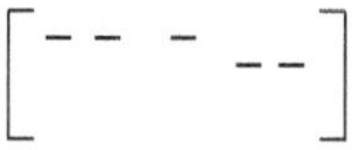

$$\begin{bmatrix} - - & - & - - \end{bmatrix}$$

dápú kìk͡píní →
hawk plan (n.)   dapʊ kik͡pini   'hawk's plan'

Despite the surface loss of this low tone, the high tones after it are clearly downstepped. Following the LOH, since both processes (high spread and downstep) are postlexical, the output of neither would be represented, and 'hawk's plan' would be written <dápú kìk͡píní>. Although there is a significant tonal difference between what people say, dápú kí �͡kpíní, and what the LOH would suggest they write, <dápú kìk͡píní>, native speakers seem to be relatively unaware of the difference.

In this next example, the floating low responsible for non-automatic downstep is the result of lexical processes.

(10) Non-automatic downstep attributable to lexical processes
    a. Downstep

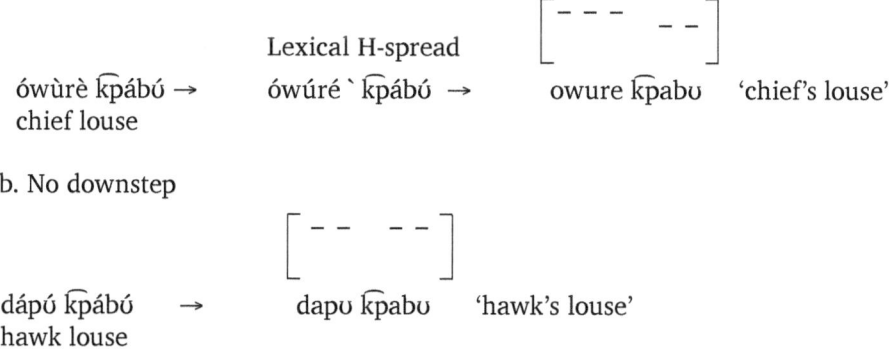

            Lexical H-spread $\begin{bmatrix} - - - & - - \end{bmatrix}$
ówùrè k͡pábú →   ówúré ` k͡pábú →   owure k͡pabʊ   'chief's louse'
chief louse

    b. No downstep

$$\begin{bmatrix} - - & - - \end{bmatrix}$$

dápú k͡pábú   →   dapʊ k͡pabʊ   'hawk's louse'
hawk louse

In (10a), the high of the prefix spreads lexically to the right edge of the stem and delinks the low, resulting in a floating low tone at the right edge of the word (viz. ówúré `). This floating low, located on the left side of the word boundary, triggers non-automatic downstep of the high tones on the right side of the boundary (viz. ówúré ᵗ k͡pábú). Although the creation of the floating

---

[1] Phonetic studies that equate the degree of high tone lowering attributable to automatic vs. non-automatic downstep include Laniran 1992 (Igbo [ibo]), Snider 1998 (Bimoba), and Snider 2007 (Chumburung).

low tone occurs lexically, the downstepping phenomenon itself is clearly postlexical since it occurs across a word boundary (cf. point B.2 in (1)). This brings us to an important question.

If non-automatic downstep is indeed a postlexical process, and if native speakers are indeed relatively unaware of the output of such processes, are native speakers aware of the pitch differences between ówúré ⁺k͡pábú and dápú k͡pábú in (10)? Having worked extensively with native speakers of many African languages including Chumburung, it is quite clear to me that they are very aware of contrasts like these.

How then does one explain this awareness, given that non-automatic downstep occurs postlexically? With respect to ówúré ⁺k͡pábú, the floating low tone of ówúré ` has arisen as the result of lexical high tone spreading and low-tone delinking, and it is this floating low tone that is contrastive here. The downstep phenomenon simply "marks" the location of the floating low by lowering the remainder of the phrase postlexically.

So how should non-automatic downstep due to lexical processes be represented orthographically? According to the LOH, since the lowering of the remainder of the phrase occurs postlexically, the contrast should not be represented on that part of the phrase (e.g., by marking any following high tones as mid). Instead, the contrast should be maintained orthographically at the location where it is realized at the conclusion of the lexical phonology. In this case, that would be at the right edge of 'chief', the first word, possibly using an apostrophe (viz. <ówúré'>). Then regardless of the different grammatical and phonological contexts in which this word occurs, it would always be spelled this way. Similarly, since downstep applies postlexically, the downstepping of the high tone on k͡pábú 'louse' should not be represented orthographically. Ignoring for now the question of whether tone should be represented exhaustively in this hypothetical orthography, here are representations that apply the LOH to the examples discussed above.

(11) Orthographic representations

Surface	Orthographic	
dápú	dápú	'hawk'
k͡pábú	kpábú	'louse'
dápú k͡pábú	dápú kpábú	'hawk's louse'
ówúrê	ówúré'	'chief'
ówúré ⁺k͡pábú	ówúré' kpábú	'chief's louse'

However one chooses to graphically display lexical outputs, when dealing with phenomena that displace phonological contrast, including non-automatic downstep, it is most important to ensure that the orthography represents the contrasts where they are located at the output of the lexical phonology. Not doing so would violate the ideal of having only one orthographic representation for each word.

6.1.6 Prepausal floating low tone docking (postlexical)

When high tones spread lexically to more than one TBU in Chumburung, a floating low tone is created at the right edge of the word.[2] In (12), compare the output of the postlexical phonology for ówúrê 'chief' when it occurs in isolation (i.e., phrase finally) with its postlexical counterparts when it occurs phrase medially before high and low tones, respectively.

---

[2] When high tones spread lexically to only one TBU, there is no evidence of a low tone at the right edge of the word (e.g., kú-ŋú 'seeing'). Only when highs spread to more than one TBU is there any evidence of a low tone (e.g., ó-ŋú-pô 'see-er').

6.1 Lexical and postlexical processes in Chumburung

(12) 'chief' in different environments

	Isolation	Before High Tone	Before Low Tone
Underlying form	/ó-wùrè/ NC-chief	/ó-wùrè kpábú/ NC-chief louse	/ó-wùrè kí-pá/ NC-chief NC-hat
H Tone dissimilation			ó-wùrè kì-pá
Lexical H- spread & delink	ówúré `	ówúré ` kpábú	ówúré ` kì-pá
Output of lexical phonology	[ówúré `]	[ówúré `] [kpábú]	[ówúré `] [kì-pá]
L tone docking	ówúrê		
Postlexical H spread			
Downstep		ówúré ` ¡kpábú	
Stray erasure		ówúré ¡kpábú	ówúré kì-pá
Output of postlexical phonology	[ówúrê]	[ówúré ¡kpábú]	[ówúré kì-pá]
Surface Pitch	⎡- -⎤ ⎣ \⎦ [owure] 'chief'	⎡- - - - -⎤ ⎣ ⎦ [owure kpabu] 'chief's louse'	⎡- - - - -⎤ ⎣ ⎦ [owure kɪpa] 'chief's hat'

In (12) H tone spreading takes place lexically, spreading the underlying high tone to the right-most TBU of 'chief'. This displaces the underlying low tone of the stem, causing it to float at the right edge of the word. When other words are added, and 'chief' does not occur pre-pausally (i.e., phrase finally), all three TBUs are phonetically realized with high level pitches. If the following word begins with a high tone, the floating low downsteps the high and subsequently undergoes stray erasure; if the following word begins with a low tone, the floating low simply undergoes stray erasure. It is important to note that crucially, stray erasure does not occur prior to postlexical H-spread; otherwise, the final high tone of 'chief' would spread onto the first syllable of 'hat'.

When 'chief' does occur pre-pausally, as it does in its isolation form, the floating low tone docks onto the end of the phrase, and this results in the last TBU of 'chief' being realized with a high falling pitch (viz. ówúrê).

That the final low tone docking process is postlexical may be deduced from the fact that the process only occurs in prepausal environments (cf. point B.3 in (1)).

6.1.7 Prepausal falling low tones (postlexical, allophonic)

In Chumburung, when words that end in a low tone and a sonorant segment (i.e., a vowel or a nasal consonant) occur in prepausal environments, the final low tone is realized as a low falling pitch. This process should not be confused with prepausal floating low tone docking, discussed immediately above. There, the final low is floating (following an associated high). In the case of a prepausal falling low tone, the phrase-final word ends in an associated low tone; in such cases, the result is a low falling pitch at the end of the phrase. Compare the examples in (13).

(13) Falling and nonfalling word-final low tones

Falling in isolation	Non-falling before high tone	Non-falling before low tone
$\begin{bmatrix} - \searrow \end{bmatrix}$	$\begin{bmatrix} - - & - - \end{bmatrix}$	$\begin{bmatrix} - - & - - \end{bmatrix}$
buni	buni kɪpʊ	buni kibu
'butterfly'	'butterfly's forest'	'butttefly's stone'

This process, like final low tone docking, is postlexical: both occur only in prepausal environments (cf. point B.3 in (1)). Also, native speakers of the language are not consciously aware of the output of the process (cf. point B.5 in (1)).

Having established the lexical/postlexical status of the different tonal processes in Chumburung, we now apply the LOH to Chumburung tone.

6.2 LOH applied to Chumburung

In chapter 4, reference was made to four different types of orthographic representations: surface, phonemic, lexical, and underlying. We now discuss the pros and cons of each in relation to the Chumburung data at hand, with a view to understanding why the lexical one works the best.

6.2.1 Surface representations

If one tried to implement a strategy of writing surface tone in Chumburung, many problems would arise. For example, writing automatic downstep (section 6.1.4) and final falling low tones (section 6.1.7) would be problematic for writers since native speakers are unaware of the output of these postlexical processes. High tone spreading across word boundaries (section 6.1.2) would also need to be represented in a surface representation, but this is something else of which native speakers are unaware.

From just the foregoing discussion, one can see that a surface representation of tone in the Chumburung orthography would result in words like *bùnì* 'butterfly' having the four different representations in (14), and this, of course, would undermine the ideal of having a single, fixed word-image for this word. Here I am using the ˷ symbol, which represents extra low tones in the IPA, to represent the low falling pitch, for which there is no IPA diacritic symbol.

(14) Four different orthographic representations for 'butterfly'
    a) <bùnḭ̀>, prepausally and either phrase initially or following words that end in low tones,
    b) <búnì>, prepausally and following words that end in high tones,
    c) <búnì>, following words that end in high tones and preceding other words in the same phrase, and
    d) <bùnì>, either phrase initially or following words that end in low tones and preceding other words in the same phrase.

The differences in these four orthographic representations for 'butterfly' are attributable to processes that produce outputs of which the native speaker is unaware (i.e., the native speaker thinks he/she is pronouncing all four forms the same). Accordingly, this would render it almost impossible to teach people how to write, short of giving them an intensive course in phonetics. Furthermore, the tone marks would provide little meaning to readers and they would most likely simply ignore them, thus defeating the whole purpose of representing tone orthographically. Hopefully this adequately demonstrates the futility of simply representing surface tone in Chumburung.

6.2.2 Phonemic representations

Writing tone phonemically in Chumburung has a major advantage over writing phonetically in that allophonic processes are excluded. In this case, phonemic writing would represent low falling tones in prepausal environments (see section 6.1.7) identically with low, non-falling tones (e.g., <bùnì> instead of *<bùnî> 'butterfly'). It would also avoid representing automatic downstep within words (e.g., <kìpá> instead of *<kì'pá> 'hat').

However, the postlexical process of high tone spreading across word boundaries (see section 6.1.2) would still be written since H is a toneme in the language. For example, a phrase like *dápú kìkpíní* 'hawk's plan', which undergoes postlexical high tone spreading and is pronounced [dápú kí'kpíní], would be written the way it is phonemically represented, i.e., <dápú kí'kpíní> (or with some other symbol to represent the downstep). The spelling of the second word would therefore be <kí'kpíní> following words that end in high tones, and <kìkpíní> elsewhere, despite the fact that native speakers do not realize they pronounce this word differently in the two different environments.

Also, the marker for non-automatic downstep in phrases like <ówúré 'dápú> 'chief's hawk' (cf. *ó-wúrê* 'chief' and *dápú* 'hawk') would be written on the word where it is realized phonetically, instead of on the word where the contrast originates. While this would at least have the advantage of maintaining the contrast, it would be almost impossible to maintain a consistent visual image for the word that undergoes the downstep (see section 6.1.5).

Finally, the output of the postlexical prepausal floating low tone docking would also be written (see section 6.1.6). This process would need to be represented in words and phrases that end in high falling contour pitches since phonological contrast exists between high falling and high level pitches.

(15) Contrast between high falling and high level pitches

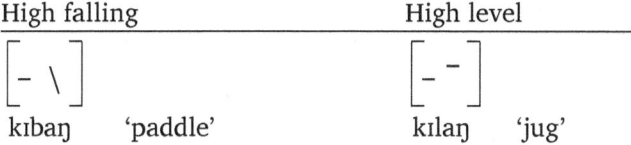

A problem for phonemic representations arises when one compares words like *kɪt͡ʃaʔ* [_ ¯] 'python', which have an underlying final floating low tone, with words like *kɪbɪʔ* [_ ¯] 'mountain', which do not.

(16) a. Words that end in floating low tones

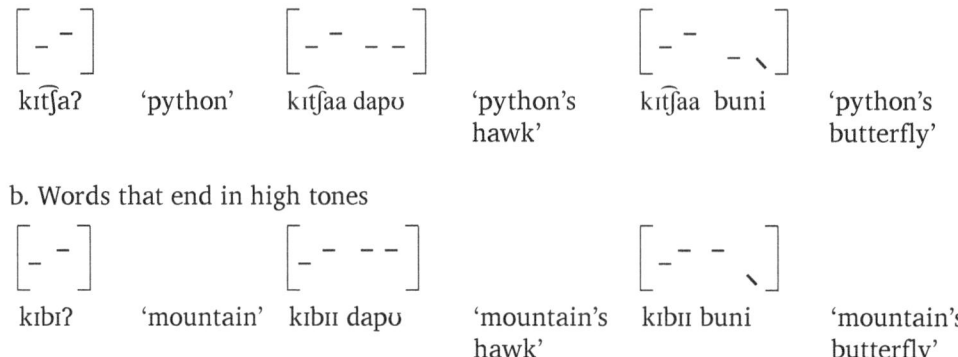

| kɪtʃaʔ | 'python' | kɪtʃaa dapʊ | 'python's hawk' | kɪtʃaa buni | 'python's butterfly' |

b. Words that end in high tones

| kɪbɪʔ | 'mountain' | kɪbɪɪ dapʊ | 'mountain's hawk' | kɪbɪɪ buni | 'mountain's butterfly' |

In (16a), the underlying tone pattern for t͡ʃaʔ, the root of 'python', is /HL/. Since the final mora of this word is voiceless when the word is spoken in isolation, the final low tone of this pattern is floating when kìt͡ʃá? 'python' is realized in prepausal environments. It is clear, though, that there is a floating low tone at the right edge of kìt͡ʃá? that appears when there are additional words to its right. When the tone to the right of the floating low is high, the high tone is downstepped, as in the form for kìt͡ʃáa ꜝdápʊ́ 'python's hawk' in (16a). When the tone to the right of the floating low tone is itself low, as in the form for kìt͡ʃáa bùnì 'python's butterfly', nothing changes in the second word, and one assumes that the floating low either undergoes stray erasure or is merged with the other low tone. On the other hand, when there is no floating low tone at the right edge of the word, as is the case for kìbí? 'mountain', in (16b), downstep does not occur on a following high tone. This may be seen in kìbíɪ dápʊ́ 'mountain's hawk'. And when the second word begins with an underlying low tone, as in kìbíɪ búnì 'mountain's butterfly', the high tone of the first word spreads rightward onto the first TBU of the second word where it displaces the low tone from the first TBU of that word. (High tone spreading onto the second word does not occur, of course, when the first word ends in a floating low tone, as in the example in (16a).)

A phonemic orthography would be forced to represent the tones of these words identically in all environments, even though it is clear that phonologically they behave very differently. This is because kìt͡ʃá? 'python' ends in a floating low tone, and kìbí? 'mountain' does not. Moreover, a phonemic orthography would be forced to represent words like dápʊ́ 'hawk' in two different ways, depending on whether they followed words like kìt͡ʃá? (e.g., <kìt͡ʃáa ꜝdápʊ́> 'python's hawk') or words like kìbí? (e.g., <kìbíɪ dápʊ́> 'mountain's hawk'). Again, following the orthographic principle of maintaining fixed word-images advocated by Nida 1954, Voorhoeve 1962, and Katz and Frost 1992, it would be better to have single representations for each word that could be used in all environments.

A final word on floating tones is in order. Although much of the present discussion focusses on the claim that lexical representations are the best phonological level upon which to base orthographic representations, the other main claim in the present work concerns the phonological entity that should be represented at that level. Most works on tone and orthography to date are based on the assumption that individual tones associated with particular TBUs should be represented in orthographies. The present work, however, claims that it is in fact the complete tonal pattern of the morpheme (as it is realized at the output of the lexical phonology) that needs to be represented orthographically.

This claim has important implications with respect to floating tones because it means that when they are part of a pattern, they must also be represented orthographically. In phonemic writing, floating tones are not indicated in any way unless they affect other tones in the phrase. When this happens, the contrasts, which are displaced onto the other words, are

6.2 LOH applied to Chumburung

orthographically represented on the affected words instead of on the words that have the floating tones. This is a logical outcome when one does not recognize the value of the complete pattern of the morpheme, but instead focusses on the individual tones of the TBUs. This makes it impossible to maintain consistent word-images because a word's orthographic form will be subject to changes as they are influenced by floating tones in adjacent words.

6.2.3 Underlying representations

Despite the potential objections, there are two major advantages in representing underlying forms compared with the other strategies discussed so far. They maintain a consistent visual image (helpful to experienced readers), and they avoid representing the output of postlexical phenomena (helpful to everyone). They do, however, have one major drawback: beginning readers need the representations of words to correspond as closely as possible to the way they perceive words to sound, and many underlying forms are just too abstract to allow them to make this connection. An orthography that represents the output of lexical processes (see section 6.2.4) is much more amenable to the needs of beginning readers.

There are two lexical processes in Chumburung that relate to tone, and it is important that the outputs of both be represented orthographically. H tone dissimilation (see section 6.1.1) and H tone spreading within words (see section 6.1.3) are both processes that have outputs of which the native speaker is very much aware. For example, if one were to represent underlying forms in the orthography, one might teach native speakers to write [kɔ̀tí] 'monkey' (no prefix) as <kɔ̀tí>, and [dápú] 'hawk' (again, no prefix) as <dápú>. So far so good. Having taught the above two forms, however, one would be hard-pressed to convince native speakers that [kìpá] 'hat' (with prefix) should actually be written <kípá>, or that [kípú] 'forest' (also with prefix) should be actually written <kípʊ̀>, as per their underlying forms.

Orthographies based on underlying forms do provide consistent visual word-images, so theoretically at least, it might be possible to teach native Chumburung speakers how to read using underlying forms. However, since the tone marks would mean almost nothing to them, writers would need to memorize the specific tone marks for each individual word—an almost impossible task. Any attempt to implement such a strategy would therefore most likely be doomed to failure.

6.2.4 Lexical representations

This brings us to what I call lexical writing, or writing the output of the final level/stratum of the lexical phonology. Lexical writing involves representing the output of lexical processes and avoids representing postlexical outputs. In the classic debate between deep/morphophonemic orthographies and shallow/phonemic ones, the tendency has been to assume that deep orthographies are more suitable for advanced readers and shallow orthographies more suitable for beginning readers. I argue that in writing lexically, this middle approach can meet the needs of both advanced and beginning readers in a single orthography. Unlike when writing underlying forms, lexical writing does not result in consistent morpheme-images, but rather in consistent word-images. In this way, word recognition process is speeded up, since a consistent visual image is key to meeting the needs of advanced readers (Katz and Frost 1992). At the same time, lexical writing also arguably represents the sounds of a language as its native speakers perceive them to be pronounced. In this way, lexical writing also meets the needs of beginning readers by enabling them to sound out words written in a way that corresponds to their perceptions.

The charts in (17)–(20) present the different tone patterns in Chumburung nouns as they are realized on the different stem syllable profiles in words from the *kI-* noun class. They also show how these patterns would be written according to each of the four different types of orthographic representation discussed above. For each chart, the lexical (ideal) representation appears in bold.[3] The diacritic ˌ, which appears at the right edge of certain lexical representations, represents a floating low tone.

(17) Simple stems with underlying /L/ pattern

	CV	CVʔ	CVN	CVCV
Surface pitch	$\begin{bmatrix} \bar{\ }\ \bar{\ } \end{bmatrix}$	$\begin{bmatrix} \bar{\ }\ \bar{\ } \end{bmatrix}$	$\begin{bmatrix} \bar{\ }\ \backslash \end{bmatrix}$	$\begin{bmatrix} \bar{\ }\ \bar{\ }\ \backslash \end{bmatrix}$
Surface	kípɔ́	kíná?	kílâŋ	kípínî
Phonemic	kípɔ́	kíná?	kílâŋ	kípínî
Lexical	**kípɔ́**	**kíná?ˌ**	**kíláŋˌ**	**kípíníˌ**
Underlying	kípɔ̀	kínà?	kílàŋ	kípìnì
Gloss	'forest'	'war'	'hip'	'mortar'

(18) Simple stems with underlying /H/ pattern

	CV	CVʔ	CVN	CVCV
Surface pitch	$\begin{bmatrix} \_\ \bar{\ } \end{bmatrix}$	$\begin{bmatrix} \_\ \bar{\ } \end{bmatrix}$	$\begin{bmatrix} \_\ \bar{\ } \end{bmatrix}$	$\begin{bmatrix} \_\ \bar{\ }\ \bar{\ } \end{bmatrix}$
Surface	kùˈwɔ́	kìˈbí?	kùˈsúŋ	kìˈk͡píní
Phonemic	kòwɔ́	kìbí?	kùsúŋ	kìk͡píní
Lexical	**kòwɔ́**	**kìbí?**	**kùsúŋ**	**kìk͡píní**
Underlying	kúwɔ́	kíbí?	kúsúŋ	kík͡píní
Gloss	'snake'	'mountain'	'work (n.)'	'plan (n.)'

(19) Simple stems with underlying /HL/ pattern

	CVʔ	CVN
Surface pitch	$\begin{bmatrix} \_\ \bar{\ } \end{bmatrix}$	$\begin{bmatrix} \_\ \backslash \end{bmatrix}$
Surface	kìˈt͡ʃá?	kìˈbâŋ
Phonemic	kìt͡ʃá?	kìbâŋ
Lexical	**kìt͡ʃá?ˌ**	**kìbáŋˌ**
Underlying	kít͡ʃá?	kíbáŋ̀
Gloss	'python'	'paddle'

---

[3] The different representations in (17)–(21) (i.e., phonetic, phonemic, lexical, and underlying) are only in reference to tone. Appropriate orthographic adaptations for the segmental aspects of the data have not been made.

6.2 LOH applied to Chumburung

(20) Simple stems with underlying /LH/ pattern

	CVʔ	CVN	CVCV
Surface Pitch	$\begin{bmatrix} -\ - \end{bmatrix}$	$\begin{bmatrix} -\ \searrow \end{bmatrix}$	$\begin{bmatrix} -\ -\ \ ^- \end{bmatrix}$
Surface	kìsà?	kìpàŋ	kùkù‘t͡ʃé
Phonemic	kìsà?	kìpàŋ	kùkut͡ʃé
Lexical	**kìsà?**	**kìpàŋ**	**kùkùt͡ʃé**
Underlying	kísá?	kípáŋ	kúkùt͡ʃé
Gloss	'nest'	'cutlass'	'oyster'

Perusing these charts, one can see that the lexical representations advocated in the present work do not differ greatly from their phonemic counterparts. Recall that both types of representations represent the output of lexical processes. Also, neither represents the output of postlexical allophonic processes. Therefore, the only difference between them is that while lexical representations do not represent the output of any postlexical processes, phonemic representations do, when the resultant sound is a phoneme in the language. Since the data presented here are all words in their isolation forms, all postlexical processes that occur across word boundaries are also excluded from the comparisons. Accordingly, the differences between the lexical and phonemic representations in the above charts are only in how each one handles the prepausal floating low tone docking process. Phonemic representations display the floating low tone when it docks onto sonorant high-toned TBUs (e.g., <kìbâŋ> 'paddle'), but do not display it when the final TBU is nonsonorant, as in <kìt͡ʃá?> 'python'. Lexical representations, on the other hand, represent both of these words consistently in all environments with a floating low tone after them (e.g., <kìbáŋˈ> and <kìt͡ʃá?ˈ>).

The differences between lexical and phonemic representations in Chumburung are more pronounced, however, when one takes into consideration phrases that consist of more than one word. Consider the examples in (21).

(21) Possessive phrases

Surface Pitch	$\begin{bmatrix} -\ -\ -\ \ \ -\ - \end{bmatrix}$	$\begin{bmatrix} -\ -\ -\ \searrow \end{bmatrix}$	$\begin{bmatrix} -\ -\ -\ \ \ -\ - \end{bmatrix}$
Surface	ówúré ˈdápú	dápú búnì	dápú kíˈk͡píní
Phonemic	ówúré ˈdápú	dápú búnì	dápú kíˈk͡píní
Lexical	**ówúréˈ dápú**	**dápú bùnì**	**dápú kìk͡píní**
Underlying	ówùrè dápú	dápú bùnì	dápú kík͡píní
Gloss	'chief's hawk'	'hawk's butterfly'	'hawk's plan'

An orthography for Chumburung developed along the lines suggested above would maintain consistent visual images for words, regardless of what comes before or after them. It would also maintain contrasts between words that end in floating tones and words that do not. And perhaps more importantly, it would represent words and phrases in a manner more consistent with native speakers' perceptions.

References

Arellanes, Francisco. 2004. La estructura silábica y la oposición fortis-lenis en el zapoteco de San Pablo Güilá. In I. Barreras Aguilar and M. Castro Llamas (eds.), *Memorias del Séptimo Encuentro Internacional de Lingüística en el Noroeste,* Vol. 1, 33–64. Sonora, Mexico: UniSon.

Arellanes, Francisco. 2009. El sistema fonológico y las propiedades fonéticas del zapoteco de San Pablo Güilá: Descripción y análisis formal. Ph.D. dissertation. El Colegio de México, Mexico City.

Arellanes, Francisco, and Mario Chávez-Peón. In preparation. On moraic typology: Syllable weight and the fortis-lenis distinction in Zapotec.

Baart, Joan L. G. 2010. *A field manual of acoustic phonetics.* Dallas, TX: SIL International.

Baart, Joan L. G. 2014. Tone and stress in North-West Indo-Aryan: A survey. In Johanneke Caspers, Yiya Chen, Willemijn Heeren, Jos Pacilly, Niels O. Schiller, and Ellen van Zanten (eds.), *Above and beyond the segments: Experimental linguistics and phonetics,* 1–13. Amsterdam: John Benjamins.

Beavon-Ham, Virginia. 2012. Consonant-tone interaction in Saxwe. In Michael R. Marlo, Nikki B. Adams, Christopher R. Green, Michelle Morrison, and Tristan M. Purvis (eds.), *Selected proceedings of the 42nd Annual Conference on African linguistics: African languages in context,* 55–69. Somerville, MA: Cascadilla Proceedings Project.

Bermúdez-Otero, Ricardo. 2011. Cyclicity. In Marc van Oostendorp, Colin J. Ewen, Elizabeth Hume, and Keren Rice (eds.), *The Blackwell companion to phonology,* Vol. 4: *Phonological interfaces,* 2019–2048. Malden, MA: Wiley-Blackwell.

Berry, Keith, and Christine Berry. 1999. *A description of Abun: A West Papuan language of Irian Jaya.* Pacific Linguistics, B-115. Canberra: Australian National University.

Bird, Steven. 1999. Strategies for representing tone in African writing systems. *Written Language and Literacy* 2(1):1–44.

Bird, Steven, and Larry M. Hyman, eds. 2014. *How to study a tone language* [Special issue]. Language Documentation and Conservation 8. Accessed September 19, 2017. http://nflrc.hawaii.edu/ldc/?p=382%20-%20tone#tone.

Blankenship, Barbara. 2002. The timing of nonmodal phonation in vowels. *Journal of Phonetics* 30:163–191.

Bradshaw, Mary. 1999. A crosslinguistic study of consonant-tone interaction. Ph.D. dissertation. *The Ohio State University,* Columbus, OH.

Brunelle, Marc. 2009. Tone perception in Northern and Southern Vietnamese. *Journal of Phonetics*. 37:79–96.

Brunelle, Marc, Duy Duong Nguyen, and Khac Hung Nguyen. 2010. A laryngographic and laryngoscopic study of Northern Vietnamese tones. *Phonetica* 67:147–169.

Cahill, Mike. 2001. Avoiding tone marks: A remnant of English education? *Notes on Literacy* 27(1):13–22.

Catford, John C. 1964. Phonation types: The classification of some laryngeal components of speech production. In David Abercrombie, D. B. Fry, P. A. D. MacCarthy, N. C. Scott, J. L. M. Trim (eds.), *In honour of Daniel Jones: Papers contributed on the occasion of his eightieth birthday, 12 September 1916,* 26–37. London: Longmans.

Catford, John C. 1977. *Fundamental problems in phonetics*. Edinburgh: Edinburgh University Press.

Chao, Yuen Ren. 1930. A system of tone letters. *Le Maître Phonétique* 45:24–27.

Chávez-Peón, Mario E. 2010. The interaction of metrical structure, tone, and phonation types in Quiaviní Zapotec. Ph.D. dissertation. University of British Columbia, Vancouver, BC.

Chen, Matthew Y. 2000. *Tone sandhi patterns across Chinese dialects*. Cambridge, UK: Cambridge University Press.

Chomsky, Noam, and Morris Halle. 1968. *The sound pattern of English*. New York: Harper and Row.

Clements, George N. 2003. Feature economy in sound systems. *Phonology* 20(3):287–333.

Clements, George N., and Kevin C. Ford. 1977. On the phonological status of downstep in Kikuyu. In Ivan R. Dihoff (ed.), *Harvard studies in phonology,* Vol. 1, 187–272. Cambridge, MA: Science Center.

Connell, Bruce. 2002. Tone languages and the universality of intrinsic F0: Evidence from Africa. *Journal of Phonetics* 30:101–129.

Connell, Bruce, and D. Robert Ladd. 1990. Aspects of pitch realisation in Yoruba. *Phonology* 7(1):1–29.

Cruttenden, Alan. 1997. *Intonation*. Cambridge, UK: Cambridge University Press.

Crystal, David. 2008. *A dictionary of linguistics and phonetics*. Sixth edition. Oxford: Blackwell.

Denes, Peter B., and Elliot N. Pinson. 1993. *The speech chain: The physics and biology of spoken language*. Second edition. New York: W. H. Freeman.

DiCanio, Christian T. 2008. The phonetics and phonology of San Martín Itunyoso Trique. Ph.D. dissertation. University of California, Berkeley.

Duanmu, San. 2000. *The phonology of Standard Chinese*. Oxford: Oxford University Press.

Ebert, Karen H. 1979. *Sprache und tradition der Kera (Tschad)*. Teil III: *Grammatik*. Berlin: Dietrich Reimer Verlag.

Ernst, Urs. 1996. *Tone orthography in Kakɔ*. Ms. Yaoundé, Cameroon: SIL. Accessed September 19, 2017. http://www.silcam.org/folder030401/page.php.

Fromkin, V., ed. 1978. *Tone: A linguistic survey*. New York: Academic Press.

Frost, Ram, Leonard Katz, and Shlomo Bentin. 1987. Strategies for visual word recognition and orthographical depth: A multilingual comparison. *Journal of experimental psychology: Human perception and performance* 13:104–115.

Gick, Bryan, Ian Wilson, and Donald Derrick. 2013. *Articulatory phonetics*. Chichester, UK: Wiley-Blackwell.

Goldsmith, John. 1976. Autosegmental phonology. Ph.D. dissertation. Massachusetts Institute of Technology, Cambridge, MA. Published by Garland Press, 1979.

Goldsmith, John. 1990. *Autosegmental and metrical phonology*. Oxford: Basil Blackwell.

Goodman, Yetta M., and Kenneth S. Goodman. 1994. To err is human: Learning about language processes by analysing miscues. In Robert B. Ruddell, Martha Ruddell Rapp, and Harry Singer (eds.), *Theoretical models and processes of reading,* 104–123. Newark, DE: International Reading Association.

Gordon, Matthew. 2005. A perceptually-driven account of onset-sensitive stress. *Natural Language and Linguistic Theory* 23:595–653.

Gordon, Matthew, and Peter Ladefoged. 2001. Phonation types: A cross-linguistic overview. *Journal of Phonetics* 29(4):383–406.

Gudschinsky, Sarah C. 1958. Native reactions to tones and words in Mazatec. *Word* 14:338–345.

Gudschinsky, Sarah C. 1970. More on formulating efficient orthographies. *The Bible translator* 21(1):21–25.

Gudschinsky, Sarah C. 1973. *A manual of literacy for preliterate peoples.* Ukarumpa, Papua New Guinea: Summer Institute of Linguistics.

Gussenhoven, Carlos. 2004. *The phonology of tone and intonation.* Cambridge, UK: Cambridge University Press.

Halle, Morris, and Kenneth N. Stevens. 1971. A note on laryngeal features. *RLE Quarterly Progress Report* (MIT) 101:198–213.

Hallé, Pierre A. 1994. Evidence for tone-specific activity of the sternohyoid muscle in Modern Standard Chinese. *Language and Speech* 37(2):103–123.

Hallé, Pierre A., Seiji Niimi, Satoshi Imaizumi, and Hajime Hirose. 1990. Modern Standard Chinese four tones: Electromyographic and acoustic patterns revisited. *Annual Bulletin of the Research Institute of Logopedics and Phoniatrics* 24:41–58.

Hansford, Keir L. 1988. A phonology and grammar of Chumburung. Ph.D. dissertation. School of Oriental and African Studies, London, UK.

Hedinger, Robert. 2008. *A grammar of Akoose: A Northwest Bantu language.* Dallas and Arlington, TX: The Summer Institute of Linguistics and the University of Texas at Arlington.

Hernández Mendoza, Fidel. In preparation. Aspectos fonológicos en el Triqui de Chicahuaxtla. Ph.D. dissertation. Universidad Nacional Autónoma de México, Mexico City.

Herrera, Esther. 2000. Amuzgo and Zapotec: Two more cases of laryngeally complex languages. *Anthropological Linguistics* 42(4):545–562.

Hirano, Minoru. 1974. Morphological structure of the vocal cord as a vibrator and its variations. *Folia Phoniatrica* 26:89–94.

Hirose, Hajime. 1997. Investigating the physiology of laryngeal structures. In William J. Harcastle and John Laver (eds.), *The handbook of phonetic sciences,* 116–136. Oxford: Basil Blackwell.

Hyman, Larry M. 1976. Phonologization. In Alphonse Juilland (ed.), *Linguistic studies offered to Joseph Greenberg on the occasion of his sixtieth birthday,* 407–418. Saratoga, CA: Anma Libri.

Hyman, Larry M. 1981. Tonal accent in Somali. *Studies in African Linguistics* 12:169–203.

Hyman, Larry M. 1984. On the weightlessness of syllable onsets. Berkeley Linguistics Society (Proceedings) 10:1–14.

Hyman, Larry M. 1985a. *A theory of phonological weight.* Dordrecht: Foris Publications.

Hyman, Larry M. 1985b. Word domains and downstep in Bamileke-Dschang. *Phonology Yearbook* 2:85–138.

Hyman, Larry M. 1992. Moraic mismatches in Bantu. *Phonology* 9(2):255–265.

Hyman, Larry M. 2014. How to study a tone language, with exemplification from Oku (Grassfields Bantu, Cameroon). *Language Documentation and Conservation* 8, 525–562. Accessed September 19, 2017. http://hdl.handle.net/10125/24624.

Hyman, Larry M., and Ernest Rugwa Byarushengo. 1984. A model of Haya tonology. In G. N. Clements and J. Goldsmith (eds.), *Autosegmental studies in Bantu tone,* 53–103. Publications in African Languages and Linguistics 3. Dordrecht: Foris Publications.

Hyman, Larry M., and William R. Leben. To appear. Word prosody II: Tone systems. In Carlos Gussenhoven and Aoju Chen (eds.), *Handbook of prosody.* Oxford: Oxford University Press.

Hyman, Larry M., and Maurice Tadadjeu. 1976. Floating tones in Mbam-Nkam. In Larry M. Hyman (ed.), *Studies in Bantu tonology,* 57–111. Southern California Occasional Papers in Linguistics 3. Los Angeles, CA: University of Southern California.

Hyönä, Jukka. 2012. Foveal and parafoveal processing during reading. In Simon P. Liversedge, Iain Gilchrist, and Stefan Everling (eds.), *The Oxford handbook of eye movements,* 819–838.

Accessed September 19, 2017. http://www.oxfordhandbooks.com/view/10.1093/oxfordhb/9780199539789.001.0001/oxfordhb-9780199539789-e-045.

International Phonetic Association. 2005. *Tones and word accents.* Accessed September 19, 2017. https://www.internationalphoneticassociation.org/content/ipa-tones-and-word-accents.

Jordan, Timothy R., Sharon M. Thomas, Geoffrey R. Patching, and Kenneth C. Scott-Brown, eds. 2003. Assessing the importance of letter pairs in initial, exterior and interior positions in reading. *Journal of Experimental Psychology: Learning, Memory and Cognition* 29(5):883–893.

Katz, Leonard, and Laurie B. Feldman. 1983. Relation between pronunciation and recognition of printed words in deep and shallow orthographies. *Journal of Experimental Psychology: Learning, Memory, and Cognition* 9:157–166.

Katz, Leonard, and Ram Frost. 1992. The reading process is different for different orthographies: The orthographic depth hypothesis. In Ram Frost and Leonard Katz (eds.), *Orthography, phonology, morphology, and meaning,* 67–84. Amsterdam: Elsevier Science.

Kenstowicz, Michael. 1994. *Phonology in generative grammar.* Oxford: Blackwell.

Kiparsky, Paul. 1982. Lexical phonology and morphology. In I. S. Yang (ed.), *Linguistics in the morning calm,* 3–91. Seoul: Hanshin.

Kiparsky, Paul. 1995. The phonological basis of sound change. In John A. Goldsmith (ed.), *The handbook of phonological theory,* 640–670. Oxford: Blackwell.

Kiparsky, Paul. 2000. Opacity and cyclicity. *The Linguistic Review* 17:351–367.

Kiparsky, Paul. 2015. Stratal OT: A synopsis and FAQs. In Yuchau E. Hsiao and Lian-Hee Wee (eds.), *Capturing phonological shades,* 1–45. Newcastle upon Tyne, UK: Cambridge Scholars.

Kisang', Philemon, and Iver Larsen. n.d. *Reading and writing Endo: A short introduction to the phonology of the Endo language.* Nairobi: Bible Translation and Literacy (E.A.).

Kutsch Lojenga, Constance. 1993. The writing and reading of tone in Bantu languages. *Notes on Literacy* 19(1):1–19.

Kutsch Lojenga, Constance. 2014. Orthography and tone: A tone system typology with implications for orthography development. In Michael Cahill and Keren Rice (eds.), *Developing orthographies for unwritten languages,* 49–72. Dallas, TX: SIL International.

Ladd, D. Robert. 2008. *Intonational phonology.* Second edition. Cambridge Studies in Linguistics 79. Cambridge, UK: Cambridge University Press.

Ladefoged, Peter. 1962. *Elements of acoustic phonetics.* Chicago: University of Chicago Press.

Ladefoged, Peter. 1971. *Preliminaries to linguistic phonetics.* Chicago: University of Chicago Press.

Laniran, Yetunde. 1992. Phonetic aspects of tone realisation in Igbo. Progress Reports from Oxford. *Phonetics* 5:35–51.

Larson, Ron, and Elizabeth Farber. 2005. *Elementary statistics: Picturing the world.* Third edition. Upper Saddle River, NJ: Prentice Hall.

Laver, John. 1980. *Principles of phonetics.* Cambridge, UK: Cambridge University Press.

Leach, Michael Benjamin. 2010. Things hold together: Foundations for a systemic treatment of verbal and nominal tone in Plateau Shimakonde. Ph.D. dissertation. LOT (Landelijke Onderzoekschool Taalwetenschap/Netherlands Graduate School of Linguistics), Utrecht.

Leben, William. 1971. Suprasegmental and segmental representation of tone. *Studies in African Linguistics. Supplement* 2:183–200.

Leben, William. 1973. Suprasegmental phonology. Ph.D. dissertation. Massachusetts Institute of Technology, Cambridge, MA. Published by New York: Garland Press, 1980.

Leben, William. 1978. The representation of tone. In V. Fromkin (ed.), *Tone: A linguistic survey,* 177–219. New York: Academic Press.

Leroy, Jacqueline. 1980. The Ngemba group: Mankon, Bangangu, Mundum I, Bafut, Nkwen, Bambui, Pinyin, Awing. In Larry Hyman and Jan Voorhoeve (eds.), *L'expansion bantoue,* Vol. 1, 111–141. Paris: SELAF.

Liberman, Isabelle Y., Alvin M. Liberman, Ignatius G. Mattingly, and Donald L. Shankweiler. 1980. Orthography and the beginning reader. In J. F. Kavanagh and R. L. Venezky (eds.), *Orthography, reading and dyslexia,* 137–153. Baltimore, MD: University Park Press.

Liu, Fang, and Yi Xu. 2007. Question intonation as affected by word stress and focus in English. In Ingmar Steiner (ed.), *Proceedings of the 16th International Congress of Phonetic Sciences,* 1189–1192.

Lombardi, Linda. 1991. Laryngeal features and laryngeal neutralization. Ph.D. dissertation. University of Massachusetts, Amherst. Published by Garland Press, 1994.

Lombardi, Linda. 1996. Restrictions on direction of voicing assimilation. *University of Maryland Working Papers in Linguistics* 4:89–155.

Lombardi, Linda. 1999. Positional faithfulness and voicing assimilation in Optimality Theory. *Natural Language and Linguistic Theory* 17:267–302.

Lukas, Johannes. 1969. Tonpermeable und tonimpermeable Konsonanten im Bolanci (Nordnigerien). In *Ethnological and Linguistic Studies in Honor of N. J. van Warmelo,* 133–138. Ethnological Publications No. 52. Republic of South Africa: Department of Bantu Administration and Development.

Maddieson, Ian, and Susan Hess. 1986. 'Tense' and 'lax' revisited: More on phonation type and pitch in minority languages of China. *UCLA Working Papers in Phonetics* 63:103–109.

McCawley, James D. 1978. What is a tone language? In V. Fromkin (ed.), *Tone: A linguistic survey,* 113–131. New York: Academic Press.

Mfonyam, Joseph. 1990. Tone analysis and tone orthography. *The Journal of West African Languages* 20(2):19–30.

Michael, Lev. 2011a. The interaction of tone and stress in the prosodic system of Iquito (Zaparoan). *UC Berkeley Phonology Lab Annual Report (2010),* 57–79.

Michael, Lev. 2011b. On the description and analysis of mixed tone-stress systems. Paper presented at the Berkeley Tone Workshop, Berkeley, CA (February 18–20).

Michaud, Alexis. 2004. Final consonants and glottalization: New perspectives from Hanoi Vietnamese. *Phonetica* 61:119–146.

Mohanan, Karuvannur P. 1982. Lexical phonology. Ph.D. dissertation. Massachusetts Institute of Technology, Cambridge, MA.

Mohanan, Karuvannur P. 1986. *The theory of Lexical Phonology.* Dordrecht: Reidel.

Munro, Pamela, and Felipe Lopez [with O. V. Méndez Martínez, R. García and M.R. Galant]. 1999. *Di'csyonaary x:tèe'n dii'zh sah Sann Lu'uc (San Lucas Quiaviní Zapotec Dictionary / Diccionario Zapoteco de San Lucas Quiaviní).* Los Angeles: UCLA Chicano Studies Research Center Publications.

Nevins, Andrew. 2012. Moraic onsets in Arrernte. Ms., University College London.

Newman, Paul. 1968. The reality of morphophonemes. *Language* 44(3):507–515.

Nida, Eugene. 1954. Practical limitations to a phonemic alphabet. *The Bible Translator* 5(1):35–39.

Odden, David. 2006. Topics in Taita tone II. *Studies in African Linguistics* 35(1):33–72.

Odden, David, and Lee Bickmore. 2014. Melodic tone in Bantu: Overview. *Africana Linguistica* 20(1):3–13.

Ohala, John J. 1978. Production of tone. In V. Fromkin (ed.), *Tone: A linguistic survey,* 5–39. New York: Academic Press.

Parker, Elizabeth. 1989. Le nom et le syntagme nominal en mundani. In Daniel Barreteau and Robert Hedinger (eds.), *Descriptions de langues camerounaises,* 131–177. Paris: ACCT and ORSTOM.

Pearce, Mary. 1999. Consonants and tone in Kera (Chadic). *The Journal of West African Languages* 27(1):33–70.

Pearce, Mary. 2007. The interaction of tone with voicing and foot structure: Evidence from Kera phonetics and phonology. Ph.D. dissertation. University College London, UK.

Pelli, Denis G., Patrick Cavanagh, Robert Desimone, Bosco Tjan, and Anne Treisman, eds. 2007. Crowding: Including illusory conjunctions, surround suppression, and attention. *Journal of Vision,* special issue 7(2).

Pierrehumbert, Janet. 1980. The phonology and phonetics of English intonation. Ph.D. dissertation. Massachusetts Institute of Technology, Cambridge, MA.

Pierrehumbert, Janet, and Mary E. Beckman. 1988. *Japanese tone structure.* Linguistic Inquiry Monographs 15. Cambridge, MA: MIT Press.

Pike, Kenneth L. 1947. *Phonemics: A technique for reducing languages to writing.* Ann Arbor: University of Michigan Press.

Pike, Kenneth L. 1948. *Tone languages.* Ann Arbor: University of Michigan Press.

Powlison, Paul S. 1968. Bases for formulating an efficient orthography. *The Bible Translator* 19(2):74–91.

Price, Norman. 1994. Mada noun class data. Ms. Jos: Nigeria Bible Translation Trust.

Pulleyblank, Douglas. 1986. *Tone in lexical phonology.* Dordrecht: Reidel.

Rayner, Keith. 1998. Eye movements in reading and information processing: 20 years of research. *Psychological Bulletin* 124:372–422.

Roberts, David. 2008a. L'orthographe du ton en kabiyè au banc d'essai. Ph.D. dissertation. Paris: Institut National des Langues et Civilisations Orientales.

Roberts, David. 2008b. Thirty years of tone orthography testing in West African languages (1977–2007). *Journal of West African Languages* 35(1–2):199–242.

Roberts, David. 2009. Visual crowding and the tone orthography of African languages. *Written Language & Literacy* 12(1):140–155.

Roberts, David, and Stephen Walter. 2012. Writing grammar rather than tone: An orthography experiment in Togo. *Written Language and Literacy* 15(2):226–253.

Roberts, David, Stephen Walter, and Keith Snider. 2015. Neither deep nor shallow: A classroom experiment testing the orthographic depth of tone marking in Kabiye (Togo). *Language and Speech* 1–26. Accessed September 19, 2017. DOI: 1177/0023830915580387.

Sabaot Bible Translation and Literacy Staff. 1990. The vowels and consonants in the Sabaot language. Accessed September 19, 2017. https://www.academia.edu/749515/Korooryo_Ku_Taay_Reading_and_Writing_Sabaot. Uploaded by Iver Larsen. Publisher: Bible Translation and Literacy (E.A.).

Saeed, John. 1993. *Somali reference grammar.* Second revised edition. Kensington, MD: Dunwoody.

Saeed, John. 1999. *Somali.* Amsterdam: John Benjamins.

Sapir, Edward. 1933. La réalité psychologique des phonèmes. *Journal de Psychologie et Pathologique* 30:247–265.

Sapir, Edward. 1949. The psychological reality of phonemes. In David Mandelbaum (ed.), *Selected writings of Edward Sapir,* 46–60. Berkeley and Los Angeles: University of California Press.

Schuh, Russell. 1971. Verb forms and verb aspects in Ngizim. *Journal of African Languages* 10:47–60.

Schuh, Russell. 1978. Tone rules. In V. Fromkin (ed.), *Tone: A linguistic survey,* 221–256. New York: Academic Press.

Silverman, Daniel. 1997. Laryngeal complexity in Otomanguean vowels. *Phonology* 14(2):235–261.

Snider, Keith. 1985. Vowel coalescence across word boundaries in Chumburung. *The Journal of West African Languages* 15(1):3-13.

Snider, Keith. 1989. Vowel coalescence in Chumburung: An autosegmental analysis. *Lingua* 78:217–232.

Snider, Keith. 1992. "Grammatical tone" and orthography. *Notes on Literacy* 18(4):25–30.

Snider, Keith. 1998. Phonetic realisation of downstep in Bimoba. *Phonology* 15(1):77–101.

Snider, Keith. 1999. *The geometry and features of tone*. Dallas and Arlington, TX: The Summer Institute of Linguistics and the University of Texas at Arlington.
Snider, Keith. 2001. Linguistic factors in orthography design. In Ngessimo M. Mutaka and Sammy B. Chumbow (eds.), *Research mate in African linguistics: Focus on Cameroon*, 323–332. Köln: Rüdiger Köppe Verlag.
Snider, Keith. 2007. Automatic and non-automatic downstep in Chumburung: An instrumental comparison. *The Journal of West African Languages* 34(1):105–114.
Snider, Keith. 2014a. On establishing underlying tonal contrast. *Language Documentation and Conservation* 8, 707–737. Accessed September 19, 2017. http://hdl.handle.net/10125/24622.
Snider, Keith. 2014b. Orthography and phonological depth. In Michael Cahill and Keren Rice (eds.), *Developing orthographies for unwritten languages*, 27–48. Dallas, TX: SIL International.
Stevens, Kenneth N. 1998. *Acoustic phonetics*. Cambridge, MA: MIT Press.
Stewart, John M. 1965. The typology of the Twi tone system. Preprint from the Bulletin of the Institute of African Studies 1, Institute of African Studies, University of Ghana, Legon, Ghana.
Stewart, John M. 1983. Review article: Downstep and floating tones in Adioukrou. *Journal of African Languages and Linguistics* 5(1):57–78.
Stewart, John. M. 1993. Dschang and Ebrie as Akan-type total downstep languages. In Harry van der Hulst and Keith Snider (eds.), *The representation of tonal register*, 1–27. Berlin: Mouton de Gruyter.
Topintzi, Nina. 2005. Word minimality in Bella Coola as evidence for moraic onsets. Talk presented at the 41st Annual Meeting of the Chicago Linguistic Society, 7–9 April 2005, Chicago, IL.
Topintzi, Nina. 2010. *Onsets: Suprasegmental and prosodic behaviour*. Cambridge, UK: Cambridge University Press.
Torres, Néstor Cuartero. 2001. Voicing assimilation in Catalan and English. Ph.D. dissertation. Universitat Autònoma de Barcelona.
Van der Hulst, Harry, and Norval Smith. 1988. *Autosegmental studies on pitch accent*. Dordrecht: Foris Publications.
Van Gompel, Roger P. G., Martin H. Fischer, Wayne S. Murray, and Robin L. Hill, eds. 2007. *Eye movements: A window on mind and brain*. Oxford: Elsevier Science.
Van Oostendorp, Marc. 2007. Incomplete devoicing in formal phonology. Ms. Accessed September 14, 2017. http://www.vanoostendorp.nl/pdf/devoicing.pdf.
Venezky, Richard L. 1970. Principles for the design of practical writing systems. *Anthropological Linguistics* 12:256–270.
Voorhoeve, Jan. 1962. Some problems in writing tone. *The Bible Translator* 13(1):34–38.
Welmers, William E. 1959. Tonemics, morphotonemics, and tonal morphemes. *General Linguistics* 4:1–9.
Welmers, William E. 1973. *African language structures*. Berkeley: University of California Press.
Wiesemann, Ursula. 1989. Orthography matters. *Notes on Literacy* 57:14–21.
Xu, Yi, and Ching X. Xu. 2005. Phonetic realization of focus in English declarative intonation. *Journal of Phonetics* 33(2):159–197.
Yip, Moira. 2002. *Tone*. Cambridge, UK: Cambridge University Press.
Zec, Draga. 1993. Rule domains and phonological change. In S. Hargus and E. Kaisse (eds.), *Studies in lexical phonology*, 365–405. San Diego, CA: Academic Press.
Zemlin, Willard R. 1981. *Speech and hearing science: Anatomy and physiology*. Second edition. Englewood Cliffs, NJ: Prentice-Hall.

Index

A

abducted position 64
Abun [kgr] 21
accent (marks) 6, 23, 41, 48, 88–90, 97.
    See also pitch-accent
acoustic study 73–77
adducted position 64
advanced tongue root (ATR) xv, 33, 102, 103,
    114, 137
Akan [aka] 3
Akoose [bss] 43, 44, 56–58
Alur [alz] 82
Arabic [ara] 86
Arellanes, Francisco 38, 48
arytenoid cartilage 46, 64, 65
Ashe [ahs] 54, 55
assimilation
    tone 5, 119
    vowel/ATR 102, 103
association patterns 14
association relationships 19
Attié [ati] 97
Autosegmental Phonology 19, 90

B

Baart, Joan L. G. xiii, 6, 64, 66
Bamileke-Dschang [ybb] 42, 43, 81
Beavon-Ham, Virginia 44
Beavon, Keith 8, 16, 44
Beckman, Mary E. 85
Bench [bcq] 12, 13
Bentin, Shlomo 92
Bermúdez-Otero, Ricardo 91, 93
Bernoulli effect 65
Berry, Christine 21
Berry, Keith 21
Bickmore, Lee 13
Bimoba [bim] 23, 24, 73–77, 161
Bird, Stephen 2, 81, 85, 87
Blankenship, Barbara 48
Bolanci [bol] 45
boundary tone 85
Bradshaw, Mary 44
breathy voice 46
Brunelle, Marc 20
Budu [buu] 88
Byarushengo, Ernest Rugwa 20

C

Cahill, Mike 86
Cantonese [yue] 19, 81
Catford, John C. 46
Chao system 22, 23, 25
Chao, Yuen Ren 22
Chávez-Peón 20, 38, 46, 47
Chen, Matthew Y. 19
Chomsky, Noam 90, 91, 92

Chumburung [ncu] ix, x, xiii, 7–12, 21–27, 29–41, 49, 50, 66–73, 81, 83, 88, 89, 101–169
Clement, Lopeok 60
Clements, George N. 53, 83
coda 7, 8, 13, 38–40, 47–49, 52, 115, 125, 126
complex stem 34–36, 40, 52, 98, 104, 113, 114, 153, 156
compound stem 34–36, 51, 53, 98, 104, 113, 114, 153, 155, 156
Connell, Bruce xiii, 72, 73
consonant-tone interaction 44–46, 52, 74, 104
contrast, tonal 6–8, 10, 11, 27, 31–33, 38, 40, 49, 50, 55, 56, 73, 82, 83, 90, 96, 97, 127, 130, 137
contrast, tone height 27
contrast, tone pattern 3, 48, 83
creaky voice 46, 48
cricothyroid muscles 65
crowding, visual 96, 97
Cruttenden, Alan 3
Crystal, David 33, 34, 63

D

database 54, 99
declination 72, 73, 74
Denes, Peter B. 64
depressor/non-depressor consonants 44, 52
Derrick, Donald 64
diacritic marking 85, 87, 88–90, 94, 96, 97, 99, 157
diacritic systems 22–25, 164
DiCanio, Christian T. 48
dock/docking 32, 38, 162–165, 169
downstep, automatic 73–77, 123, 155, 160, 161, 164, 165
downstep, non-automatic 73–77, 124, 142, 156, 161, 162, 165
Duanmu, San 65

E

Ebert, Karen H. 44
Endo [enb] 88
energy peak 70, 72
Engenni [enn] 88
English [eng] 1–3, 17, 22, 26, 34, 79, 80, 83, 86, 89, 92–96, 137, 153
Ernst, Urs 88
Ewe [ewe] 87

eye movement 96

F

Farber, Elizabeth 76
Feldman, Laurie B. 92
fields, database 31
Ford, Kevin C. 53
fortis 38, 47
French [fra] 80, 83, 86
Fromkin, Victoria xi
Frost, Ram 85, 92, 166, 167
fundamental frequency 2, 63, 64, 67

G

Gick, Bryan 64
glottalized 45, 46, 48, 52
glottal stop 10, 40, 48, 103, 116, 125
Goldsmith, John 15, 49, 90
Goodman, Kenneth S. 83
Goodman, Yetta M. 83
Gordon, Matthew 38, 46
grammatical tone. *See* tone, grammatical
Gudschinsky, Sarah C. 83, 86, 87, 92, 94
Gussenhoven, Carlos xi, 3

H

Halle, Morris 65, 90–92
Hallé, Pierre A. 65
Hansford, Keir L. 101
Haya [hay] 20
Hedinger, Robert xiii, 43, 56
Hernández Mendoza, Fidel 48
Herrera, Esther 48
hertz (Hz) 63, 67
Hess, Susan 46
high tone spreading. *See* tone spreading
Hirano, Minoru 64
Hirose, Hajime 64, 65
Huautla [mau] 83
hum 20, 26, 27, 71
Hungarian [hun] 3
Hyman, Larry M. xiii, 2, 3, 5, 7, 13, 20, 26, 38, 42, 49, 59, 60, 94
Hyönä, Jukka 96

I

Igbo [ibo] 161

implosive 44–46, 66
International Phonetic Alphabet (IPA) 24
International Phonetic Association (IPA) 22–24
intonation 2, 3, 25, 26, 63, 68, 97
Iquito [iqu] 6, 8, 48, 49
Italian [ita] 3

J

Jingpho [kac] 46
Jordan, Timothy R. 96

K

Kabiye [kbp] 88, 94
Kako [kkj] 11, 12, 88
Kasem [xsm] 87
Katz, Leonard 85, 92, 166, 167
Kenstowicz, Michael 93
Kenyang [ken] 3–5, 81, 82, 89, 90
Kiparsky, Paul 90, 93, 94
Kisang', Philemon 88
Kutsch Lojenga, Constance xiii, 83–84, 88, 97–98

L

Laarim [loh] 60, 61
Ladd, D. Robert 3, 72
Ladefoged, Peter 46, 67
Laniran, Yetunde 161
Larsen, Iver 88
Larson, Ron 76
larynx 64, 65
Laver, John 46
Leach, Michael Benjamin 88
Leben, William x, xiv, 3, 13–15, 49, 90
lenis 38, 47–48
Leroy, Jacqueline 43
lexical processes 93–96, 99, 158–169
lexical phonology (process or level) 93, 94, 96–98, 157, 162–163, 166, 167
Lexical Phonology (theory) 90, 91, 93, 94, 157
lexical tone. *See* tone, lexical
Liberman, Isabelle Y. 92
Liu, Fang 3
logarithmic 64
Lombardi, Linda 93
Lopez, Filipe 46, 47

Lukas, Johannes 45
low tone spreading. *See* tone spreading

M

Maddieson, Ian 46
Mandarin [cmn] 1, 3
Maninkakan, Western [mlq] 88
Marlett, Steve 7
Mattingly, Ignatius G. 92
Mazatec, Soyaltepec [vmp] 94
McCawley, James 1, 6
McKendry, Inga xiv, 88
mels 63
Mende [men] xiv, 13–16, 20, 21, 37, 91, 98
metrical foot 49
Mfonyam, Joseph 87
Michael, Lev 6, 48, 49
Michaud, Alexis 20
minimal pair 8, 31, 80–85, 87–88
modal voice/phonation 46–48, 52
Mohanan, Karuvannur P. 90, 93, 94
Moloko [mlw] 44
mora(s)/moraic 7–8, 38–40, 47–49, 52, 56, 59, 103, 115, 125, 146, 151, 166
Munro, Pamela 46, 47

N

Nawuri [naw] 7–8, 19
Nevins, Andrew 38
Newman, Paul 92
Ngizim [ngi] 45–46
Nida, Eugene 85, 92, 96, 166
Njyem [njy] 8, 9, 16–18, 37, 38
noun class 9, 31, 32, 34–36, 38, 40–43, 88, 101–102, 104, 114–115, 120, 125, 129, 136–137, 150–151, 153–158, 167

O

obstruents 44–46, 69, 70, 73
Odden, David 1, 13
Ohala, John J. 64
onset 38, 46

P

Parker, Elizabeth 43
Pearce, Mary xiv, 44, 45, 87

Pelli, Denis G. 96
perturbation 70, 71, 72
Pierrehumbert, Janet 72
Pike, Kenneth L. ix–xi, xiv, 13, 22, 23, 25, 84, 92
Pinson, Elliot N. 64
pitch ix, x, 1–3, 5–8, 10–16, 18–20, 22–24, 26, 27, 29, 31–34, 36, 38–41, 43–46, 48, 49, 52, 55, 63–73, 84, 98, 113, 115, 116, 119, 120, 122–125, 128, 136, 139, 140, 143, 145–147, 151–153, 155, 160, 162–164, 168
   contour 2, 3, 8, 11, 13, 15, 19, 20, 23, 24, 68–70, 142, 165
   falling 2, 3, 5, 7, 8, 11, 14–16, 22, 24, 27, 32, 36, 39, 40, 47, 98, 116, 119, 123, 125, 135, 139, 140, 142, 149, 152, 153, 163, 164, 165
   level ix, 2, 3, 7, 11–13, 18, 20, 23–27, 32, 37, 39, 40, 63, 68, 69, 119, 143, 153, 155, 163, 165
   rising 2, 3, 14, 15, 19, 22–24, 38, 45, 47
pitch-accent 6, 48, 49
pitch pattern, contrastive 6, 14, 52, 55
pitch trace 26, 27, 68, 69, 70–72
polar tone 153
postlexical processes 93–96, 99, 100, 158–169
Powlison, Paul 83
Price, Norman 43
prosodic foot 49
prosodic word 48, 49
psychology of reading 79, 96
Pulleyblank, Douglas 94

R

Rayner, Keith 96
register 4, 24, 25, 44, 123, 160, 161
Roberts, David xiii, 88, 93, 94, 96–98
root, definition 33, 34
roots
   disyllabic 16, 56
   monosyllabic 15, 16, 20, 47
   trisyllabic 16

S

Sabaot [spy] 88, 89, 97
Saeed, John 5
Sapir, Edward 92
Schuh, Russell 45

Shankweiler, Donald L. 92
Shimakonde [kde] 88
Silverman, Daniel 48
simple stem 7, 16, 34–37, 40, 49, 52, 55–57, 98, 104, 115, 118–121, 128–134, 136–137, 140, 144, 146, 153, 155, 156, 168–169
Smith, Norval 6, 48
Snider, Keith ix, x, xi, 2, 8, 43, 73, 87, 90, 93–95, 103, 121, 155, 161
Somali [som] 3, 5, 6
Spanish [spa] 86, 97
Speech Analyzer 26, 68, 74
spreading 5, 17, 19, 44–46, 59, 122, 123, 125, 140, 142–144, 147, 151–153, 156, 159–167
stem, definition 33, 34
Stevens, Kenneth N. 64, 65
Stewart, John M. 123, 124
Stirtz, Timothy M. 60
Stratal Optimality Theory 90, 92–94, 157
stress ix, 6, 26, 31, 38, 48, 49, 52
surface tone. *See* tone, surface
syllable 37, 48, 52, 91
syllable profile 7, 37, 52

T

Taita, Mbololo [dav] 1
Tadadjeu, Maurice 42
Terena [ter] 83
Thai [tha] 18, 19
tone-bearing unit (TBU) xi, xiv, 8, 18, 20, 40
tone delinking 19, 161, 162
tone, floating 11, 13, 17, 19, 32, 38, 43, 51, 59, 115, 120, 126, 144, 161, 166, 167, 169
tone, grammatical 6, 81, 82, 88, 89, 99, 100
tone language ix, 2, 3, 13, 20, 25, 49, 83, 86, 96, 98, 156, 157
toneless 3–5, 56, 86, 130, 159
tone, lexical 48, 49, 81–83, 87–89, 99
tone melody xiv, 13
tone, metrical 48, 49
tone neutralization 9, 11, 41, 52, 151, 152
tone pattern xiv, 3, 13, 18–20, 26, 31, 34, 37, 38, 40, 41, 44, 48, 51, 81, 83, 91, 97, 98, 121, 126, 136, 139, 147, 156, 166
tone pattern inventory 13, 21, 157
tone spreading 5, 17, 19, 44–46, 59, 122, 123, 125, 140–144, 147, 151–153, 156, 159, 160–167
tone-stress systems. *See* stress

tone, surface xiv, 31, 33, 35, 40–46, 59, 69, 84–85, 115, 141, 164
tone, underlying xiv, 6, 7, 9, 11, 13, 15, 20, 21, 29, 31, 33, 36, 38, 40, 41, 44, 48, 81, 90, 91, 99, 101, 104, 115, 117–120, 126, 136, 139, 147, 150, 158, 166
Topintzi, Nina 38
Torres, Néstor Cuartero 93
transcription ix, 24–26, 41, 58, 63, 160
transitional TBUs 71
trochee 49

U

upstep 24, 25

V

Van der Hulst, Harry 6, 48
Van Gompel, Roger P. G. 96
Van Oostendorp, Marc 93
Venezky, Richard L. 85, 92
Vietnamese, Northern [vie] 20
vision
   foveal 96
   parafoveal 96, 97

vocal folds xiii, 2, 39, 46, 63–68
vocalis muscle 64, 65, 66
Voorhoeve, Jan 85, 96, 166
vowel assimulation 102, 103

W

Walter, Stephen 88
Welmers, William E. 3, 86
whistle 20, 26, 27, 71, 98
Wiesemann, Ursula 87

X

Xu, Ching X. 3
Xu, Yi 3

Y

Yip, Moira xi, 18, 46, 81

Z

Zapotec, Quiaviní [zab] 20, 38, 46–48
Zec, Draga 94
Zemlin, Willard R. 65
Zulu [zul] 3

About the Author

Keith L. Snider (born in Jos, Nigeria) is a Senior Linguistics Consultant with SIL International® and an Affiliate Professor at Trinity Western University in British Columbia, Canada, having directed their M.A. in Linguistics program for five years. He began his linguistics career in Ghana, working with the Chumburung people, which sparked a lifelong interest in phonology, especially tone analysis. After his years in Ghana, Snider also served as SIL's Linguistics Coordinator in Cameroon. Now an SIL International Senior Consultant, Snider has conducted over a dozen phonology and tone workshops throughout Africa, covering more than 50 languages, and presented key papers at the historic Berkeley Tone Workshop and at the Australian National University Tone Workshop. He has taught courses in phonology and historical linguistics, and developed a course in tone analysis that has been replicated elsewhere and was part of the foundation for this volume. Snider has a special interest in applying tone studies to new orthographies in under-researched languages. He was granted a Doctor of Letters in African Linguistics degree from Leiden University (1990), with a dissertation titled *Studies in Guang Phonology*.

Select Bibliography

Snider, Keith. 2014. On establishing underlying tonal contrast. *Language Documentation and Conservation* 8:707–737. http://hdl.handle.net/10125/24622.
Snider, Keith. 2014. Orthography and phonological depth. In Michael Cahill and Keren Rice (eds.), *Developing orthographies for unwritten languages*, 27–48. Dallas, TX: SIL International.
Snider, Keith. 2013. Orthography. In Carole A. Chapelle (ed.), *The encyclopedia of applied linguistics*. Oxford: Blackwell.
Snider, Keith. 1999. *The geometry and features of tone*. Dallas, TX: Summer Institute of Linguistics and University of Texas at Arlington.
Snider, Keith. 1998. Phonetic realisation of downstep in Bimoba. *Phonology* 15(1):77-101.
Snider, Keith, and Harry van der Hulst (eds.). 1993. *The representation of tonal register*. Linguistic Models 17. Berlin: Mouton de Gruyter.
Snider, Keith. 1990. Tonal upstep in Krachi: Evidence for a register tier. *Language* 66(3):453–474.

www.ingramcontent.com/pod-product-compliance
Lightning Source LLC
Chambersburg PA
CBHW080539300426
44111CB00017B/2795